Christiane Lütge, Max von Blanckenburg (Eds.)

Drama in Foreign Language Education

Fremdsprachendidaktik in globaler Perspektive

herausgegeben von

Prof. Dr. Christiane Lütge
(Ludwig-Maximilians-Universität München)

Band 7

LIT

Drama in Foreign Language Education

Texts and Performances

edited by

Christiane Lütge and Max von Blanckenburg

LIT

Cover photo: iStock.com/Orbon Alija

This book is printed on acid-free paper.

Bibliographic information published by the Deutsche Nationalbibliothek
The Deutsche Nationalbibliothek lists this publication in the Deutsche Nationalbibliografie; detailed bibliographic data are available in the Internet at http://dnb.dnb.de.

ISBN 978-3-643-91469-9 (pb)
ISBN 978-3-643-96469-4 (PDF)

A catalogue record for this book is available from the British Library.

© LIT VERLAG GmbH & Co. KG Wien,
Zweigniederlassung Zürich 2021
Flössergasse 10
CH-8001 Zürich
Tel. +41 (0) 76-632 84 35
E-Mail: zuerich@lit-verlag.ch   https://www.lit-verlag.ch
Distribution:
In the UK: Global Book Marketing, e-mail: mo@centralbooks.com
In North America: Independent Publishers Group, e-mail: orders@ipgbook.com
In Germany: LIT Verlag Fresnostr. 2, D-48159 Münster
Tel. +49 (0) 2 51-620 32 22, Fax +49 (0) 2 51-922 60 99, e-mail: vertrieb@lit-verlag.de

Table of Contents

Drama in Foreign Language Education. Texts and Performances – An Introduction..7
Christiane LÜTGE & Max VON BLANCKENBURG

Part I – Dramatic Texts, Textualities and Literacy Perspectives

A Multiliteracies Approach to Teaching Plays 15
Maria EISENMANN

'Hemel op die Platteland' – Reading Lara Foot's Play *Reach* in the EFL Classroom..33
Christian LUDWIG

'We Can't Make It Ours, Unless We're in It' – Contemporary Young Adult Drama and Political Education in EFL Learning 55
Frauke MATZ

Theatricality of Visual Literature – EnACTing Picturebooks............................79
Grit ALTER

Drama and Performance in Digital Spaces...97
Christiane LÜTGE & Max VON BLANCKENBURG

Part II – Drama Pedagogy, Language Learner and Teacher Performance

Taking Literature off the Page: Drama, Drama Techniques and the Performative Turn in EFL 119
Laurenz VOLKMANN

German English Teacher Trainees' Drama-Based Instructions: Exploring the Status Quo 137
Christiane KLEMPIN

Exploring Shakespeare in the Multilingual Classroom 155
Annette DESCHNER & Lisa PETER

Dialogue, Drama Pedagogy and English Language Education 169
Werner DELANOY

CHRISTIANE LÜTGE & MAX VON BLANCKENBURG (LUDWIG-MAXIMILIANS-UNIVERSITÄT MÜNCHEN)

Drama in Foreign Language Education. Texts and Performances – An Introduction

The foreign language classroom has been a space to explore all kinds of stagings: Learners investigate dramatic texts, get to know theatre productions or take on roles themselves, be it in improvised dialogues or enactments of scenes from a play. Yet, neither is there a static canon of dramatic texts seen as unquestionably relevant for language education, nor exist any unchallenged interpretations of widely known or newly published plays.

On the contrary, traditional plays appear in various redesigned shapes and adaptations both analogue and digital, hence allowing for new readings and requiring new forms of literacies. Contemporary interpretations and retellings of dramatic texts are hereby always embedded in new discourses in literary and cultural studies. When it comes to foreign language education, normative assumptions about what should or could be done in classrooms serve as an additional filter, which applies to both text selection and task design.

Consequently, new teaching paradigms, concepts and topics are strongly interrelated with the choice of texts, methods and modes of performative practice. Also, performances are, more than ever, composed in digital text formats and viewed in digital spaces, which goes along with new forms of production and reception of drama and theatre. This is in accordance with an extended notion of drama and performance that applies not only to theatre plays in a strict sense but also to everyday forms of communicative and symbolic action.

This volume sets out to explore such developments and reflect them with regard to the goals of and methodological approaches to foreign language education. Within the following two parts of the book, the first set of contributions focuses on dramatic texts and textualities whereas the second zooms in on language learners and teacher performances with a special focus on the concept of drama pedagogy.[1]

---

[1] We would like to thank our student assistant, Hannah Jahner, very much for her help with this volume.

Part I – Dramatic Texts, Textualities and Literacy Perspectives

The first part of the volume aims to investigate developments in research and teaching concerning various dramatic texts in printed, multimodal and digital formats, including canonical and popular literature. In light of a diversification of text types, communication platforms and subsequent concepts of literacies, the role of drama in foreign language education may need to be renegotiated by addressing some guiding questions as the following ones – without claiming to fully account for all aspects:

- How does the changing and expanding notion of 'text' impact on the dramaticity of literary works?
- How do 21st century dramatic texts represent, encourage or even require instances of performance?
- How may the status and (educational) relevance of canonical texts be reformulated by taking into account their multifaceted versions and adaptations available?
- What makes for competent and critical readers (or: produsers) of dramatic texts in light of multimodality and digitalisation?

In the first contribution, **Maria Eisenmann** suggests a multiliteracy approach to teaching plays by emphasising the potential of production-oriented tasks in which learners transform dramatic texts into new designs. She thereby intertwines fostering performative competence with the development of (critical) media literacy. Next to grounding her argument in multiliteracy pedagogy and discourses around new media in TEFL, Eisenmann also provides detailed reflections for practical implementation in the classroom through preparatory, supporting and follow-up phases.

In addition to an extension of dramatic text and task formats, a point has been made to reconsider and broaden the cultural spaces drawn on to select theatre plays for foreign language learning. **Christian Ludwig** makes a case for reading a play by the South African author Lara Foot in the EFL Classroom. The drama *Reach* provides multifaceted insights into linguistic, sociocultural and political dimensions of everyday life in the Eastern Cape, a rural South African province. Ludwig embeds his discussion of the play's learning potential in a wider reflection of the country's past and present with a special view to the relevance of South African theatre. The contribution concludes with an illustration of various classroom activities encompassing close reading and contextualisation tasks as well as pathways for creative and media-supported engagement with the play.

In the following chapter, **Frauke Matz** explores political dimensions of drama, too – yet she lays the focus specifically on how young adults can find and negotiate their own or an adopted (political) position through performance. Taking Stef Smith's play *Remote* as an example, Matz argues that foreign language learners need to be equipped to become competent critical performers and producers of YA theatre plays whereby they develop the performative competences required to participate in today's globalised societies. Furthermore, she calls for a critical evaluation of current approaches to political education in EFL learning and, in doing so, highlights the benefits of a human rights and cosmopolitan perspective.

Engaging in performative activities can likewise be encouraged with younger EFL learners already and it can take various text types as a starting point. **Grit Alter** illustrates this in suggesting a performative approach to the picturebook *Yo! Yes!* by Chris Kaschka. She argues for recognising a profound sense of theatricality in visual literature, and, against this background, emphasises the benefits of an action-oriented exploration of picturebooks, ranging from dramatic readings to performances. In order to cater such an approach to pre A1/A1 learners, Alter discusses characteristics of suitable visual literature, reflects on opportunities for competence development, and sketches out concrete ways of using the picturebook in a primary EFL context.

Concluding the first part of this volume, **Christiane Lütge** and **Max von Blanckenburg** draw attention to various forms of drama and performance taking place in digital spaces. They discuss the changing role and shape of drama and performance within digital text formats as well as in relation to digitally rendered aesthetic re-enactments. In doing so, the authors particularly focus on performative dimensions of digital literature, autobiographical self-staging as well as on political and sociocultural performances. On this basis, Lütge and von Blanckenburg argue that digital practices and their performative dimensions need to be scrutinised much more thoroughly in the context of media literacy and require the development of a 'performative gaze'.

Part II – Drama Pedagogy, Language Learner and Teacher Performance

The second part of the volume is concerned with notions of language learner and teacher performance in the context of drama pedagogy, both historically as well as with regard to current developments. The following contributions will therefore reflect on concepts and approaches that allow and encourage learners to 'perform' in the classroom, and will reflect on implications for teaching practice and teacher education. More specifically, these questions are of central interest, again without necessarily providing final answers:

- How can drama pedagogy be understood and how can it be harnessed today against the background of historical developments in performative teaching and learning?
- How can empirical research as well as best practice examples be of benefit to teacher education and professional development in drama pedagogy?
- Where does drama pedagogy open up spaces for participation, creativity and holistic learning in multilingual learner groups?
- In what ways may drama pedagogy bring together playful and explicit cognitive language learning, and hence allow for multifaceted and differentiated forms of learner performance in the classroom?

Opening the second part of the volume, **Laurenz Volkmann** provides an overview of four different, yet intertwined paradigms of drama-oriented teaching and learning in EFL. In characterising the historical development and interrelatedness of these traditions, he traces different ways how literature has been taken off the page, each of them grounded in particular theoretical frameworks and schools of thought. With this survey, Volkmann contextualises and elucidates recent calls to foster performative competences in the foreign language classroom and invites teachers to select from the wide array of activities these paradigms comprise.

While dramatic texts and activities have long played a role in classroom practice, researching the impact of drama-oriented teaching empirically remains a desideratum of research. The chapter by **Christiane Klempin** hence focuses on the effectiveness of drama-based instruction in EFL and ESL learning contexts. Her quasi-experimental study investigates the use of drama methods by teacher trainees in different school types. The results of the study indicate that there may be a need for in-depth training in drama pedagogy as part of teacher education courses. She further sketches out research perspectives for evaluating the effects of drama-based approaches on both teachers and learners of English.

In addition to empirical research, the field of drama in EFL learning also benefits from practice-oriented reports and reflections. In their contribution, **Lisa Peter** and **Annette Deschner** present the EU-funded project *CultureShake* in which multilingual students explore Shakespeare through drama techniques. After discussing advantages of treating multilingualism as a resource in language classrooms, the authors showcase a range of activities aimed at engaging learners with plays such as *A Midsummer Night's Dream* and *The Tempest*. These interactive and creative approaches encourage students to make their linguistic and cultural backgrounds and experiences an integral part of the learning process and lead to different forms of multilingual performance.

With the aim of drama-oriented teaching to open up spaces for participation and cooperation, such an approach can be regarded as dialogic in nature. **Werner Delanoy** explores this line of thought in the last chapter of this volume by drawing on a normative concept of dialogue, serving as a foundation to explore a play by the Irish writer Brian Friel and to design performative activities around the text. In the course of creating and implementing a drama-based project for university students, Delanoy, moreover, shows how assemblage theory can be harnessed as a tool to promote dialogue-friendly learning and teaching.

Drama-oriented and performative language teaching are facing new challenges in the digital age and they need to constantly readjust to new textualities and literacies, to emerging trends in pedagogy and to educational discourses in general. The role of literary texts and of reading practices seems to be undergoing major changes in foreign language classrooms. However, with the advent of new technologies and text formats, well-established teaching practices and traditions will also develop dynamically, ideally adapting to classroom affordances regarding interactivity, creativity, communication and collaboration. Drama-oriented and performative approaches offer the potential to frame this process and foster the development of multiple literacies for the futures of teaching.

Part I – Dramatic Texts, Textualities and Literacy Perspectives

MARIA EISENMANN (JULIUS-MAXIMILIANS-UNIVERSITÄT WÜRZBURG)

A Multiliteracies Approach to Teaching Plays

In light of multimodality and digitalisation this contribution will focus on the benefits of transforming dramatic texts into Internet-based products not only to educate competent and critical readers, but also to develop critical media literacy. The article will show how multiliteracy pedagogy offers a very helpful approach, which allows students to transform plays into their own designs such as computer adventures, short films or other forms of adaptations.

1. Multiliteracy pedagogy

The multiliteracies concept sees itself as a pedagogical answer to the manifold changes resulting from the consequences of globalisation and those brought by digital technology and the computer, which since the turn of the 20th century is causing an enormous change in almost all areas of life. The common denominator of 'multiple literacies' as developed by the New London Group (2000) and elaborated on by other scholars, especially more recently by Kalantzis and Cope (2012), is plurality and diversity. As a result of worldwide migration societies can be characterised by increasing ethnic, linguistic and cultural heterogeneity. At the same time, the technical possibilities of computer-based communication have grown tremendously, many different (e.g. hybrid) textual forms have been produced, making traditional literacy and a teaching concept based on a monolingual, monocultural pupil outdated. This means that it is no longer enough for literacy teaching to focus solely on the rules of standard forms of language and literature. The basic challenge is to preserve the diversity on the one hand and to enable active participation in social life on the other hand.

The growing importance of other semiotic systems and new forms of communication also entail new demands for EFL teaching such as an extended definition of text, flexible and interlinking use of the foreign language, integration of various media and modal forms of presentation as well as the development of further competences. Very often multiliteracies are associated with the skills of dealing with nonlinear texts, with visual or hybrid encodings in more than one semiotic system. And because language use today arises in part from the characteristics of the new information and communications media, meaning is made in ways that are increasingly multimodal, i.e. written-linguistic modes of meaning interface with oral, visual, audio, gestural, tactile and spatial patterns of meaning. Learners do not only have to be able to read and write in the classical sense, they also have to be able to decode and produce all kinds of combinations of different semiotic systems. This means that the range of multiliteracy pedagogy has to be extended so that it does not unduly privilege alphabetical representations, but brings multimodal representations into the classroom, particularly those typical of the new, digital media. This makes multiliteracy pedagogy all the more engaging for its manifest connections with today's communications contexts. It also provides a powerful foundation for a pedagogy of synaesthesia or mode switching, i.e. the process of shifting between modes and re-representing the same thing from one mode to another.

However, visual media are absolutely nothing new in teaching English, but their functions have changed over time. Historically, the use of pictures and images has always had a firmly established position in the EFL classroom (for a detailed historical outline see Hecke / Surkamp 2015: 19ff.). "In the 19th century and in the first half of the 20th century, pictures were mostly regarded as an integral part of making learning more vivid and interesting. Images were seen as conducive for motivation, repetition of information and greater attentiveness. After the communicative turn in the 1970s and 1980s, pictures primarily served to create speaking and writing incentives in the foreign language. In the 1990s with the advent of intercultural learning focusing on intercultural communicative competence, images have primarily been used to provide insights into other cultures" (Eisenmann / Meyer 2018: 11).

Today, new media and the digitalisation of everyday life have had an impact on dealing with pictures and images in the EFL classroom. Images are increasingly viewed under semiotic aspects and perceived as independent meaningful 'texts', which give insights into 'external', always already highly mediatised realities and must be decoded in an interpretative way. Today the variety of genres, the multimediality and the multimodality of text and material combination reflect the large number of forms of representation and symbolisation involved in the development of cultural ideas, interpretive paradigms, and ways of acting (see Kress 2010; Hallet 2011: 107ff.). According to the present state of research, multiliteracy pedagogy approaches are implemented in the following materials:

- Course books, where pictures have numerous functions, e.g. illustrative, instructive or aesthetic functions.
- Picture books because in a picture book illustrations are as important as the words in telling the story (e.g. Bland 2013; Bland / Lütge 2013).

- Multimodal novels, in which the textual world that is created and the narrative world that the reader constructs are fed from a variety of semiotic resources perceived through different senses (Hallet 2015; Eisenmann / Meyer 2018).

- Comics, graphic novels, mangas, which are nowadays an integral part of EFL teaching (e.g. Dong 2012; Ludwig / Pointner 2013).

- Films which have been employed in EFL teaching contexts for more than fifty years (e.g. Blell et al. 2016; Lütge 2012; Viebrock 2016).

- Internet which has strongly shifted attention to multiliteracies in the EFL classroom (Heim / Ritter 2012; Marenzi 2014).

- Gamification: While using games for supporting education and enhancing language learning is not a new phenomenon, the use of digital games is comparatively recent. Since the 1990s, there has been digital game-based learning (cf. Prensky 2001) and didactically prepared language learning games (cf. Seidl 2015: 294f.), whose affective added value should help the learning progress (Farber 2015; Gee 2007; Reinders 2012).

All these teaching materials somehow relate to multimodal literacies even if many of the publications do not explicitly use the terms 'multimodality' or 'multiliteracies'.

2. The potential of new media in the EFL classroom

Media-based language learning has always had the potential to cross the classroom's boundaries and create authentic, up-to-date learning situations. Computer-assisted e-learning has developed further into blended learning, so to speak a combination of online and face-to-face instruction. Nowadays, due to technical simplification digital media can be easily used without specific know-how. And there is a variety of resources for interaction for language acquisition, such as apps, tools or free mp3-downloads. This way digital learning is developing towards mobile learning, which promotes self-responsible and autonomous learning independent from time and place.

By virtue of the computer's ability to present content in a multimodal manner, different sensory channels and combinations of these modes of perception can be included, or as Baier et al. (2015: 288) put it: "Die Potentiale neuer Medien für den Unterricht werden bereits aus ihren psychologisch-pädagogischen

Kennzeichen der Multimodalität, Multicodierung und Multimedialität deutlich." In other words, multicoding enables the integration of several semiotic systems such as text, spoken language, sounds and music, pictures, animation and film. As web-based multimedia production and distribution tools are continuously growing, today's classrooms are faced with ever expanding opportunities to integrate new technologies into teaching and learning processes. This is closely linked to multimediality which allows quick access to an extensive online material selection in different medial forms. Thus different learning channels can be addressed, a variety of learning strategies considered and students' interests taken into account.

As online learning environments for today's learners make use of Internet sources with adaptable and adaptive software, the learning processes can be better individualised and differentiated. The concept of student-centered, self-directed and self-regulated learning has long been a pursuit of education and the integration of Web 2.0 tools and educational applications (edu apps) into learning designs seems to make a qualitative difference as it gives students a sense of ownership and control over their own learning and planning. Furthermore, there is also greater recognition of the potential of communication technologies to foster dialogue, networking and team skills among learners. Current research also points to a growing appreciation of the need to support and encourage learner control over the entire learning process (cf. Dron 2007; Eisenmann / Strohn 2012). In the context of individualised instruction, but also learner autonomy, the following range of practical and pedagogical affordances and potential advantages have been mentioned in recent publications (e.g. Eisenmann 2018: 76f.; Reinders / Hubbard 2013; Reinfried / Volkmann 2012):

- **Independence from time and place**: technology facilitates learners easy access to various kinds of resources at any time
- **Flexibility**: contents can easily and quickly be altered and offer new types of activities
- **Storage and retrieval**: technology allows for easy storage and retrieval of learning and teaching materials
- **Recyclability**: contents can be taken over by other learning contexts and environments
- **Distributions**: easy distributions of contents and sharing with others
- **Authenticity of materials**: learners use real-world materials that are relevant to their individual interests

- **Interaction**: opportunity of language usage in settings outside formal education, e.g., through email, chat and social networking sites; allows all participants to change the parameters, thus influence the learning process
- **Situated learning**: focus on the relationship between learning and the social situation of the learner, which is enabled by the use of technology that allows access to real-world settings
- **Multimediality**: with regard to their learning styles, learners decide about the fashion of input resources, e.g., film, text, listening example, etc.
- **Non-linearity of information**: contents can be displayed dynamically
- **Hypertextuality**: updating, networking and linking up information online
- **Feedback**: possibility to get feedback from the teacher and to connect with other learners to obtain peer-feedback

If teachers specifically select tools for their learners' purposes, new media offer a great potential for EFL teaching, including lessons on dramatic texts. Here, common features of new media and dramatic staging such as interactivity, cooperation and multimodality play a fundamental role. It is important to emphasise the myriad of possibilities the new media offer for presentation and staging which can be implemented in a relatively easy, varied and imaginative way. Through their unlimited and consistent availability and dissemination a wider audience can be reached. Moreover, due to the interactive elements the products of the digital stage offer, they are no longer just purely receptive but invite for collaboration.

3. Fostering performative competence through the use of dramatic texts

In view of the great variety of media, particularly the advent of new media, the theatre has long since ceded its leading role to film, television and, in recent years, to the digital media (see e.g. Waldmann 2008: 117f.; Baier et al. 2015: 291). Visiting the theatre or even reading dramatic texts does not seem to have high priority among young people today. Although no one seriously questions the cultural value of plays, the relevance of teaching dramatic texts in the EFL classroom is subject of controversial debate in foreign language learning (see e.g. Ahrens et al. 2008; Nowoczien 2012). The treatment of dramatic texts has a unique position in the field of literary texts. Nevertheless, in traditional and modern foreign language literature classes the genre is well-established and is used in the sense of aesthetic education as well as in the context of intercultural learning. This applies to plays as dramatic instruction in primary and secondary teaching as well as to didactically processed, adapted and authentic texts in more advanced learner groups.

Due to the dual nature of plays, i.e. two different forms of representation as printed text and as a performance, dramatic texts hold a special position compared to narrative and lyrical texts. Different to narrative or lyrical texts, plays should be read as scripts (see e.g. Gibson 2016) for scenic performance. This is particularly relevant for foreign language teaching with its goal of action-orientation (cf. Bach / Timm 2013: 11). A drama is not a text to read, but a score, a game design, an instruction for an active and productive scenic realisation (see Waldmann 2008: 2), which attributes the plurimedial character. Thus, dramatic instructions, aspects such as gestures, facial expressions, body posture, but also setting, equipment, props and dialogue structures play an essential role in the EFL classroom. Both in productive as well as in receptive approaches these aspects are central to the performance dimension. However, particular attention has to be paid to affective components and emotional involvement of the learners in acting out the play, or as Carola Surkamp explains: "Since the staging of dramatic texts is not a purely cognitive matter, but also challenges learners emotionally by stimulating different senses and activities (reading, listening, viewing, representing, feeling, explaining, etc.), it supports the formation of affective learning objectives. Performance-oriented approaches also contribute to pupils becoming aware of their own experiences, values, feelings, and imaginations, and encourage them to integrate these in the process of reception" (Surkamp 2015: 143f.). Moreover, acting allows learners to express their emotions and their personality through non-verbal communication, to train their spontaneity, creativity, and ability to associate, and therefore to strengthen their self-confidence.

What is more, by playfully adapting different identities while acting out, learners can also develop performative competence, an important real-life ability which has increasingly been discussed in foreign language teaching contexts (see e.g. Hallet 2008). Wolfgang Hallet calls this "staging lives" (Hallet 2008: 387ff.) and further explains that real-life situations are characterised by self-representations and stagings, which contribute significantly to the identification and development of students' identity in the sense of positioning the self in social space as well as the constitution of social interaction. Thus, everyday life self-staging / self-dramatisation (Selbstinszenierung) can be compared to social interaction in literary dramatic performances. These can be seen as a positive or negative model of personal and social productions and as models of interpersonal configurations with a view to the development of a performative real-life competence. This way the EFL classroom can function as a place to contribute to the formation of the performative competences (cf. Hallet 2008).

All these playful forms of dramatic work with texts in foreign language classes can be successfully implemented especially with the new media. The multifaceted functions of digital media open up almost infinite dimensions for creative and productive drama lessons. Digital media are particularly suitable because of being interactive, communicative, multimodal, multicodal, multimedial, involving students (flow experience) and audience (e.g. via Internet presentation) (see Baier et al. 2015: 293f.). Through their technical possibilities, new media open up a digital stage, because they not only preserve performances, but also make changes, post-processing and editing possible. Moreover, digital productions require different roles for the students comparable to theatre performances, such as screenplay, directing, dramaturgy, lighting, stage design, props, costumes etc. All roles require cooperative student interaction to ensure a successful production.

This approach can also play an important role for differentiation and individualisation in the EFL classroom because students are able to utilise and actively contribute their creativity and media skills obtained in any other context. This differentiation according to the students' readiness, learning styles, and interests not only serves to individualise the dramatic work, but it can also foster cooperative learning if the teacher decides to let students work together in pairs or small groups. This is an individualising teaching strategy which not only addresses learners who like to deal with literary texts or have an acting talent, but also those who prefer to work with the technical side of the implementation. All of the scenic-dramatic work with media should be carried out in small groups working autonomously and collaboratively, which strengthens the students' self-confidence.

4. Practical implementation – Suggestions for the EFL classroom

When looking at the characteristics of digital media and dramatic texts with regard to a scenic-dramatic implementation in the classroom, parallels can be seen that indicate a high degree of compatibility. The current evolution of the combination of theatrical performances with new media on traditional stages supports this hypothesis. For instance, in 2016 William Shakespeare's *The Tempest* was staged in Stratford (and transferred to the Barbican) by using a digital avatar who embodied the character of Ariel (see online references). This way the avatar was brought into the world of Shakespeare's play to work seamlessly in real time, interacting with live actors and bringing a unique modern update to the production. The active uptake of such elements in a process-oriented teaching approach can be implemented by a **preparatory phase**, a **supporting phase** and a **follow-up phase**. This systematisation makes it particularly easier to see how and where scenic-dramatic processes with digital media can be taught according to a tight curriculum. In the following my choice fell on some examples of Shakespeare because of the level of recognition his plays enjoy.

Preparatory phase

As part of preparatory procedures, the students are being prepared to engage to the text and to their own associations accordingly. A media-based start to scenic-dramatic processes can be a classic Internet-based research which might be overtaxing for some students by getting lost in hyperspace. To avoid this, students and teachers can also make use of already existing conversions or adaptations of the respective plays via portals such as YouTube (e.g. "Romeo and Juliet in 3 minutes", "Macbeth in 96 seconds" or "Hamlet in 60 seconds", see online references).

Based on digital media, computer quests or computer adventures related to the text can also arouse students' interest and curiosity on the subject and give first insights into setting, time and character constellations. A computer adventure based on a drama enables the learners to put themselves into the position of others and to empathise with a character. An adventure game is a game story in which the player usually guides a hero/protagonist through complex virtual worlds. Adventure games are all about unravelling stories, exploring worlds and solving puzzles, usually within a narrative framework, generally with few or no action elements.

In adventure games the players experience themselves as fictional characters of a fictive world, which they can freely explore and which offers multiple options for action and thus meets the constructivist requirements of a complex learning environment. Students immerse themselves in the special game world that have their own inherent set of rules and laws, which are first revealed in the exploration of this world. Such an approach corresponds to the methodology of exploratory and action-oriented learning. Above that, there is an emotional involvement of the players through their attachment to the avatar, who as a representative interacts directly with the world of the game. By means of digital technology action and decision options of the characters can be experienced. In the computer's secure simulative space an authentic testing of role behaviour takes place, which creates a bridge between gaming and playing. In interacting with other characters of the play, attitudes, beliefs and inclinations are constantly negotiated on the one hand. On the other hand, the conflicts of interest created in the drama also come into focus and can be experienced in terms of the characters' relationships. The sensitivity for crucial scenes and key situations in the drama is trained, connected with questions about alternative endings of the text.

In the context of dealing with Shakespeare, a very suitable tool is the literary computer adventure series called "The Chronicles of Shakespeare", produced by Daedalic Entertainment, which is devoted to the work of William Shakespeare (see online references). In 2013, the series began with "Romeo & Juliet", which tells the story of the couple of love in verses, and lets the players become part of the story themselves. Using the computer game "The Chronicles of Shakespeare – Romeo & Juliet" consists of the task to play the story of *Romeo and Juliet* on the computer. The students are expected to find different objects within the frame story with the help of detailed, unmoved or slightly animated pictures in order to continue the story. The access to the game is almost self-explanatory and can quickly be grasped and understood. The actual story is not unnecessarily lengthened and a pleasant narrative flow is possible, which is continued in short video sequences between the searching tasks. This gamification approach is very beneficial because students are turned into problem solvers and the game allows them to engage in friendly competitions. Above that, it helps them to analyse and decode multimodalities, which enhances multiliteracies.

Supporting phase

This gamification approach can, of course, also be used while actually working with the text. Moreover, in this phase digital media can generally help to implement or support different forms of performative, scenic work. This is equally true for scenic reading as well as role and acting out elements. Scenic-dramatic processes with new media can be developed, for example, by creating websites. In a modified way, you can create a profile of drama characters or character profiles of classic drama figures in social computer networks such as Facebook or Twitter. By setting up a Facebook or Twitter account for a character the students have to deal intensively with the literary creation of characters in order to develop a sustainable profile. Moreover, they inevitably have to think about character traits which are not explicitly elaborated in the text. The filling of these blank spaces thus requires the ability to change perspectives, which has become increasingly important for EFL teaching in the last decades. Short characterisations of different dramas and characters can be found on Facebook in large numbers. All you need to do is enter the name of a character and the name of the text to refer to numerous profile pages. For example, you will find over 200 profiles for Lady Macbeth or profiles for Hamlet. Reactions of other users to such character profiles come from all around the world, which might lead to stimulating classroom discussions. As a result, it can be expected that well-prepared character profiles of various dramas created in the classroom will encourage in-depth authentic discussions. Already in 2010 the Royal Shakespeare Company London developed a Twitter-based version of *Romeo & Juliet* named "Such Tweet Sorrow", where Twitter users can follow the storyline by subscribing to the actors' tweets. In this version the story is retold and set into the 21st century (see online references).

Another digital option beyond social media is to encourage students to produce short films on their own. The continuation of given scenes (preferably the core parts of the text) through the production of short film sequences builds equally on both the creativity of the students and the exchange possibilities that digital media offer. In practical terms, this means learners may be asked to fill in gaps and breaks in the storyline on their own after having been provided with various sets of drama excerpts as film clips on a learning platform (e.g. the opening scene and the final scene of a play). The task for the learners is to fill the gap between the given scenes with their own productions and to transfer them into a video format.

The use of digital technology significantly expands the manifold possibilities and the creative potential for the EFL classroom. This can be implemented by making the learners act out scenes by themselves or by hand puppets assuming the role of actresses and actors. Equally conceivable is the creation of brick films with stop-trick elements or to choose Barbie or Playmobil figures as well as sock-puppets in their life action short films. There are many types of short films pupils can produce as well as manifold techniques and a range of computer software for the production process. Students can use mobile phones, digital photo or video cameras to shoot their films. Most students use mobile phones for photography and filming in their daily lives and, hence, may be used to the filming process and motivated to apply their knowledge in school (cf. Matz / Rogge 2014: 324).

As an inspiring example, pre-existing scenes on YouTube can be viewed. Afterwards, the video scenes created by the students can also be displayed on the learning platform uploaded and presented, substantiated and discussed in the process of plenary discussions. Through this process the tension between theatre performance, literary, aesthetic and cultural knowledge as well as linguistic-communicative competences is systematically explored. (cf. Baier et al. 2015: 300f.).

It has to be pointed out that it should always be the students' choice whether they prefer to act out scenes themselves or whether they would rather use other resources. A great option for the students' own productions are animated short films which are usually produced by photographing a series of gradually changing drawings, single images or frames, which give the illusion of movement when played back in a fast sequence. Among computer animated films there are many different animation techniques such as cartoons, finger or sock puppet, silhouette animation, clay motion or Shakespeare in Lego (cf. Matz / Rogge 2014: 324; Henseler et al. 2011: 147). After importing these images (Lego figures, puppets or paper cut-outs) into a computer, they can then be sequenced into a film with the help of free film software such as Windows Moviemaker or iMovie.[2] It is also possible to add a soundtrack in which students insert sound effects or music and read out dialogues from the play. Adding theme music, sound effects, and/or voiceovers is crucial in the success of any stop motion animation. Sound sets a mood, adds to a story, and supports the viewers in understanding the action. Students can find plenty of theme music and sound effects online or in apps to use throughout their project.

But teachers should not forget that most of the students are not experienced users of film software and should be allowed to practice before they actually start with filming their stop motion animations. The pupils can use this practice period to animate everyday objects such as books, papers, scissors, pencils, etc. The students should have time to get used to the equipment and experiment with making objects disappear and reappear in a different place.

And what is more, the transformation of knowledge based on a literary text into new contexts still seems to be a highly demanding task for most students, both cognitively and linguistically. Therefore, the students' own film productions require temporary support structures provided by teachers, such as situated

---

[2] For creating stop motion animation with an iPad, an app has to be installed. There are plenty of stop motion animation apps on the Internet to choose from. Two of them – Stop Motion Studio and iStopMotion – work well for any in class stop motion animation lesson.

learning and scaffolding, in order to equip them with the necessary knowledge and skills to successfully carry out the task. From a multiliteracies' perspective, teachers need to help students to understand the design of dramatic texts and assist them in transforming these forms of meaning into their own interpretation of the text (cf. Cope / Kalantzis 2012: 214). This very special way of dealing with literature is considered an active construction of new understanding by transforming knowledge, taking on new perspectives and critically assessing prior understanding. Scaffolding, in this perspective, provides the necessary support that learners need to successfully accomplish such complex learning tasks (cf. Matz / Rogge 2014: 319). Next to learning how to deal with the technical equipment, the teacher can help with the following guideline questions concerning the setting, the characters and the plot:

Setting	Characters	Plot
Where does the scene take place? Why/How do you know that? Which props do you need?	Who of the characters should be in your film? What do the characters look like? How do they feel? Are they scared / happy / angry/...?	What happens in your scene? What do the characters do? First... then... finally...

In order to create their own animated video with images, video clips, and music, students can also engage in digital storytelling by using Internet tools such as e.g. Animaker (see online references). It allows students to develop videos in which characters speak with lip-synchronization and move around. They can choose from character models, backgrounds, properties, sound effects and other elements to create their videos easily and quickly, without having to draw or download anything. This kind of graphic adaptation offers students the opportunity to make their own animated films. The technical simplicity of Animaker should convince even the most reluctant teachers that using this digital tool will improve lessons and learning without demanding much technical experience.

It is a very creative approach that can facilitate a better understanding of the plays' language, the characters as well as a practical application of media literacy, or as Nancy Grimm and Julia Hammer posit: "Digital storytelling pushes students beyond creating simple slide shows or presentations about the text, requiring them to incorporate their own opinions and perspectives" (Grimm / Hammer 2015: 334f.).

If carefully prepared and planned, digital storytelling can make literary texts come alive. In terms of scaffolding, productive, meaningful and stimulating tasks activate and motivate students as well as develop their critical awareness. The tool caters to creative approaches to understanding a dramatic text by inviting students to discuss their creative choices and collaborate in creating the animated film. Furthermore, students can publish their digital stories on a blog and encourage classmates to view and comment on them. This way tools such as Animaker offer a wide range of creative options for students to select and discuss and thus facilitate media literacy.

Another very creative as well as useful tool is toondoo (see online references) which helps students to create their own cartoons. It can be used on several levels (beginners, intermediate or advanced) and allows students to get deeper into the play's plot, setting and characters. The tool offers a vast variety of characters, props and backgrounds categorised into specific galleries. Students can either make use of this choice or create their own characters by uploading images from their own mobile devices or from anywhere else.

Transforming a script or play into a performance like this not only visualises the plot structure of the text, but recreates it using the imaginations of the pupils, thus moving beyond the textual base. The so-called toons can later be embedded in blogs, websites or forums, the comic strips can be shared, mailed, tagged, recommended and bookmarked. Moreover, the tool invites students to discuss their creative choices and collaborate in combining multiple toons into a toonbook.

Generally, while-reading as well as post-reading activities should not only help students' comprehension of the entire play, but also concentrate on their personal reaction to the text. In re-writing the plot using a different viewpoint or even genre, students demonstrate not only their understanding of the plot, characters, and message of the play they have read, but also train their literary competences. The multiliteracies approach as developed by the New London Group, especially more recently by Kalantzis and Cope (2012), suggests that a learning process is only really successful when students transform a text into another genre (or design) as they will only then create their own meaning, making the learned knowledge their own.

Follow-up phase

In case there is no need for re-work and the production has already been finalised, in a follow-up phase the manifold products can be shared in the classroom. This post-production phase can be done by a general viewing lesson where the students watch all the videos, digital stories and cartoons created. Since the films are relatively short (usually no longer than about five minutes), their presentation does not last long, all films can be viewed and discussed in one go.

After each film the whole class as well as the teacher should be given a few minutes to ask questions and/or comment on what they have just seen. Before moving on, the film producers should also have the possibility to review and reflect on their own projects. In terms of evaluation and assessment the following questions can be discussed:

- How are the characters presented?
- What is indicated about their relationship, their feelings, their states of mind?
- Which part of the extract is emphasised?
- How is this scene designed? How does the design fit to the action?
- What effect do music, light, colours and props have in this scene?
- Is it an informative reproduction of the scene?
- How would I judge the extent and value of creativity in this film version?
- Does the transfer of the scene work in this context?
- Comment on the interpretation of the passage.

(cf. The New London Group 2000: 248)

By contrasting different ways of adapting a text into another design, such reflection phases can also be used in the classroom to demonstrate various interpretations of a play.

5. Conclusion

Transforming a text into a new, individualised digital form is suitable for a multiliteracies approach and for competence-oriented teaching that aims to prepare students for digital discourse in times of the Internet. New meanings are created by transforming available resources into new, individual and often multi-modal designs. At the same time narrative, audiovisual and media-critical competences are being enhanced with this method. With the enormous changes in communication technologies that have been taking place since the early 1990s now allow for oral, audio, visual and gestural meaning in a way that was not possible with the written word. The multiliteracies approach to dramatic texts takes into account not only changing technical innovations but also globalisation processes by providing students with the relevant skills that are firmly grounded in the students' lifeworlds.

Multi-channeling and interaction are hallmarks of modern digital media as well as traditional theatre. By using these media scenic-dramatic realisations can be set into the students' lifeworlds and thus be very beneficial for enhancing receptive as well as productive skills. The exchange of texts in the broadest sense enlarge and deepen literary-aesthetic insights, cultural knowledge and communicative skills. As a result, different perspectives on theatre and drama can playfully be explored within this method pool.

Bibliography

Ahrens, Rüdiger / Eisenmann, Maria / Merkl, Matthias (eds.) (2008). *Moderne Dramendidaktik für den Englischunterricht*. Heidelberg: Winter.

Bach, Gerhard / Timm, Johannes-Peter (eds.) (^{5}2013). *Englischunterricht. Grundlagen und Methoden einer handlungsorientierten Unterrichtspraxis*. Tübingen: Francke.

Baier, Jochen / Buhrle, Jasmin / Gecius, Melanie (2015). Szenisch-dramatische Verfahren und Aufführungen mit digitalen Medien und Internetformaten. In: Hallet, Wolfgang / Surkamp, Carola (eds.). *Handbuch Dramendidaktik und Dramapädagogik im Fremdsprachenunterricht*. Trier: WTV, 287-304.

Bland, Janice (2013). *Children's Literature and Learner Empowerment. Children and Teenagers in English Language Education*. London: Bloomsbury.

Bland, Janice / Christiane Lütge (eds.) (2013). *Children's Literature in Second Language Education*. London: Bloomsbury.

Blell, Gabriele / Grünewald, Andreas / Kepser, Matthias / Surkamp, Carola (eds.) (2016). *Film in den Fächern der sprachlichen Bildung*. Baltmannsweiler: Schneider Hohengehren.

Dong, Lan (2012). Introduction. Reading and Teaching Graphic Narratives. In: Dong, Lan (ed.). *Teaching Comics and Graphic Narratives: Essays on Theory, Strategy and Practice.* Jefferson, NC: McFarland, 5-10.

Eisenmann, Maria (2018). Differentiation and Individualisation through Digital Media. In: Van de Poel, Kris / Ludwig, Christian (eds.). *Collaborative Language Learning and New Media: Insights into an Evolving Field.* Frankfurt: Lang, 73-86.

Eisenmann, Maria / Meyer, Michael (eds.) (2018). Multimodality and Multiliteracy. *Theme Issue of ANGLISTIK* 1.

Eisenmann, Maria / Meyer, Michael (2018). Multimodality and Multiliteracies. In: Eisenmann, Maria / Meyer, Michael (eds.). Multimodality and Multiliteracy. *Theme Issue of ANGLISTIK* 1, 5-23.

Eisenmann, Maria / Strohn, Meike (2012). Promoting Learner Autonomy in Mixed-ability Classes by Using Webquests and Weblogs. In: Heim, Katja / Rüschoff, Bernd: *Involving Language Learners: Success Stories and Constraints.* Duisburg: Universitätsverlag Rhein Ruhr, 145-158.

Farber, Matthew (2015). *Gamify Your Classroom: A Field Guide to Game-Based Learning.* New York: Lang.

Gee, James Paul (2007). *What Video Games Have to Teach Us about Learning and Literacy.* New York, NY: Palgrave Macmillan.

Gibson, Rex (2016). *Teaching Shakespeare. A Handbook for Teachers.* Cambridge: CUP.

Grimm, Nancy / Hammer, Julia (2015). Performative Approaches and Innovative Methods. In: Delanoy, Werner / Eisenmann, Maria / Matz, Frauke (eds.). *Learning with Literature in the EFL Classroom.* Frankfurt: Lang, 321-339.

Hallet, Wolfgang (2008). Staging Lives: Die Entwicklung performativer Kompetenz im Englischunterricht. In: Ahrens, Rüdiger / Eisenmann, Maria / Merkl, Matthias (eds.). *Moderne Dramendidaktik für den Englischunterricht.* Heidelberg: Winter, 387-408.

Hallet, Wolfgang (2011). *Lernen fördern. Englisch: kompetenzorientierter Unterricht in der Sekundarstufe I.* Seelze: Klett-Kallmeyer.

Hallet, Wolfgang (2015). Teaching Multimodal Novels. In: Delanoy, Werner / Eisenmann, Maria / Matz, Frauke (eds.). *Learning with Literature in the EFL Classroom.* Frankfurt: Lang, 283-298.

Hecke, Carola / Carola Surkamp (eds.) (^{2}2015). *Bilder im Fremdsprachenunterricht: Neue Ansätze, Kompetenzen und Methoden.* Tübingen: Narr.

Heim, Katja / Markus Ritter (2012). *Teaching English: Computer-Assisted Language Learning.* Paderborn: Schöningh.

Henseler, Roswitha / Möller, Stefan / Surkamp, Carola (2011). *Filme im Englischunterricht. Grundlagen, Methoden, Genres.* Seelze: Klett/Kallmeyer.

Kalantzis, Mary / Cope, Bill (2000). A Multiliteracies Pedagogy: A Pedagogical Supplement. In: Cope, Bill / Kalantzis, Mary (eds.). *Multiliteracies: Literary Learning and the Designs of Social Futures*. London: Routledge, 239-248.

Kalantzis, Mary / Cope, Bill (2012). *Literacies*. Cambridge: CUP.

Kress, Gunther R. (2010). *Multimodality: A Social Semiotic Approach to Contemporary Communication*. London: Routledge.

Lütge, Christiane (2012). *Mit Filmen Englisch unterrichten: [Sekundarstufe I/II]*. Berlin: Cornelsen.

Ludwig, Christian / Frank Erik Pointner (2013). *Teaching Comics in the English Language Classroom*. Trier: WVT.

Marenzi, Ivana (2014). *Multiliteracies and E-learning 2.0*. Frankfurt am Main: Lang.

Matz, Frauke / Rogge, Michael (2014). Shakespeare in Shorts: A Multiliteracy Approach to Teaching Shakespeare. In: Eisenmann, Maria / Lütge, Christiane (eds.). *Shakespeare in the EFL Classroom*. Heidelberg: Winter, 315-330.

Nowoczien, Jessica (2012). *Drama in the Classroom: Dramenarbeit im Englischunterricht der Sekundarstufe I im Hinblick auf Gendersensibilisierung und interkulturelle Kommunikation*. Frankfurt am Main: Lang.

Prensky, Marc (2001). *Digital Game-Based Learning*. New York: McGraw-Hill.

Reinders, Hayo (2012). *Digital Games in Language Learning and Teaching*. Basingstoke: Palgrave Macmillan.

Reinders, Hayo / Hubbard, Philip (2013). CALL and Learner Autonomy: Affordances and Constraints. In: Thomas, Michael / Reinders, Hayo / Warschauer, Mark (eds.). *Contemporary Computer-Assisted Language Learning*. New York: Continuum, 359-375.

Reinfried, Marcus / Volkmann, Laurenz (eds.) (2012). *Medien im neokommunikativen Fremdsprachenunterricht: Einsatzformen, Inhalte, Lernerkompetenzen*; Beiträge zum IX. Mediendidaktischen Kolloquium an der Friedrich-Schiller-Universität Jena. Frankfurt am Main: Lang.

Seidl, Monika (^{2}2015). 'SlashSit' und andere Geschichten vom Sitzen: Geschlechtertsreotype in Bildermedien und Computerspielen und ihre Untersuchung im Fremdsprachenunterricht. In: Surkamp, Carola / Hecke Carola (eds.). *Bilder im Fremdsprachenunterricht: Neue Ansätze, Kompetenzen und Methoden*. Tübingen: Narr, 294-311.

Surkamp, Carola (2015). Playful Learning with Short Plays. In: Delanoy, Werner / Eisenmann, Maria / Matz, Frauke (eds.). *Learning with Literature in the EFL Classroom*. Frankfurt am Main: Lang, 141-156.

The New London Group (2000). A Pedagogy of Multiliteracies. Designing Social Futures. In: Cope, Bill / Kalantzis, Mary (eds.). *Multiliteracies. Literacy Learning and the Design of Social Futures*. London, New York: Routledge, 9-37.

Viebrock, Britta (eds.) (2016). *Feature Films in English Language Teaching*. Tübingen: Narr Francke Attempto.

Waldmann, Günter (^{5}2008). *Produktiver Umgang mit dem Drama. Eine systematische Einführung in das produktive Verstehen traditioneller und moderner Dramenformen und das Schreiben in ihnen. Für Schule und Hochschule.* Baltmannsweiler: Schneider Hohengehren.

Online References

The Tempest: https://edition.cnn.com/style/article/shakespeare-the-tempest/index.html (04/07/21)
Romeo and Juliet in 3 min: https://www.youtube.com/watch?v=sbxAwDauDwo (04/07/21)
Macbeth in 96 seconds: https://www.youtube.com/watch?v=F5nlx2XzP-4 (04/07/21)
Hamlet in 60 seconds: https://www.youtube.com/watch?v=74Jr7IhWJTs (04/07/21)
Daedelic Entertainment http://www.daedalic.de (04/07/21)
Such Sweet Sorrow (@Such_Tweet): https://twitter.com/such_tweet?lang=de (04/07/21)
Othello in Lego: https://www.youtube.com/watch?v=fFxTa-92Hk4 (04/07/21)
Sock Puppet Shakespeare: https://www.youtube.com/watch?v=6pgE3LFAR98 (04/07/21)
Animaker: https://www.animaker.com (04/07/21)
Toondoo: http://www.toondoo.com (04/07/21)

CHRISTIAN LUDWIG (FREIE UNIVERSITÄT BERLIN)

'Hemel op die Platteland' – Reading Lara Foot's Play *Reach* in the EFL Classroom

South Africa held its first multiracial democratic elections in 1994, bringing the ANC to power. Since then, the country has been attempting to overcome the legacy of colonial exploitation and racial oppression, particularly present during the time of apartheid from 1948 until the early 1990s. The historical burden of more than five decades of mutual hatred and violence, however, continues to resonate today. Nevertheless, South African literature in general, and theatre in particular, are increasingly freeing themselves from the country's past and have come to produce complex, multilayered texts which not only have changed in content but also in style. Against this background, the present article introduces its readers to the cultural and historic context of South Africa, particularly emphasising the political, cultural, social, and linguistic challenges the New South Africa is facing. The major part of the contribution then focuses on contemporary South African drama and its relevance for the EFL classroom. Laura Foot's highly acclaimed play 'Reach' explores the lives of two entirely contrasting individuals both trying to come to terms with their traumatic experiences and the fundamental and radical transformations of a country they still call home. Practical suggestions for dealing with South African plays in the EFL classroom with the support of digital media conclude the article.

1. Introduction

English as a foreign language teaching is no longer restricted to the former core English cultures and literatures of the United States and the British Isles (cf. Eisenmann / Grimm / Volkmann 2010; Delanoy / Eisenmann / Matz 2015) but has come to include countries as diverse as New Zealand, Singapore, India, and Jamaica. One of the results of this is that the complexity of 'the African experience' has become an attractive gateway for discussing a plethora of critical issues such as gender, religious and ethnic diversity, distribution of resources, ecological destruction, and many others in the English as a foreign language (EFL) classroom.

This contribution focuses on South Africa, which has undergone extensive reform in its attempt to overcome the legacy of colonialism and apartheid. South Africa as a topic can be deemed particularly suitable for the EFL classroom as its linguistic, cultural, and socio-economic diversity offers considerable scope for students to address perennial trends and issues. In addition to this,

South African stories are more than just South African stories as they illustrate the lived realities of millions of people around the globe (cf. Feuerle 2010: 43-58). Thus, dealing with these stories in the classroom can help to enhance students' inter- and transcultural competence (cf. Anton 2019: 233-252) as well as raise their awareness of global issues.

Since the official end of apartheid (from the Afrikaans word for apartness), the institutionalised social and spatial segregation of racial and ethnic communities, in 1994, South Africa has undergone several transformative processes, attempting, at least superficially, to bring the people of this vast multiethnic, multicultural, and multilingual country closer together. This troubled past and its influence on the present are also reflected in the country's diverse body of literature, which has gained increasing international popular and scholarly attention in recent years (cf. Heywood 2004). This is particularly true for literature written by and for the younger generation. As Partridge (2011: n.p.) has it: "[i]t is an interesting time to be a youth writer in South Africa. […] Our writers have their fingers on the pulse". In a similar vein, Stadler (2017: 5) points out that

> [t]heir texts tackle the new hot spots of South African society, which are located in both the public sphere (education, youth unemployment, economic policies, etc.) and the private sphere (family, lack of adult role models, identity, sexually transmitted diseases, value orientation, importance of peer groups, etc.).

This contribution suggests moving away from the vibrant South African film (cf. Bartosch 2017: 207-220; Ludwig 2020) and novel scene and paying closer attention to South African theatre. This promises particularly worthwhile as "[i]nnumerable performances in a diversity of South African theatre settings have confronted crises in the social order" (Heywood 2004: 72). This is not only true for theatre in the past but also more recent plays written and performed in South Africa.

The article commences by briefly establishing a historical framework, particularly focusing on the decades of (post-)apartheid. The ensuing section then provides an overview of the current challenges South Africa is facing in the light of a weak economy, corruption, poverty, and discrimination. The next section then takes a closer look at both apartheid and contemporary theatre, exploring the fractures in contemporary South African society (cf. Peimer 2013: 131-144). Lara Foot's *Reach*, which sketches the lives of two entirely different individuals who share an emotionally charged history, then serves as an example of the new directions contemporary South African theatre is taking. The contribution concludes by providing practical ideas for approaching the play in the EFL classroom, allowing students to experience the harsh but hopeful realities of life in contemporary South Africa and relate them to their own contexts.

Here, the focus is on how digital media can help to increase the students' engagement with both the text and its cultural context.

2. A rather brief history of South Africa

The complex and precarious situation in South Africa is closely intertwined with its long and troublesome history, particularly the period of colonialism and the era of apartheid (for a more detailed discussion of South Africa's history see Thompson 2001). Especially for (post-)secondary EFL students it is important to gain a basic understanding of South Africa's history as the country's current situation cannot be understood without making references to history. Thus, it helps to address (global) questions such as:

- Why are South Africa's cultures not only different from each other but also different from our own?
- Why does South Africa struggle to overcome the legacy of racial oppression and economic exploitation?
- Why is finding a shared or national identity so difficult for contemporary South Africans?

Thus, engaging with multifaceted historical, social, and political processes of South Africa's ongoing nation building project can ultimately lead students towards becoming more aware and developing a better understanding of their own culture(s) and other cultures across the world.

The colonial history of what today is South Africa goes back to when the Dutch East India Company under the leadership of Jan van Riebeeck established a permanent, secure camp at the Cape. This was not only followed by a long period of immigration from the European mainland but also skirmishes, wars, and mutual land seizures (cf. Stapleton 2010: 1-86) among the Dutch and the British colonial powers as well as between the settlers and the native population. The Union of South Africa (*Unie van Suid-Afrika*) came into being in 1910 when the former British colonies and the territory of the former Boer republics unified for the first time. In 1925, English and Afrikaans became the two official languages, with Afrikaans being the language for the social engineering project of a society based on white supremacy. While the Union of South Africa was largely autonomous from the United Kingdom, it only gained independence in 1931. Thirty years later, in 1961, South Africa became a republic under the name of Republic of South Africa (*Republiek van Suid-Afrika*).

After many years of often already institutionalised racial segregation and discrimination, apartheid was officially introduced in South Africa in 1948 by the right-wing National party, which was ruling at the time, to 'stop the spread of communism in the region' and to 'secure the equal development of the different cultural groups'. The main and real reason for introducing apartheid, however, was to protect the white status quo. These racist sentiments among the Afrikaners, the descendants of the early Dutch settlers, were deeply engrained in white culture, partly due to the survival of the traditional, ultra-conservative form of Calvinistic theology (cf. Washington Jr. 1987). Apartheid itself was based on a collection of laws which cemented a de facto racial segregation, for example prohibiting mixed marriages (1949), freedom of movement and settlement among the non-white population (1950) as well as equal education (1953). The pass laws may serve as an example here to illustrate the perfidity of the apartheid system. Passbooks represented a form of internal passport system which required most African men to carry around a little booklet, when being outside their designated areas, stating exactly which areas their bearers were granted or denied access to. Violating the law entailed a fine or, if the person was unable or unwilling to pay the money, arrest. It was only in 1986 that the law was repelled in the attempt to avoid a regime change by removing some of the apartheid laws.

While by far not all white South Africans supported the system of segregation, resistance came largely from black and coloured resistance groups such as the African National Congress (ANC), which has been in power uninterruptedly since 1994. Formed in Bloemfontein in 1912, the principles of the ANC were initially dialogue, petition and direct opposition without involving any armed struggle. After 1949, however, the ANC took a more militant path, increasing their strike actions, protests, and other forms of non-violent resistance. The main faces of the ANC were Oliver Reginald Tambo (1917-1993), Nelson Mandela (1918-2013), and Walter Sisulu (1912-2003). In 1969, the black consciousness movement (BC), led by Steve Biko, a medical student from East London, started and continued even after his death in 1977. After 1973, apartheid was drawing even more international attention than before when it was labeled a crime against humanity in the very same year. In 1976, a mandatory UN embargo prohibited the sales of weapons to South Africa, followed by sanctions by the United Kingdom and the United States. With a growing resistance inside the country and in the attempt to appease the international community, many of the apartheid laws were abolished under the government of Pieter Willem Botha (1916-2006), who was President from 1984 until 1989. This, however, came too late to calm down the broad masses and the country found itself on the brink of civil war until the state of emergency was declared in 1985. When

Botha stepped down in 1989, F.W. de Klerk became South Africa's last white President until today. In 1990, Mandela was released from prison and together with de Klerk he negotiated the end of apartheid and a peaceful transition, commonly referred to as the Negotiated Revolution. In 1994, the first free elections led to a coalition government with a nonwhite majority, marking the official end of the apartheid system. Until today, apartheid has remained one of the most shaping periods of South Africa's history.

3. The new South Africa — Clouds over the Rainbow Nation?

Today's multiethnic South Africa faces a number of problems, most of which have a strong racial dimension. Poverty and unemployment among large parts of the population remain two of the most pressing ones, making South Africa one of the most unequal countries in the world. In addition to this, violence, discrimination, and harassment remain constant challenges to the project of building of a more equal society. For example, according to a recent 2018 survey by Statistics South Africa on crime perpetrated against women, females remain one of the main target groups of rape and murder. The report states further that 68,5% of victims of sexual offences were women, resulting in a number of 138 women raped per 100,000 inhabitants. To quote Statistics Africa: "This figure is among the highest in the world. For this reason, some have labelled South Africa as the 'rape capital of the world'" (ibid.: n.p.). The situation of women is only one of the many examples of the clashes between (African) tradition and (Western) modernity in contemporary South African society which affect all areas of life and interact to produce a hybrid culture.

Notwithstanding the country's intention to overcome segregation and racism during the years of transition from apartheid to democracy, both issues still play a large role in South African society today. Despite affirmative action in form of the often criticised BBBEE, i.e. Broad-Based Black Economic Empowerment, aiming at diminishing the prosperity gap between the different ethnic groups, racism is still tangible in many areas of life. In addition to this, (perceived) reverse racism, a not empirically grounded discrimination of white South Africans by people of colour has become a major problem in today's society (cf. Garner 2017). According to the South African Reconciliation Barometer, an annual public opinion survey conducted by the Policy and Analysis Programme at the Institute for Justice and Reconciliation in Cape Town, less than half of South Africans do socialise with people from another race while only one fifth of white South Africans live in integrated communities. The institute paints an even gloomier picture for racial integration at a school level with only a small number of both white and black children attending racially integrant schools. Many of the issues described in the previous section play a role in contemporary South African literature in general and theatre in particular, a topic which will be discussed in the ensuing section.

4. Theatre in South Africa

As Orkin (1991: 2 as qtd. in Heywood 2004: 72) posits for theatre in South Africa: "[t]he attempt to engage with the social order, the presentation of the subject within the South African space on stage, has never been easy". Suffice it to say that South African theatre, both in English and Afrikaans, before apartheid, has a long history which, due to its complex and entangled history, cannot be discussed here in greater detail (cf. Orkin 1991: Heywood 2004 for a more detailed discussion). Anti-imperial theatre, for example, goes back to the English occupation of the Cape area. As Heywood (ibid.: 74) points out:

> Unlike the English theatre tradition, which focused on classics and commercials from the London stage, the Afrikaans tradition focused on crises in national history, notably the achievement of independent identity beyond Dutch colonial administration, and the Trek, which sought liberation from the military style of the British administration.

During apartheid, plays were often staged under difficult circumstances such as small budgets and a draconic censorship. Theatre was often seen as a weapon against the state and the oppression of the apartheid regime which is reflected in the different forms of protest theatre, a form of theatre which had developed under the white government, such as the Black Consciousness Theatre and theatre by members of the white minority, an insurgency against the privileges they possessed. Many of the plays of that time had been produced in mixed workshops, which often led to highly stereotyped characters and simplified narratives (cf. Peimer 2009: viii-x). Thus, in the almost entire absence of *l'art pour l'art*, many plays lacked subtle characters and depth, drawing the viewers' attention to the binaries of race and justice versus injustice, inherent to society at that time. One of the most popular South African plays from that period is *Woza Albert!* (transl. *Come Albert!*) by Percy Mtwa, Mbongeni Ngema, and Arena Simon (1981), which also gained wide international recognition. The satirical play imagines that Christ comes to apartheid South Africa. In order to kill Jesus, the apartheid government launches a nuclear bomb but some of the leaders of the fight against apartheid rise again from the destroyed country. Athol Fugard, John Kani, and Winston Ntshona's *The Island* (1973) is another example of a play which was successfully performed in South Africa despite the strict censorship during the 1970s (cf. Heywood 2004: 178-193; Peimer 2009: viii-x). The play is set in a prison which closely resembles Robben Island, where Nelson Mandela was kept in a small cell for many years. The cellmates, one of them hoping for an early release from the prison, work hard during the day, while at night they rehearse for a performance of Sophocles' *Antigone*, drawing parallels between the prisoners' situation and Antigone.

Almost 20 years after the Negotiated Revolution and the resolution of the Truth and Reconciliation Commission (TRC), which commenced in 1996 to give victims and culprits the opportunity to come to terms with their traumatic experiences,

> [...] new methods of capturing and conveying the subjective and societal revelations of truth, the discovery of the 'Other', the collective and individual trauma are being explored by artists and theatre-makers. Additional important themes include the complexities of new-found freedom and a sense of belonging. But there is no false euphoria: removing the claws of totalitarianism has also revealed feelings of abandonment, revenge, and anger. Since the late 1990s, fear, a disillusionment with certain ideals of the revolution, corruption, and extremely violent crime have also formed part of the South African experience. (Peimer 2009: VIII)

In the light of these difficult realities, contemporary post-apartheid South African theatre attempts to reflect on these issues, not in a "single dominant aesthetic style, but, rather, a paradigm of evolving forms and eclectic functions" (ibid.). Most plays are still informed by the aftermath of (apartheid) history and ideology as well as influenced by the legacy of protest theatre but no longer dictated by either of them. Today's South African theatre produces often complex and multilayered plays in which the question of human existence is gradually becoming stronger. Also, it put the writer and not the workshop group in the focus of production. As Peimer (2009: X) emphasises:

> The writers then investigate ways of building on the 'township' tradition of employing song, dance, heightened physicality, satire, and leaps in space and time. This is done because they are interested in reflecting current radical changes. The result is that the plays combine the aesthetics of non-realism and realism, multidimensional characters and simple comedic caricature, crafted dramatic situations and narrative, and the visual pleasure of more abstract, majestic design.

This brief overview of the history and status quo of South African theatre illustrates the multifacetedness of this literary form, which also becomes visible in Sara Foot's *Reach* which will be discussed in the following section.

5. Lara Foot's *Reach* (2007)

Lara Foot is a South African writer, director, and producer who has co-written more than 20 plays, with *Reach* being her third stand-alone piece. This nationally and internationally highly acclaimed two act play brings together two unlikely individuals from completely different ethnic, cultural, social as well as generational backgrounds, exploring the theme of spatial and social isolation in the wider context of the country's past and present. Thus, the play draws on the experiences of the Truth and Reconciliation Commission which revealed the pain and brutality of apartheid. Ordinary people gathered day after day in bare community halls throughout the country, to face their perpetrators across a table as millions watched on TV. The nation was gripped by the painful, but mysterious power of truth and the glimpses of humanity it engenders. Revealing the truth did not lead to an acquiescent sense of redemptive forgiveness but aspired to help humanise a traumatized society (Peimer 2013: 132 f.).

Foot's *Reach* equally explores South Africa's past, present, and future. The two protagonists Marion and Solomon slowly come to terms with their multiple collective and individual traumas through revelations of the past which enable them to overcome their struggles with the "racially determined, binary identities of colonization (civilized/primitive, master/servant/inferior/superior/self/other) they have inherited" (ibid.: 134). Nevertheless, at the same time, the process of truth and reconciliation also sheds light on the lawlessness of contemporary South Africa and its indefinite future.

The play is set near Port Alfred, in the Eastern Cape, the most rural and poorest of all South African provinces, one year before the Football World Cup, an event which raised the (unfulfilled) hopes for a better life in many South Africans. 63-year-old Marion Banning, a white South African with English heritage, lives alone and impoverished in an isolated, dilapidated Victorian cottage near a former 'black township' after the death of her beloved son several years ago, the subsequent divorce, and the emigration of her daughter and grandchildren to Australia. Instead of living with her daughter, she has decided to spend her final days in her utterly transformed home country and die on her own soil. One day, she receives an unexpected visitor, the young rural Xhosa man Solomon Xaba who, equally lonely, is on the mission to unravel the truth behind the death of Marion's son. About the origin of the play, Foot states (2007: n.p.):

> The play was inspired by conversations with psychoanalyst Tony Hamburger. It was born in a time of depression in our country and was motivated, in a sense, by a time in Cape Town when South Africa felt desperate both politically and

socially. Sifting through all this, I found a symbol of life which exists in unlikely relationships. It is that relationship which I explore in *Reach*.

Mostly stuck in the happier days of the past, Marion has come to accept the monotony of her days and quite openly yearns for death. As she writes in a letter to her estranged daughter right at the beginning of Act I:

> Things are the same here, the mountain still cuts the sky in half, and it still has its many colors of orange, purple, and gray. Still no rain, and still major power cuts. [...] I don't walk much anymore, neither does anyone else it seems. (Foot 2009: 131)

Marion's lethargic state is suddenly interrupted when the young but terminally ill Solomon, the grandson of Marion's former laundress, arrives. While he pretends that he is only there to paint her house, it becomes evident as the play progresses that his real intention is to deliver the final words from Marion's deceased son, who was killed while Solomon secretly watched the crime. Through their conversations, Solomon and Marion both little by little learn to overcome their traumas and face life again.

The play, however, not only explores the stage relationship of two completely different characters but, through discovering their lives, confronts the reader with the harsh realities of life in (post-)apartheid South Africa and the ongoing "struggle" (ibid.: 137) people endure, including the exodus of younger, mostly white South Africans, the AIDS epidemic, the fragile security situation, the lack of power and supplies, land redistribution, or the precarious situation in the townships. Marion's overt prejudices against people of other colour may serve as an example here. Although she was not a strong supporter of racial segregation during apartheid, she did not openly question the system:

> I have seen this country go through good and bad and good and bad. I was even a little involved in the struggle. No bravely so, but involved. The struggle — isn't that a haphazard sort of term? — the struggle as if it was finite. With a beginning and an end. How I wish that were the case. (ibid.: 138)

When Solomon arrives, however, she assumes that he is there to kill her. Yet, these and other topics are not discussed 'on the big stage' but rather become evident through the unhappiness of the protagonists. Solomon's parents presumably died of AIDS, while he is suffering from a fatal liver problem which was not treated with conventional medicine, but herbs given to him by his aunt, a traditional healer (*sangoma*). Or, he lived most of his life in townships and lost his job at Woolworth when a white customer spuriously complained about him. Marion, on the other hand, lives alone on an unsecured farm, threatened with losing everything either through the new land distribution legislation or the protests related to them. Her son was killed by township criminals who were not punished for the crime while the reasons for her son's killing were never revealed:

> Marion: Please! And open all that up again. The newspapers, the television. The photos of my boy on the front page. Lying naked in the scrapyard. The speculation: was he gay? Was he involved in drugs? anything to make it not arbitrary. Anything to substantiate why he was asking for it. Why it could happen to him but not to someone else. Are they all fucking blind? This country has been breeding murderers for the past century. Isn't that clear. There doesn't need to be a reason. Anger, despair! That's the reason" That's the motivation. Isn't it obvious? (ibid.: 160)

Learning more about the nature of her son's death and developing a closer relationship with Solomon enable Marion to slowly escape from her paralysis while also Solomon learns to come to terms with his feeling of guilt and powerlessness. The characters fail to fully overcome their differences and mutual accusations, but they make concrete steps towards each other as the closing scene, in which Marion attempts to convince Solomon to borrow and not steal an extension cord for her television, elucidates:

> Solomon: Yes, Mies Marion, I'll borrow one.
> Marion: Solomon, my boy, do you have to continually use that old subservient term "Miss Marion?" It's what your grandmother called me.
> Solomon: Mies is not always a subservient term, Mies Marion. Mies can also be a term of ... Of care. Of caring.
> Marion: What, Solomon? Are you saying you care about me?
> Solomon: I'm not sure what I'm saying, Mies Marion.
> Marion: Solomon?
> Solomon: Yes, Mies Marion?
> Marion: Thank you!
> Lights fade to black. (ibid.: 164)

The following section will discuss the role of dramatic texts in the EFL classroom with Foot's *Reach* serving as an example.

6. Reading *Reach* in the EFL classroom

As Ahrens (2013: 181; cf. also Eisenmann 2018: 138-139) points out, the reasons for reading foreign language literature in the classroom are manifold and

> [...] include scientific literary analysis such as aesthetic education, genres and types of texts, stimulus to imagination, textual analysis, as well as important components of EFL teaching such as media competence, student motivation and creativity.

While dramatic texts have been an essential part of the classroom for centuries, today they appear to be increasingly considered an alternative rather than the standard. Yet, they provide a number of advantages, particularly with more advanced students of English that should not be ignored (cf. Ahrens / Eisenmann / Merkl 2008; Peterson / Volkmann 2010, I, II; Hallet / Surkamp 2015). One of the major benefits is that dramatic texts allow students to follow the transformation of a text, e.g. from drama text to stage text, often requiring dialogical and creative approaches. One example of this is the work with stage directions, offering first-hand information on what the stage looks like, or how the characters are dressed. Engaging with these directions in depth helps students not only to learn how to navigate a script but also to shift between text and meta-text. Thus, especially inexperienced readers can gradually get a feel for the many ways in which a dramatic text can be (re-)imagined on stage.

Especially dramatic texts from other cultures provide students with opportunities to look at the alien culture(s) from an insider's perspective by using the foreign culture and not their own as their frame of reference (cf. Bredella 2008: 179-180). Moreover, dramatic texts offer the opportunity to analyse and experience everyday language (cf. Ahrens 2008: IX). This appears to be particularly true for plays from South Africa as they, more often than not, reflect the multilingual everyday lives of their characters. With regard to the classroom, dramatic texts have usually not been written to be read but for the purpose of being performed on stage (cf. Ludwig / Pointner 2019: 143-162). This offers ample opportunity for hands-on activities in the classroom, especially when it comes to creative action- and product-oriented approaches to learning English (cf., for example, Sambanis / Walter 2019).

At first glance, *Reach* presents a challenging read for sixth-form students of English, mainly for two reasons: it requires at least some knowledge of South Africa's past and present as the play consistently alludes to the country's apartheid history and the challenges of post-apartheid society (cf. section 2 and 3). Moreover, while the play's language is generally very accessible, it frequently uses South African English, Afrikaans, and African words, reflecting the multilingual approach many South Africans take to language. Nevertheless, the cultural and linguistic alienness of the play combined with its emancipatory power make the play worthwhile for students of English. Closely related to this, a close analysis of selected text passages combined with creative classroom approaches supports students in better understanding the protagonists' struggles and enables them to transfer them to their own contexts.

Digital media are gradually transforming the nature of traditional theatre concepts such as storytelling, stage, and audience, as an increasing number of multimedia performances vividly illustrates. For example, technological devices such as live screenings blur the boundaries between audience and stage and turn the spectator into an active participant of performance. As Jensen (2011: 227) points out:

> Digital technologies are important in the theatre world because many conceptions of the present-day theatre space have been shaped by these technologies. […] Like earlier media technologies, digital technologies influence the non-linear presentation of theatrical materials, the fragmentation of time and space and invite contemporary spectators to reconsider what live performance means.

In a similar vein, Jensen also emphasises the potential relevance of technology in theatre and drama education (cf. also Cameron / Carroll / Anderson 2009; Jensen 2012):

> Drama/theatre education practitioners have an impetus to engage in digital environments because these technologies and tools have a direct impact on conceptions of time and place, and those new conceptions bring new possibilities for creative constructs and representations that new / young audiences can identify with. (ibid.: 231)

To summarise, digital technology not only alters the nature of theatre itself but also provides new opportunities for drama education. The same is true for the foreign language classroom as the diverse possibilities of digital media can change the traditional way of perceiving and understanding literary texts (cf. Ludwig 2021). This trend is particularly worthwhile in the light of Reader Response Criticism which posits that the meaning of any text does not lie in the text itself but in the mind of the readers. In other words, the use of (educational) technology tools can support more learner-centred and creative engagements with literary texts, encouraging students to examine their personal reactions to a text and negotiate their individual responses with others (cf. Ludwig 2021). The purposes of digital media in the literature classroom are manifold (cf. Webb 2011) and include, among many others, reading 'new' forms of literature, such digital narratives (cf., for example, Lütge 2018: 299-310; Lütge / Merse 2018; Lütge / Merse / Stannard 2018: 4-7), opportunities for researching information, collaborating via digital media (Ludwig / Van de Poel 2017: 13-22) as well as producing digital texts (cf., for example, Owczarek 2018: 11-14).

With regard to working with dramatic texts, digital media can change the traditional way of perceiving and understanding dramatic texts in foreign language learning contexts. By doing so, students not only gain a deeper understanding of the text itself and develop their foreign language skills but also train their general media competences. The following overview shows selected key advantages of digital media when working with dramatic texts (based on Jenkins 2006: 4).

Students

- adopt and discover new identities,
- discover and learn to respect multiple perspectives,
- simulate real-word processes,
- discover how form, style, and content interact to create meaning,
- remix content and ideas in a mixed-media approach,
- collaborate with others and pool knowledge and insights,
- evaluate the reliability of sources.

The use of virtual reality systems may serve as an example to illustrate how students not only learn with but co-create a dramatic text by using digital media. Augmented and virtual reality systems have started to change the landscape of foreign language learning as they are increasingly being used for various purposes (cf. Johnson-Glenberg / Birchfield / Tolentino / Koziupa; Bonner / Reinders 2018; Ludwig 2021b; Ludwig 2021a for a more detailed discussion). In contrast to other digital tools, virtual reality allows students to fully immerse in an environment or even help co-construct it themselves, which, as preliminary research indicates, can have a motivating effect (cf. Freina / Ott 2015, 7; Hellriegel / Čubela 2018: 67).

With regard to *Reach*, students could, depending on the school's technical equipment, for example,

- go on a virtual field trip and explore the location in which the play takes place,
- physically participate and interact in key scenes from the perspective of different characters, allowing them to feel part of the scene by looking in any direction, walking around, or taking on the role of any of the characters,
- explore selected themes of the play, e.g. the role of women or cross-ethnic conflicts as they collaborate with other students in discussing VR representations of the written text,
- change selected scenes accordingly to their own readings of the play.

By doing so, students not only gain a deeper understanding of aspects such as setting or characters but also to get a feeling for the multivocality of literary texts.

On a more cautious note, virtual reality systems may have detrimental effects especially with younger students who are not yet able to fully distinguish between the virtual reality of the system and the real world (cf. Southgate 2018). While this is not the case with older learners, a limited use of VR systems seems recommendable as motion sickness can appear among all age groups (cf. ibid.).

In the following, a sample lesson for working with Foot's *Reach* in a virtual reality setting will briefly be elaborated on. The aim is to support students in actively engaging with the play, i.e. content, form, and style, allowing them to gradually develop a deeper understanding of the characters' feelings and motives and to put their actions in the historical, political, and social context of South Africa.

Suggestions for the classroom

The following ideas illustrate how the play can be approached in the advanced EFL Classroom with the help of digital media.

Approaching the play

The main aim of the following lesson sequence is to activate students' prior knowledge and thus make connections to the new information later on. Getting a first taste of south Africa should also create curiosity and arouse interest in the play.

In her 2008 article, "Djanet Sears' Harlem Duet als zeitgenössische Shakespeare-Adaptation", Sandten suggests approaching critical issues such as racism, interracial relations, and racial stereotypes through a so-called 'picture kiosk' (*Bilder-Kiosk*). This activity not only activates students' prior knowledge but also helps them to find out more about the other students' attitudes towards the topic (cf. ibid.: 165-166). The teacher creates a *Padlet* wall on which they post selected pictures of South Africa. The students are then given the task to look at the pictures and post their ideas on the *Padlet* wall. While there is a cornucopia of (iconic) images relating to South Africa's past and present, students may not be able to personally relate to all images. In this case, the activity can be slightly adapted, providing brief explanations on the back of the pictures. Images could, for example, show one of the following: the 2010 Football World Cup, Nelson Mandela, an AIDS ribbon, a township, an apartheid passbook, a farm, or Hector Pieterson.

Alternatively, students go on a Virtual Reality trip to South Africa, for example exploring its apartheid history (based on Ludwig 2021a).

Steps	**Tasks**
Preparation (teacher)	• open *Google Expeditions* • download, for example, the Nelson Mandela Museum or Robben Island trip • make sure that you are in guide mode • ensure that all devices (teacher tablet and student headsets) are on the same network
Pre-task phase	• tell learners that they are going to explore the South apartheid past and its struggle for freedom • revise some important facts about South Africa's apartheid past • introduce key vocabulary used in the scripts • ask learners to put on their headsets (headsets connect automatically but check number of all connected headsets to make your that all of your students are connected) • tell them to raise their hand if they feel dizzy
While-task phase	• begin guided tour (compass indicates place of focus) • use scripts for additional information • ask learners to complete a see (*What do you see?*), think/feel (*What do you think/feel?*), wonder (*Which questions do you have?*) chart, for example using Padlet
Post-task phase	• place learners in groups and ask them to collect what they learned about apartheid and/or answer the questions provided by Google Expeditions, depending on the level, students can either answer all the questions or just the ones on their level • discuss questions from the 'wonder' column • reflect on VR experience

Engaging with the play

While-reading activities should encourage students to focus on selected aspects of the text itself and to understand it better, they also help them to become more involved in the text that they read. Reading, examining, and reflecting the text should be an enjoyable experience. Furthermore, deep-level engagement should support students in analysing, understanding, and reproducing the characters' emotions, thoughts, and motivations. Thus, students can gradually learn to examine their thoughts and feelings and compare them with those of fictional characters. In the following, reading logs serve as an example of how to encourage students to see the world from other perspectives.

Written or spoken reading diaries provide many opportunities for deeper level engagement with the text and active participation in classroom discussions as it helps students to remember important things they read and reflect from their reading experience (cf. Sandten 2008: 164ff.). This could be done in four stages: during the first stage, students are asked to speculate about the title of the play. Here, the word 'reach', implying that the characters 'reach out' for or cannot 'reach' something, could be used as a prompt. During the second stage, students read the first part of Act I up to "Where are your manners?" (Foot 2009: 132) and are asked to discuss the following questions:

What do you learn about Marion's past and present? What do you think has caused her lethargic state of mind?

What do think Solomon is doing on Marion's farm? Does he really intend to kill her?

For the third stage, the class is divided into groups A and B. Both groups continue reading the play, writing their impressions, feelings, ideas, and thoughts in their reading logs. All students are also asked to write down and research unknown words (alternatively to be collected in a class language wiki) and make a list of the challenges the protagonists face in contemporary South Africa, such as poverty, unemployment, and power shortages. Moreover, each group is asked to particularly focus on one of the protagonists, i.e. Marion or Solomon:

Make notes on the major events in your character's life. Also write down their feelings and how they are described in the play. For Marion, you should also pay attention to the following:

What has caused Marion's depression?

What are the functions of Marion's letter to her daughter which she continues writing during the play?

Why is Marion not safe on her farm?

For Solomon, you should also pay attention to the following:

Which jobs did Solomon have in the past and why did he lose the jobs?

What are the major problems of Solomon and his family?

Why did he not report earlier what he had seen when Marion's son died?

The following questions can serve as additional guiding questions either while reading the play or for the group discussions afterwards:

How is the play structured?

Where does the play take place? Why is the setting relevant?

What do the stage directions say?

After having finished reading the play, the students from group A and B respectively form groups of four, sharing their information on the other character. Once the students have exchanged their information, each group should be asked to complete the ensuing task:

Create a graphic representation of Marion and Solomon's relationship in form of a relationship model, including people, objects, places, concepts, or events which are important either to one or both of them.

During the last stage, students should be encouraged to engage in more creative approaches and to relate the messages of the play to their own contexts. Here, the following task could, for example, be set:

Choose one of Solomon and Marion's central discussions and reenact the scene.

In order to do this, students have to put themselves in the character's positions, imagining how the character not only reacts verbally but also physically. Alternatively, students could play fictional conversations, for example between Marion and her daughter, based on the information they can deduct from Marion's letters to her daughter. In order to identify more easily with the protagonists, students could present their characters in form of a rehearsal: "I, Marion …" or "For me, Solomon is …" (cf. Bredella 2008: 207). To practise, students can record their texts on their phones.

Stepping out

Last but not least, follow-up tasks should encourage students to transfer what they have learned about South Africa to their own contexts. Here, the reconstruction of stereotypes or the awareness of their own multilingual contexts are potential connecting points. Here, one possible activity would be to ask students to pick one conversation between Marion and Solomon and translate it into a WhatsApp chat between the two characters. Afterwards students should reflect on how the medium potentially changes their perception of Marion and Solomon's dialogue.

8. Conclusions

This article explored the potential of contemporary South African theatre for the EFL classroom, focusing on working with the play with the support of digital tools. It has been shown that digital media can play a vital role when it comes to literature in the EFL classroom in general and dramatic texts in particular. While reading Sara Foot's play *Reach* requires sound background knowledge of the country's history and present challenges, it also shows vast potential for students to explore the southernmost country of the African continent.

Bibliography

Ahrens, Rüdiger (2013). Teaching Literature. In: Eisenmann, Maria / Summer, Theresa (eds.). *Basic Issues in EFL Teaching and Learning.* Heidelberg: Winter, 181-189.

Ahrens, Rüdiger / Eisenmann, Maria / Merkl, Matthias (eds.) (2008). *Moderne Dramendidaktik für den Englischunterricht.* Heidelberg: Winter.

Anderson, Michael / Carroll, John / Cameron, David (2009). *Drama Education with Digital Technologies.* London: Continuum.

Anton, Daniela (2019). Getting Engaged with South Africa's Culture and History through Authentic Materials. In: Summer, Theresa (ed.). *Culture and Literature in EFL Education: Relating Theory to Practice.* Frankfurt: Peter Lang, 233-252.

Apartheid Museum Resources, https://www.apartheidmuseum.org/resources (23/06/21).

Avert, Global Information and Education on HIV and AIDS (2018). HIV and AIDS in South Africa, https://www.avert.org/professionals/hiv-around-world/sub-saharan-africa/south-africa (23/06/21).

Bartosch, Roman (2018). Framing the Alien. In: Bergthaler, Hannes / Mortensen, Peter (eds.). *Framing the Environmental Humanities.* Leiden: Brill / Rodopi, 207-220.

Bonner, Euan / Reinders, Hayo (2018). Augmented and Virtual Reality in the Language Classroom: Practical Ideas. *Teaching English with Technology,* 18(3), 33-53.

Bredella, Lothar (2008). Dramatische Texte im Interkulturellen Fremdsprachenunterricht: Alternatives von Drew Hayden Taylor. In: Ahrens, Rüdiger /

Eisenmann, Maria / Merkl, Matthias: *Moderne Dramendidaktik für den Englischunterricht*. Heidelberg: Winter, 177-210.

Cameron, David / Anderson, Michael (2009). Potential to Reality: Drama, Technology and Education. In: Anderson, Michael / Carroll, John / Cameron, David (eds.). *Drama Education with Digital Technology*. London: Continuum.

Carroll, John / Cameron, David (2009). Drama, Digital Pre-Text and Social Media. In: *Research in Drama Education: The Journal of Applied Theatre and Performance*, 14/2, 295-312. doi: 10.1080/13569780902868960 (September 2018).

Delanoy, Werner / Eisenmann, Maria / Matz, Frauke (2015). *Learning with Literature in the EFL Classroom*. Frankfurt: Peter Lang.

Eisenmann, Maria (2018). The Potential of Young Adult Dystopian Fiction in the EFL Classroom. In: Maruo-Schröder, Nicole / Ludwig, Christian (eds.). *Issues in Contemporary Young Adult Dystopian Fiction*. Heidelberg: Winter, 137-170.

Eisenmann, Maria / Grimm, Nancy / Volkmann, Laurenz (2010). *Teaching the New English Cultures and Literatures*. Heidelberg: Winter.

Feuerle, Gisela (2010). Teaching South African Literatures: A Diversity of Writings and Experiences. In: Eisenmann, Maria / Grimm, Nancy / Volkmann, Laurenz (eds.). *Teaching the New English Cultures & Literatures*. Heidelberg: Winter, 43-58.

Foot, Laura (2009 [2007]). Reach. In: Peimer, David (ed.). *Armed Response – Plays from South Africa*. In: London: Seagull, 127-164.

Freina, Laura / Ott, Michela (2015). A Literature Review on Immersive Virtual Reality in Education: State Of The Art and Perspectives. *eLearning & Software for Education* 1, 133-141.

Fugard, Athol/Kani, John / Ntshona, Winston (1973). The Island. In: Fugard, Athol / Kani, John / Ntshona, Winston (1986). *Statements*. New York: Theatre Communications Group, Inc.

Gabriel, Peter (1980). Biko. YouTube: https://www.youtube.com/watch?v=H1G8nVMg6Io (September 2018).

Garner, Steve (^{2}2017). *Racisms: An Introduction*. Los Angeles, Calif.: SAGE Publications.

Hallet, Wolfgang / Surkamp, Carola (2015). *Dramendidaktik und Dramenpädagogik im Fremdsprachenunterricht*. Trier: WVT.

Hellriegel, Jan / Čubela, Dino (2018). Das Potential von Virtual Reality für den schulischen Unterricht – Eine konstruktivistische Sicht. *Zeitschrift für Theorie und Praxis der Medienbildung*, 58-80. doi.org/10.21240/mpaed/00/2018.12.11.X)

Heywood, Christopher (2004). *A History of South African Literature*. Cambridge: Cambridge University Press.

Jensen, Amy Petersen (2011). Theatre Education and New Media / Digital Technologies. In: Schonmann, Shifra (ed.). *Key Concepts in Theatre / Drama Education*. Rotterdam: Sense Publishers, 227-234.

Jensen, Amy Petersen (2012). Digital Culture, and the Viewing/Participating Pre-Service Teacher: (Re)envisioning Theatre Teacher Training for a Social Media Culture. In: *Research in Drama Education: The Journal of Applied Theatre and Performance*, 17/4, 552-568. Doi: 10.1080/13569783.2012.727626

Jenkins, Henry (2006). Confronting the Challenges of Participatory Culture: Media Education for the 21st Century. New York: MacArthur Foundation.

Johnson-Glenberg, Mina C. / Birchfield, David A. / Tolentino, Lisa / Koziupa, Tatyana (2014). Collaborative Embodied Learning in Mixed Reality Motion-capture Environments: Two Science Studies. *Journal of Educational Psychology*, 106(1), 86-104.

Ludwig, Christian / Pointner, Frank Erik (2019). Of Ghosts and Daggers: Using Comic Adaptations of Macbeth in the EFL Classroom. In: Eisenmann, Maria (ed.). *Teaching Shakespeare in the Classroom*. Frankfurt am Main: Peter Lang, 143-162.

Ludwig, Christian / Van de Poel, Kris (2017). Collaborative Learning and the New Media. In: Ludwig, Christian / Van de Poel, Kris (eds.). *Collaborative Language Learning and New Media: Insights into an Evolving Field*. Frankfurt am Main: Peter Lang, 13-22.

Ludwig, Christian (2020). This Land Is Your Mand. This Land Is My Land. – Developing Students' Film Literacy with Neill Blomkamp's *District 9*. In: Ludwig, Christian / Shipley, Elizabeth (eds.). *Mapping the Imaginative: Teaching Fantasy and Science Fiction in the University EFL Classroom*. Heidelberg: Winter, 113-144.

Ludwig, Christian (2021a). 'The Future Is Now' – Virtual Reality im Englischunterricht. In: Bündgens-Kosten, Judith / Schildhauer, Peter (eds.). *Englischunterricht in einer digitalisierten Gesellschaft*. Weinheim: Beltz Juventa, 175-187.

Ludwig, Christian (2021b). Teaching Literature with Digital Media. In: Lütge, Christiane / Merse, Thorsten (ebs.). *Digital Teaching and Learning: Perspectives for English Language Education*. Tübingen: Narr, 207-230.

Lütge, Christiane (2018). Digital, Transcultural and Global? Reconsidering the Role of Literature in the EFL Classroom. In: Zwierlein, Anne-Julia / Petzold, Jochen / Boehm, Katharina / Decker, Martin. (eds.). *Anglistentag 2017 Regensburg. Proceedings*. Trier: Wissenschaftlicher Verlag Trier, 299-309.

Lütge, Christiane / Merse, Thorsten / Stannard, Michelle (2018). Digital Narratives. Exploring New Practices of 'Reading' and 'Play'. In: *Praxis Fremdsprachenunterricht Englisch* 4/2018, 4-7.

Lütge, Christiane / Merse, Thorsten (2018). Digitale Literatur – Überlegungen zur Typologie und Modellierung. In: Falkenhagen, Charlotte / Volkmann,

Laurenz (eds.). *Tagungsband DGFF-Kongress 2017*. Baltmannsweiler: Schneider Verlag Hohengehren, forthcoming.

Mtwa, Percy / Ngema, Mbongeni / Simon, Arena (1981). *Woza Albert!.* London: Bloomsbury.

Orkin, Martin (1991). *Drama and the South African State*. Johannesburg: Witwatersrand University Press.

Owczarek, Claudia (2018). Producing Digital Texts. Das Potential von Digital Storytelling im Englischunterricht nutzen. In: *Praxis Fremdsprachenunterricht* 4/2018, 11-14.

Partridge, Sally (2011). Youth Lit in South Africa. Sunday Times Books LIVE. http://sapartridge.bookslive.co.za/blog/2011/04/18/youth-lit-in-south-africa/ (23/06/21)

Peterson, Roland / Volkmann, Laurenz (2010). *Shakespeare didaktisch I: Neue Perspektiven für den Unterricht*. Tübingen: Stauffenburg.

Peterson, Roland / Volkmann, Laurenz (2010). *Shakespeare didaktisch II: Ausgewählte Dramen und Sonette für den Unterricht*. Tübingen: Stauffenburg.

Peimer, David (2013). A Brief Moment in the Great Postcolonial Story: Representations of Crime in Contemporary South African Theatre. In: Bray, Suzanne / Préher, Gérald (eds.). *Fatal Fascinations Cultural Manifestations of Crime and Violence*. Newcastle: Cambridge Scholars Publishing, 131-144.

Peimer, David (2009). Introduction. In: Peimer, David (ed.). A*rmed Response – Plays from South Africa.* London: Seagull Books.

Sambanis, Michaela / Walter, Maik (2019). *In Motion – Theaterimpulse zum Sprachenlernen: Von neuesten Befunden der Neurowissenschaft zu konkreten Unterrichtsimpulsen*. Berlin: Cornelson Scriptor.

Sandten, Cecilie (2008). Othellos schwarze Frau: Djanet Sears' Harlem Duet als zeitgenössische Shakespeare-Adaptation. In: Ahrens, Rüdiger / Eisenmann, Maria / Merkl, Matthias: *Moderne Dramendidaktik für den Englischunterricht*. Heidelberg: Winter, 155-174.

Southgate, Erica (2018). Immersive Virtual Reality, Children and School Education: A Literature Review for Teachers. https://ericasouthgateonline.files.wordpress.com/2018/06/southgate_2018_immersive_vr_literature_review_for_teachers.pdf. (23/06/21)

Stadler, Sandra (2017). *South African Young Adult Literature in English 2000–2014*. Heidelberg: Winter.

Stapleton, Timothy L. (2010). *A Military History of South Africa: From the Dutch-Khoi Wars to the End of Apartheid*. Oxford, England: Praeger.

Statistics South Africa (2018). Crime Against Women in South Africa. http://www.statssa.gov.za/publications/Report-03-40-05/Report-03-40-05June2018.pdf. (23/06/21)

South African South African Reconciliation Barometer Survey (2019). https://www.ijr.org.za/south-african-reconciliation-barometer-survey-2019/ (23/06/21).

Thompson, Leonard (³2001). *A History of South Africa*. Yale: Yale University Press.
Washington Jr., Joseph Reed (1987). *Puritan Race Virtue, Vice, and Values 1620-1820: Original Calvinist True Believers' Enduring Faith and Ethics Race Claims*. New York: Peter Lang.
Webb, Allan (2011). *Teaching Literature in Virtual Worlds: Immersive Learning in English Studies*. Abingdon: Routledge

Online References

Expeditions: https://apps.apple.com/de/app/expeditions/id1131711060 (23/06/21)
Padlet: https://padlet.com/dashboard (23/06/21)

FRAUKE MATZ (UNIVERSITY OF MÜNSTER)

'We Can't Make It Ours, Unless We're in It' – Contemporary Young Adult Drama and Political Education in EFL Learning

Contemporary dramas written for young adults offer valuable opportunities for political education: These texts not only address political issues, but they also invite students to 'play' with different roles and perspectives, to take a stance without it having to be their own. As these learners are young members of performative societies, attempting to find their own (political) positions in society, they can be encouraged to become competent critical performers and producers of such young adult plays, while developing their own performative (discourse) competences in today's global society. This theoretical contribution will not only look at current approaches to political education in EFL learning in the European context and discuss models of democratic, human rights, global and cosmopolitan education, but it will also illustrate how Stef Smith's drama Remote *(2015) could be used to foster discourse competence in these respects.*

1. Introduction: Cultural actors and performative societies

In a democratic society, one key aim of school education is to enable students to participate (socially and politically) within it. This is based on the idea that society can only be constituted through the democratic participation of all individuals (cf. for example Council of Europe 2010 & 2017, Hallet 2011, KMK 2004 & 2012, Starkey 2015). To achieve this, educators need to aid students in becoming critically aware, respectful and tolerant communicators – not only in their first language(s) but also in the foreign languages (cf., for example, KMK 2004: 6). The subject of English as a foreign language plays a special part within political education, since "with the spread of globalisation and the concomitant growing importance of English as an interplanetary lingua franca" (Volkmann 2015: 22), students' discourse competences need to be fostered, so that they can partake in discourses (global and digital) regarding political and social issues that might concern them. In line with the *New London Group* (2000), Hallet stresses the importance of discourse competence (*Diskursfähigkeit*), pointing out that the lack of this vital competence might lead to the exclusion from discourses that are relevant for society, therefore otherwise resulting in the marginalisation of the individual (cf. Hallet 2011: 55).

At the end of secondary school, teenage students are on the verge of becoming adult citizens with the right to vote – within the borders of both our own democratic society and the European Union. Furthermore, they are also becoming citizens within an interconnected global world. This article takes the stance that this has direct consequences on the scope of political education, especially in connection with English language learning, as it also needs to aid students in developing "a consciousness that we are vulnerable human beings living in a relatively fragile interdependent world society" and that "[s]olidarity and reciprocity are essential for our protection" (Starkey 2015: 1). This article will thus focus on ways in which EFL education can help young adults to become responsible citizens in the European and global context. It will also take a closer look at education policy proposals, provided by the European Council, to guide teachers in implementing political and democratic education and question whether they factor in "the development of a global awareness, an understanding of and commitment to human rights, and opportunities to act with others to make a difference locally and in the wider world" (ibd.: 24).

A frequently used term within the context of democratic participation is that of a cultural actor or player (*kultureller Akteur*), who is aware of the conventions and rules of the corresponding society. This coincides with concepts that depict societies as *performative*, in which scripts and schemata need to be learned and 'acted out', in order to be able to participate effectively and successfully (cf., for example, Hallet 2011 & 2015, Nicholson 2009). For students to become successful cultural and social actors, it is therefore important for them to develop symbolic competence (cf. Kramsch 2006) and understand the scripts and schemata of cultural and political *performance*. They also need to understand in how far these are used in a political context, how these can be used to effectively take a stance in a critically reflected way. Political and social issues such as discrimination, segregation, unfair treatment and exclusion are already part of an English language education, and students are required to read texts, take part in discussions or write comments on these. But this might still prove to be a challenge for many teenagers who have never experienced the above-mentioned scripts, who have never actively participated in a democratic context. Following Nicholson's idea that "[e]lements of performance have permeated many areas of life" and that young adults "growing up in performative societies inevitably absorb the imagery they see", drama could serve as a powerful tool to support students in their effort to become cultural actors, as it can help them "to interrogate how performances of power have been constructed and find different ways to imagine and symbolise experience" (Nicholson 2009: 44-45). This is why this article suggests drama learning as a way into and as a part of political learning in the EFL classroom.

2. Contemporary young adult drama

2.1. Young adult literature – Teenage texts for teenage readers

Since the turn of the millennium, young adult fiction has constantly developed and expanded, and it still continues to do so. However, despite the fact that it offers an immense variety in terms of subgenres and literary trends, the genre-defining features could be described as follows: YA texts are written for a teenage audience and "revolve around adolescent main characters that face similar questions, issues, problems, fears and joys of youngsters of that age", addressing topics such as the coming of age and the forming of their own personalities and relationships (Matz / Stieger 2015: 122). Due to this closeness, both in age of the protagonists and the life-world relevance of the topics discussed, it seems that YA fiction can also serve as a helpful resource for cultural learning in the EFL classroom (cf. for example Alsup 2010, Hesse 2012, Henseler / Surkamp 2007).

Currently, though, there is little statistical evidence that shows that EFL students in secondary school classrooms are offered YA texts as class readers and, if given the opportunity, that they enjoy reading YA texts or even prefer them to adult texts.[1] This article follows the assumption that the closeness in age and the similarity in their life-world experiences aid young adult readers in suspending disbelief, allowing them to enter fictional worlds in inherently transcultural settings. To state it in the words of the American Young Adult Library Services Association (YALSA):

> […] to see oneself in the pages of a young adult book is to receive the reassurance that one is not alone after all, not other, not alien but, instead, a viable part of a larger community of beings who share a common humanity. (Cart 2008)

YA fiction has set its own trends and greatly influenced the international book markets (cf. Matz / Stieger 2015), with the most noticeable trends, since 2000, initially being publications within the genre of fantasy and with waves of dystopian and science fiction publications to follow. And, while bloggers and book journalists were waiting for the 'next big thing' in the Anglo-American publishing YA book industry, a new trend seems to have already taken off: that of political activism, i.e. "[b]ooks focussed on giving tools to aspiring activists and would-be protest leaders […], turning a spotlight on double standards, dis-

---

[1] A recent study conducted in Northrhine-Westphalia suggests, however, that if teenage students had to read fictional texts at all, they would prefer texts written for a young adult audience (see Matz / Rumlich 2020).

crimination, or inequality" (Corbett 2018). While this article will not attempt to look more closely at the origins and reasons for the rise in politically motivated YA fictional and non-fictional texts, it does seem important to point out, though, as the demand for and interest in such texts appear to exist. Suffice it to note that, in the course of secondary education, political education plays an increasing role in terms of European curriculums in general and German curriculums in particular, which encourage political education through literature (cf. KMK 2012: 2).[2]

2.2. *New Plays for Young People* – British contemporary young adult drama

The trend of focusing on political activism, on calling out double standards and discrimination, on speaking out against bullying and injustice has also been observable in the publication of YA plays, i.e. plays written for both a young adult audience and young adult performers. There is no shortage of such plays. In Britain alone, over 160 plays dealing with political, controversial and current themes were published from 1995 to 2015 (Banks 2015: v). In its *Connections*-series, the *National Theatre* launches ten plays every year, following the principle of "established playwrights create short plays for young actors to perform" (ibid.). Hence, this series can also serve as a rich resource for EFL classrooms all over Europe. Furthermore, while other fictional and non-fictional texts also have their merits within the context of political education, plays particularly offer specific learning opportunities:

> In contrast to poetic texts, which place sensations of the lyrical I in the foreground, or narrative texts that tell of past events, one of the main features of a play is the direct action of the characters [...]. This action-related dimension of plays strongly suggests that they should be dealt with in an active and productive way in class [...]. Hardly any other literary genre offers so many possibilities for – and even necessitates – the use of action-oriented methods of text work as part of student-centered teaching (Surkamp 2015: 141).

YA plays lend themselves to the playful learning of English as a foreign language, as also discussed in this volume: They invite students to speak the language, to memorise and repeat chunks, to contextualise new words and phrases, and they aid in learning turn-taking, etc. (see, for example, Walter 2012, Sur-

---

[2] In the national education standards (*Bildungsstandards*) for both middle and upper secondary school, it is clearly stated, even though not further explained, that EFL students should be enabled to take on social responsibility and partake in democratic society (*Kultusministerkonferenz* 2004: 6 & 2012: 5).

kamp 2015, Surkamp / Elis 2016). In the context of political education, however, it is mainly the *performative* competence that is in the foreground:

> Acting brings the real world to life and models social situations. Pupils can thereby learn to take their place in the social and public sphere [...]. They also gain the insight that social realities as well as individual and social identities are not given, inherent, and permanently fixed, but that they are rather products of continuously updated and modified actions that can be negotiated and therefore changed. This reflection on the social staging of their own life world empowers them to participate in society (Surkamp 2015: 143).

This could be a suitable learning opportunity in terms of identity formation, especially for students who have not yet found their place in the social and political sphere: In acting out roles in a play that deals with political issues, they can take a stance without it necessarily being their own, see how it 'fits', how they can argue their point, and how they can interact with differing positions. In this article, one of those plays, Steph Smith's *Remote* (2015), will be looked at more closely in this context.

Nevertheless, after having looked at a suitable text choice and before discussing teaching methodology, it seems important to examine models of political education in this context: On closer inspection, there appears to be very little agreement on what is meant by political and/or democratic education in the educational guidelines on a regional level. Hence, it may pose a challenge for teachers to foster political and democratic awareness in an EFL context, as the guidelines could be interpreted in different ways. Therefore, in the following, the scope of what political education might entail within the European context will be discussed.

3. From national to regional to global: Education for a cosmopolitan citizenship?

3.1. Democratic education and human rights education – European perspectives

When considering democratic principles in language education from a teaching perspective, it is vital to be critically aware of the current models, concepts and frameworks, as they will inevitably influence the teaching and learning processes. If teachers aim to enable their students to partake in political discourses and deal with global issues in their EFL classes, they should be clear about what these competences entail, which school of thought they originate from and, hence, which values and allegiances they impart. Using the example of Stef Smith' *Remote*, it will have an impact on students' learning experience if teachers give their lessons an intra-national, international, regional or even global focus, if matters of individual rights in one specific country, in one specific region will be discussed, or if universal rights play an important role. Looking at the European documents, it appears that all of the above are to be encouraged (cf. for example European Council 2008, 2010 & 2017).

In essence, European models of democratic education have been closely connected to concepts for human rights education (HRE), which – in turn – are based on the *Universal Declaration of Human Rights* (UDHR) (cf. Council of Europe 2010). This may seem logical and understandable, but – as Freeman (2002) and Osler and Starkey (2010: 47) have pointed out – it is not unproblematic, as "human rights and democracy have independent and potentially competing theoretical foundations". Osler and Starkey clearly state that:

> Democracy is a political construct based on the premise that the people should rule. Human rights is a moral and legal concept that provides a set of principles against which the performance of government can be judged. They therefore limit the power of governments since even democratically elected law-makers may overturn human rights. (ibd.: 47-48)

This may be the issue at the heart of these theory-building processes, as will be discussed later. There have been different models in the course of the last 20 years, which, in turn, are based on very different theoretical, philosophical assumptions. These differences are striking and are therefore the reason for going back to the history of their origin, to critically question if further developments can indeed be viewed as progress. In the following, an attempt is made to outline the historical development of what is meant by democratic education, according to the relevant European documents.

3.2. The first project: Embracing human rights, global perspectives and cultural hybridity

The first of its kind, the European Council project for *Education for Democratic Citizenship* (EDC) ran from 1997 until 2000 and declared HRE as "the core and an indivisible part of EDC" (Bîrzéa 2000: 32). As this appears to be the foundation and starting point of all following concepts, this particular aspect deserves closer attention. One of the authors of this first project, Bîrzéa, formulated three distinct aspects of HRE as part of EDC:

- acquisition of knowledge **about** human rights of freedoms; learning about the functioning of national and international instruments of protection (education about human rights),

- acquisition of attitudes and skills for promotion and protection of human rights (education **for** human rights),
- development of an environment that promotes learning and teaching in human rights (education **within** human rights" (ibid, emphasis in the original).

The classification into a cognitive, cultural and participative dimension is, one could argue, the foundation of all subsequent models, as will be illustrated later. It is important to note, however, that this first project was not based on the concept of intercultural communicative competence (ICC), as put forth by Byram around the same time (Byram 1997). Whereas the latter is firmly rooted within the notion of a relatively common cultural heritage and shared national identities, which it continues to promote today, this first European project has very different theoretical foundations: The project was undertaken, as Bîrzéa states, in a "period of challenges and uncertainties, caused by the depreciation of the basic values of modernity, i.e. work, the mass society and the Nation-State", which was also "the beginning of new optimism" and the revival of citizenship virtue (2000: 7). The "*citizenship ideal* was invoked as a hope, a solution or a new civilization project" (ibid.) in the global and early digital age and therefore embraced human rights as part of a new social contract. Both globalisation and cultural hybridisation played an important role in this first project: Globalisation was understood as "the opposite of homogeneity" and as being connected to cultural hybridisation (ibid.). This indicates that globalisation calls for a newly defined, inherently transcultural understanding of culture and cultural learning that allows for hybridity.

In this document, citizenship is thus seen as "less and less linked to a particular territory" but viewed as both a status and a role:

> The former refers to civil, political and social rights guaranteed by a state to its citizens. The latter aspect takes into account the identities and mental representations that each individual designs with respect to public life and politics. These subjective representations may be attached to a particular region or nation, as well as to an organization, a network or a supranational entity (Europe, World Village, Cosmopolis). In most cases, individuals create several identities simultaneously […] (ibid.).

In its essence, it becomes clear that this document shares the same origins as the concept of transculturality (cf., for example, Doff / Schulze-Engler 2011, Delanoy 2006). The 'traditional' categories to help define culture(s) ("i.e. national, cultural, religious communities", Freitag-Hild 2018: 167) are thought of as not being universally applicable. Instead, the document appears to be based on a notion of culture that is shaped by "inner differentiation, polyphony, cultural complexity, hybridity, external networking and entanglements with other cultures" (ibid.). It does not view citizenship and democratic education in the context of nation states but as a "context-related issue" (Bîrzéa 2000: 7): "Economic, cultural and political globalization is the new context of democratic citizenship" (ibid.: 9). In the learning and teaching context, this indicates a very complex, inherently transcultural approach to political education, as it not only takes HRE into consideration but also the merits and challenges of the globalised world, thereby recognising a shared responsibility of all global citizens.

3.3. Weakening the strong connection: Democratic education without notions of hybridity

A decade later, Gollob, Krapf and Weidinger (2010) continue the strong connection between democratic education and HRE. In their material collection *Educating for democracy*, which was also published by the *Council of Europe*, they state that the goal of democratic education is to help students to be young citizens who:

- know their human rights and have understood the conditions they depend on (**learning 'about'** democracy and human rights);
- have experienced school as a micro-society that respects freedoms and equality of its students, and have been trained in exercising their human rights and respecting the rights of others (**learning 'through'** democracy and human rights);
- are therefore competent and confident to exercise their human rights, with a mature sense of responsibility towards others and their community (**learning 'for'** democracy and human rights)" (Gollob et al. 2010: 29, emphasis F.M.).

Hence, as part of the foundation of their model of EDC, Gollob et al. also view democracy and human rights as being connected to one another. It is curious to note, however, that concepts and notions such as 'hybridity' or 'hybridisation', 'post-nation' or 'cosmopolis' are not mentioned in the document. The authors state that "for a people is government within the confines of a nation state" but list this under a section entitled "Problems and weaknesses": "Increasing global interdependence, such as in economic and environmental developments, limits the scope of influence of democratic decision making in a nation state" (ibid.: 17). Yet, a solution for these 'problems and weaknesses' is not offered.

The following model was later adapted in the German context by Knippertz and Möller (2015) for the EFL classroom, to illustrate the interconnectedness of the different dimensions, but which should be viewed as fluid and mutually dependent:

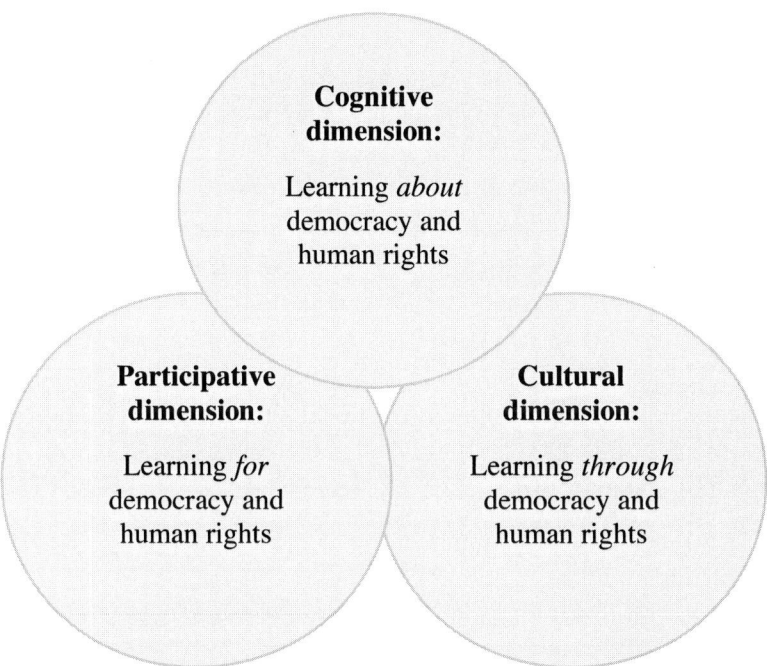

Table 1: Three Dimensions of Democratic Education adapted from Knippertz / Möller 2015: 138.

While this model lends itself to a practical application within the context of EFL learning, it is noteworthy to observe that not much is left of a concept that critically discusses the vision of a global political community which is hybrid and interconnected. Instead, it focuses on democratic education within a nation state, which is problematic, as it thus "aims to transmit a particular view of national identity and culture, rather than enabling reflecting on plural identities" (Starkey 2015: 21). The two models discussed here are thus rooted in an educational policy based on the notion of a national homogeneity and cultural identity (cf. Olser / Starkey 2010: 88).

This retrogression on the European level, as it were, is astonishing in a time in which concepts of transculturality, global education and cosmopolitanism are widely discussed and continually further developed for the educational context (cf., for example, Gaudelli 2016, Jackson 2019). Surprisingly, this retrogression appears to persist, as these concepts did not play a role in the development of the current model, the *Reference Framework of Competences for Democratic Culture*, which will be discussed in the following.

3.4. The intercultural turnaround: Competences for democratic culture and (global) cultural issues

In April 2018, the *Council of Europe* published the recently developed *Reference Framework of Competences for Democratic Culture*, which "is offered as an instrument to help inspire individual approaches to teaching competences for democratic culture" (Council of Europe 2018: 8). Since language teachers are very familiar with the binding *Common European Framework of Reference for Languages* (CEFR) (Council of Europe 2001), it would only be logical for teachers to turn to this new framework, when looking for guidance in addressing political issues and encouraging critical discourses in language education. This, however, may not prove to be helpful for teachers who wish to encourage their students to view themselves "as a member of the human family, all of whose members have equal entitlement to dignity and defined human rights" and to promote "solidarity with those denied their rights locally, nationally, and internationally" (Starkey 2015: 21).

At first glance, the shortcomings of this document do not appear to be obvious, as it claims to be based on the "belief that education systems, schools and universities should make preparation for democratic citizenship one of its key missions" (Council of Europe 2018: 7) and which was also designed to be a tool for teaching across all subjects. Like the EDC, the described competences for democratic culture (CDC) are also based on the three dimensions of learning. Unlike the EDC, it does not connect those dimensions with HRE and even excludes Human Rights:

> First, self-efficacy can develop when learners are given opportunities to solve tasks, being encouraged to persevere and acknowledged for even the smallest success. This experienced-based and affective dimension of the learning process is **'learning through'** democracy. Second, the acquisition of knowledge and critical understanding is **'learning about'** democracy. Third, the ability to use one's capabilities in a given context or situation is **'learning for'** democracy" (ibid.: 16, emphasis F.M.)

The heart of the *Framework* is a model of the CDC, which, according to its authors, "need(s) to be acquired by learners if they are to participate effectively in a culture of democracy and live peacefully together with others in culturally diverse democratic societies" (ibid.: 11):

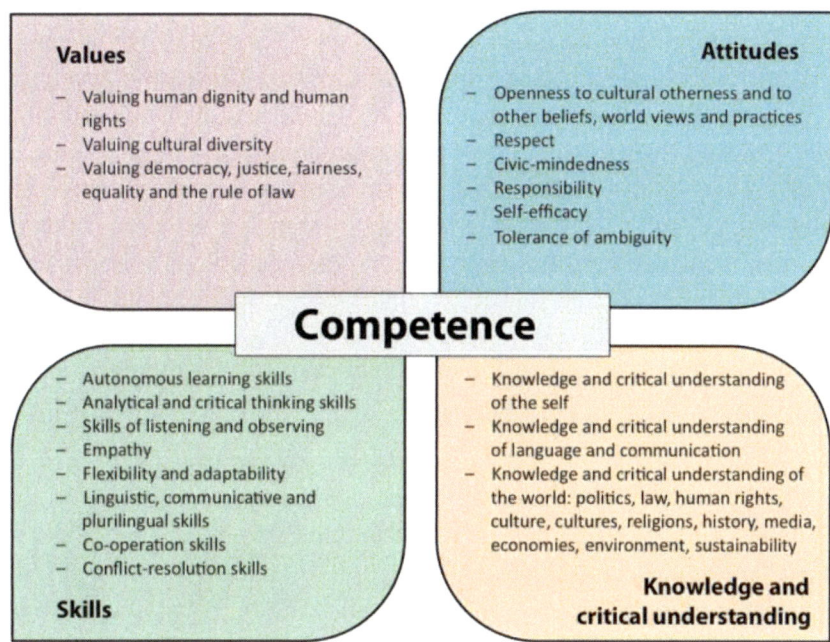

Table 2: *Model of CDC* (Council of Europe 2018: 38)

Human Rights are referred to, but not as explicitly as in the previous projects and guidelines by the same institution, nor can they be found at the heart of the model. Also, globalisation and global education, though briefly mentioned in the document (see descriptors for *Knowledge and critical understanding of economies, the environment and sustainability*, ibid.: 57), are not part of the model itself. This may come as no surprise, as this *Framework* is firmly rooted in an intercultural understanding, which becomes explicitly clear in its reference to the *White Paper on Intercultural Dialogue* (Council of Europe 2008). Furthermore, it defines the term intercultural dialogue as "an open and respectful exchange of views between individuals, groups with different ethnic, cultural, religious and linguistic background and heritage on the basis of mutual understanding and respect" (ibid.: 10), suggesting that there might be a "European identity to be realised", which will, for example, be based on "shared fundamental values" and "respect for common heritage" (ibid.: 4). In this respect, this *Framework* shares an understanding of culture, which is also the basis of the CEFR. However, considering all the critique on the concept of intercultural learning and/or intercultural (communicative) competence, since the publication of the CEFR, this is not only somewhat curious but also a clear sign that current research into concepts of cultural learning has been ignored.

In contrast to the 1997-2000 project, culture is defined as a "set of distinctive spiritual, material, intellectual and emotional features of society or a social group" (Council of Europe 2018: 70). Although it states that "any social group can have a culture and all cultures are dynamic and constantly changing over time" and that "[c]ultural affiliations are also fluid and dynamic" (ibid.), it is still far removed from a transcultural understanding, which views culture not as separate entities but as a "fluid cluster of different individual practices" (Doff / Schulze-Engler 2011: 7)[3]. It therefore leaves educators wondering if this model can truly prove to be helpful in preparing "the next generation and those beyond it for inhabiting this complicated and troubled world" (Gaudelli 2016:3).

3.5. Global citizenship education and cosmopolitan citizenship

In summary, whereas globalisation, hybridisation and the issue of global citizenship play an important role in the first project by the *European Council*, these issues remain absent from its most recent project. Considering the advancement of globalisation and digitalisation since the year 2000, the *Framework* leaves a rather conservative impression: It appears to place the idea of nation states in the foreground, rather than allowing the idea of a post-national citizenship (cf. Bîrzéa 2000: 10). In 2000, it was discussed that a political community may not be based on "kinship and origin":

> On the contrary, it is gradually arranged alongside concentric circles of political socialization, directed from the local to the general, from particular to universal, from proximal to global identities, from state to supranational entities. From this perspective, the members of a community may choose any political entity for their own identification. Since global issues are increasingly worrying, supranational identities (e.g. European citizenship) become major attraction poles for identification processes (ibid.: 10-11).

It is unclear as to what led to this development within the *European Council*, but, when considering on which model one should base one's teaching, it is important to be aware of this shift in perspective. On an even wider transnational level, UNESCO published a very different concept: the Global Citizenship Education (GCED), which "aims to empower learners of all ages to assume active roles, both locally and globally, in building more peaceful, tolerant, inclusive and secure societies" and which is based on very similar dimensions as

---

[3] As Appiah states: "We do not need, have ever needed, settled communities, a homogenous system of values, in order to have a home. Cultural purity is an oxymoron. The odds are that, culturally speaking, you already live a cosmopolitan life, enriched by literature and art, and film that come from many places, and that contains influences from many more" (2007: 113).

the aforementioned models, namely "cognitive, socio-emotional and behavioural" (UNESCO 2019):

- Cognitive: knowledge and thinking skills necessary to better understand the world and its complexities;
- Socio-emotional: values, attitudes and social skills that enable learners to develop affectively, psychosocially, and physically and to enable them to live together with others respectfully and peacefully;
- Behavioural: conduct, performance, practical application and engagement.

Reverting to the original idea that political education and learning for democracy could and should be based on Human Rights, it may be helpful to turn attention back to the importance of HRE as being the basis for an "education for cosmopolitan citizenship," (Osler / Starkey 2010: 113) since the

> human rights project is a cosmopolitan one and effective education for our global age requires a cosmopolitan vision, based on a shared understanding of human rights and an exploration of citizenship on all levels, from the local, encompassing the national, but extending to the global.

4. Young adult drama and political education: Performative societies and performances of power

Learning/Teaching with YA drama, in the context of political education, this article suggests an inherently transcultural approach based on an understanding of cosmopolitan citizenship, as put forth by Osler and Starkey (2010: 45):

> The compelling attraction of the UDHR derives from its capacity to provide an alternative account of what binds human beings together, beyond theories of nationalism. Cosmopolitan perspectives do not inevitably negate the emotional ties of nationhood that many people espouse. Instead, they encourage us to reconceptualise all communities, including the local and national, as cosmopolitan. Cosmopolitanism challenges perspectives that privilege national solidarities over all others.

Secondary school students, who may be taught in this context, are invited to 'play with' portrayals of power, to 'act' in a performative society; they are encouraged to take a stance, even if it is not for a specific cause. This article is based on the assumption that cultural action is always connected to performance (cf. Hallet 2015: 63). For this context, cultures are understood as essentially transcultural and hybrid, as "thought of as a chance to critically question essentialist and assimilatory concepts of culture in the interest of a more democratic society", as "a diverse set of cultural practices, which may serve highly divergent ends" (Delanoy 2006: 233). It is important that students try out different roles to help them understand various performances of power and political scripts and that they not only 'have a role to play' but that their opinions also matter, and they can learn to be heard.

For teachers, then, it is the question as to which educational concepts for democratic and political education should be the basis of such lessons. The performances of power, as described by the Council of Europe's current *Framework* (2018), takes a national and regional stance. The aforementioned discrepancy between democratic and human rights education (Olser / Starkey 2010: 47) seems to be mirrored in this new framework, as it moves away from the global, universal and cosmopolitan perspective to an intercultural, nation-based approach. Yet, if teachers aim to enable their students "to work together with others to challenge the ongoing injustices and inequalities which continue today and to identify with the struggles of strangers" (ibid.: 143), the first project by the European Council might prove to be a more constructive starting point.

5. Steph Smith's *Remote*: A very practical example of HRE in English language education

5.1. Characters, setting and discourse – A short introduction

The Scottish playwright Stef Smith wrote the play *Remote* in the context of the *Connections-Series* by the National Theatre. In essence, it is not a political play but a play about how to be(come) political. In this sense, the play is transcultural and globally relevant since it deals with universal issues and challenges of adolescents. This focus hence invites educators to open up discourses concerning "human vulnerability" (Osler / Starkey 2010: 29).

The play itself is written for a cast of seven main characters and a chorus, consisting of two or more members, and allows for hybridity amongst the cast itself. In terms of gender, some roles are rather fixed: the main character (Antler) and her sister (Crystal), as well as two more characters (Skin, Finn), are constructed as female, whereas two characters are envisaged as male (Oil, Blister). One character (Desk) and the members of the chorus, however, are not fixed in terms of gender. All characters could be played by teenage-actors of any age and background. Although the age suitability is given at 13+, in terms of language ability in a German EFL classroom, it may already be suitable from about year 9 onwards.

In terms of setting, the stage direction allows room for interpretation and is not related to any national context. Only two aspects are important: The play itself is set in a park; the main character needs a tree tall and strong enough to sit in. Apart from this, the "staging can be simple or complex and is open to interpretation of the group. There are no scenes, but rather this play is one long moment, flicking back and forward between moments" (Smith 2015: 483). Smith emphasizes that she wishes for the performing group to "imagine their own world within *Remote*" (ibid.).

The characters' names are somewhat unusual and appear rather abstract. Also, the way in which the play is written may be both a challenge and a chance for the producers of this play: There are only very few stage directions and the text for the chorus is written in single, mostly unconnected lines, so that they can be spoken abruptly or in a connected way, only by a few or by many performers. Hence, performers need to be competent in critically interpreting setting, plot and discourse for their purpose and be very clear in the meaning they would like their performance to convey. Furthermore, although the play's author is Scottish, the play itself does not offer any distinct cultural features or noticeable trace in terms of language variety. In summary, it is an essentially transcultural play that allows for hybridity and encourages students' cognitive and socio-emotional engagement.

5.2. A play about (how to) protest

On the content level, Smith describes *Remote* as "a play about protest, power and protecting yourself" (ibid.: 480). In essence, it deals with the main character's inability to really voice her concerns, to express the anger and the teenage *angst* she feels. It also deals with the coldness and detachment that can be part of human relationships, which can be distant and shaped by the lack of interest in the (emotional) well-being of others. This could very well be a familiar setting to students who have an indistinct feeling that something in their surroundings is not quite right, who are unable to put these feelings into words or pinpoint exactly what makes them feel uneasy, or that human beings (including themselves) are not being treated fairly. Also, it might help students who are aware of this but who are uncertain whether they want to, or, respectively, how they could take action. As a lead-in and pre-acting/pre-reading activity, students could voice three things that make them angry, whether it be everyday things or political, social and/or environmental issues. If done sensibly, this could be a first step in helping students to create what Bîrzéa calls "education **within** human rights", i.e. the "development of an environment that promotes learning and teaching in human rights" (2000: 32).

At the opening of the play, Antler destroys her mobile phone, in order to cut herself off from her family and friends, and climbs up into a tree, where she plans to hide. Angry and confused, she states, "My name is Antler. And I will not be part of the world. Not this world. Not any more" (ibid.: 500). She does this as part of a protest but can neither really understand herself nor explain to others why exactly she is protesting. She is trying to find the appropriate words, concepts or ideas, but all that comes to her mind are isolated images, individual pieces of a larger context that she is unable to fathom. Sitting in the tree, she is "[l]ooking out for change" (ibid.: 490) and battles with vague images that could be interpreted as symbols of political protest and environmental catastrophes:

" – And flags in the air

– And police throwing gas canisters" (ibid.: 489)

"– And she is fine

– As she thinks about earthquakes

– And flooding

– And fires tearing down forests" (ibid.: 500)

Secondary school teenage students might be able to relate to this emotional chaos, as they are at a time of their (individual) development in which they are not only attempting to make sense of the world but also the political landscape in which they are growing up, as well as dealing with/developing human relationships. Also, the statements Antler makes about exam results (ibid.: 492), money, future plans, saving up for a flat and car (ibid.: 511) are symbolic for the *teenage angst* she feels and with which other teenage students might empathise. Hence, this presentation of her feelings offers learning opportunities within the socio-emotional domain (cf. UNESO 2019), by helping students to voice not only her but also their own *angst*. The chorus spells out clearly that Antler isn't "a child anymore. [...] The world had made it clear that there was nothing childish about her" (ibid.: 511). She neither has the carefreeness of childhood, nor does she really know how to take responsibility for herself, how to find her position in society. It might seem childish to hide in a tree, but this is the only temporary solution Antler can think of. Hence, the first 'while-reading' task for students could be to 'take on' Antler's role, by acting as if they would be slipping into a coat (see Elis / Von Blanckenburg / Haack 2016). They can try out how it feels to make these statements out loud, to hear the chorus' words describing her. Moreover, students could choose a quote that they like and 'pose' this quote to see if they, in fact, can identify with it (ibid.). This also paves the way for the cognitive domain of learning, since – using Antler as a role – students learn to voice these concerns (cf. UNESO 2019).

A significant moment for later reflection is the scene in which Desk sees Antler in the tree: She tells him that she is sitting there because she is protesting and that one is "not supposed to know how long a protest is" (Smith 2015: 492). Desk, rather surprised to hear this, responds: "Shouldn't people know why you are protesting so they know what it is you want done?" (ibid.: 492). This clearly shows that Antler is not at all familiar with the schema of a protest and thus offers students the opportunity to learn **about** democracy and human rights (cf. Bîrzéa 2000:32, Gollob et al. 2010: 29, Knippertz / Möller 2015: 138); they can learn about the right to protest, about the freedom of opinion.

Antler appears as a character who has never learned to express her feelings and thoughts in a (for her) meaningful way. In a time in which the European-wide *Fridays for Future* protests – initiated and mainly organised by young adults – have both gained momentum and the attention of international media, this can be used to discuss the unwritten scripts of political action and performance of young adult power. In looking at these recent (and still ongoing) protests, talking about them and maybe even finding own ways of engagement, students can "experience school as a micro-society that respects freedoms and equality", training them "in exercising their human rights and respecting the rights of others (**learning 'through'** democracy and human rights)" (Gollob et al. 2010: 29, emphasis F.M.). Hence, they can also begin to **learn 'for'** democracy and human rights and become "competent and confident to exercise their human rights, with a mature sense of responsibility towards others and their community" (ibid.). In terms of political education, though, it is also important to discuss the nature of the process and the regional, national or global perspectives a protest could have, and which effects students would expect. The play's stance on the role of the individual in politics (regional, national and global) is clear: "look at everyone around us. All the power in the world and they don't care about nothing, don't fight for anything. We are being cowards by not fighting" (ibid.: 534).

5.3. Remoteness – or 'Perspective is Everything'

Remote – the title of the play – mirrors Antler's initial indistinct emotions about the society she lives in: She does not feel part of it, nor, so she claims, does she want to be part of it. In climbing the tree, she also attempts to create this remoteness in a physical way. Smith herself comments on this distancing, this remoteness, as follows:

> [...] it juxtaposes the fact that the title has connotations of a technical device (a TV remote) with its opening image of the destruction of a similar device (a mobile phone), and then is entirely set outside any technology – but thematically explores the idea of the remoteness of its characters, especially Antler, who chooses to be remote from the world. It is also about how it feels to be an adolescent and to feel remote from being either an adult or a child" (ibid.: 541-542).

As another 'while reading' task, individual students can take on Antler's role and consciously remove themselves physically from the rest of the group, to see how it feels. This encompasses all three dimensions of learning (cognitive, socio-emotional and behavioral), as they can also (learn to) describe reasons for wanting to remove themselves from a situation or moments in which they (unwantedly) feel remote from the people around them. Although they appear to be rather close, later in the play it becomes clear that Antler was upset by her sister Crystal, who seemed not to care about Antler's emotional life. This triggered an indistinct feeling, which is symptomatic for the world surrounding her: "It's apathy. It's everywhere. You said you didn't need me. I mean, what can I do? How can I change any of this? If I can't even get my own sister to care about me" (ibid.: 535). This feeling of being powerless leaves her frustrated and paralysed: "I can't change the world and I definitely can't save it. I can't do nothing" (ibid.: 524). The aspect of powerlessness could also be subject of discussion in class. It is juxtaposed by a different position: Desk decides that, by sitting up in this tree, Antler "is doing the exact thing she hates other people doing": "Us, down here, on the ground. We care. We've got no choice. [...] You've got to care about something. Everybody knows that. [...] It's one thing to count yourself out, but it just seems stupid to count yourself out because others are counting themselves out" (ibid.: 536). This is an illustration of what Starkey calls the dimension of "practice", which – along with the dimensions of feeling and status – characterises citizenship: Students can learn to see themselves as having "a sense that they are entitled and empowered to act in the world, in order to defend their own rights or the rights of others." (Starkey 2015: 21). With this "sense of agency", they can learn to grasp their "identity as a citizen" (ibid.). The very different roles – Antler as the confused, hurt and disappointed character, as well as Desk as the rather clear-headed, distant and critical character – can serve as means to change perspectives. When playing these roles, it might be helpful to use the 'thought tap' (see Elis / Von Blanckenburg / Haack 2016): While acting these two roles, they are tapped on the shoulder by a third person who asks them to voice the characters' feelings, thoughts and perspectives, aside from the script, to help students get into the character, on the one hand, while, at the same time, they continue to try out the different perspectives.

The play is not without hope, though. The solidarity Antler wishes for actually develops throughout the play and deepens between the characters. Especially Antler and Crystal are finally starting to talk and listen to one another, thereby mending their relationship. The other characters, particularly Desk, Finn and Oil mediate between them and – seemingly –between Antler and her relationship to the world. One of the most significant and remotely cosmopolitan quotations in the course of the play is the following: "This is ours. All of this is ours. But we can't make it ours, like truly properly ours, unless we're in it. We can't fix anything by being above it" (Smith 2015: 537). Instead of Antler climbing down, Desk, Crystal, Finn and Oil all climb the tree and watch the sunset, claiming, "Perspective, after all, is everything" (ibid.: 540).

Leading out of the play, students can 'slip out of' their role again, as if they were taking off a coat. After discussing the play and how it felt to become (cultural) actors within it, there can then be room for students to start 'looking for change' in the real-life world – whether it be their own or that of their contemporary counterparts such as Emma Gonzales (*March for Our Lives Movement*), Xiuhtezcatl Martinez (the indigenous environmental YA activist who gave a speech in front of the UN in 2015 at the age of 15), or Greta Thunberg (*Fridays for Future Movement*), just to name a few. In any case, if taught in line with the principles of HRE, the play can aid students in understanding that "[c]itizenship is a valuable way of understanding one's association with and connections to others", beyond national borders (Starkey 2015: 21). It offers plenty of opportunities to learn about, for, within and through Human Rights and democracy, while embracing the cognitive, socio-emotional and behavioral domain of learning.

6. Conclusion

This article started out by claiming that *Remote* and other YA dramatic texts may offer valuable opportunities for political education: They not only represent instances of performances; they also encourage them. These instances of performance are especially suitable, as they invite teenage students to engage in various performances of power. Learning through *Remote* allows students to 'play' with Antler's search for her own stance; they can take on Desk's role or just simply take any stance, without it having to be their own. Moreover, they can stage a protest, as absurd as it may seem, just to see how it feels, or learn the script of a protest. The play offers plenty of opportunity for learners to foster and practice their critical discourse competence, to learn about, for, through and within human rights and democracy, as it is open to interpretation and direction.

It is universal, hybrid and transcultural in its very essence. Yet, teachers who choose to teach with this play (or others similar to this) have to be certain as to which model of political education (democratic – national or regional –, global / cosmopolitan) they will use as their base. Since the students they teach are young members of performative societies attempting to find their own (political) positions in society, they will be – consciously and/or unconsciously, critically reflected or not – influenced by the direction the lessons take. This article argues that a larger view (global and cosmopolitan) needs to be taken into consideration, when helping students to develop their own performative (discourse) competence in today's global society. In line with Jackson, this article hence takes the stance that

> [c]ivilisational discourse is not simply one way of seeing and understanding the social world. It is also a political performance of cultural identification and allegiance. [...] Young people should be directively taught *against* the notion that there is an easy fit among concepts of culture, race, and civilisation, as they learn to *question* and not assume a sense of loyalty to groups describing themselves as civilisations for political aims (2019: 25)

Bibliography

Alsup, Janet (2010). *Young Adult Literature and Adolescent Identity Across Cultures and Classrooms: Contexts for the Literary Lives of Teens*. New York: Routledge.

Appiah, Kwame Anthony (2007). *Cosmopolitanism. Ethics in a World of Strangers*. London: Penguin.

Banks, Anthony (2015). Introduction. In: The National Theatre (ed.). *National Theatre Connections 2015 – New Plays for Young People*. London: Bloomsbury, v-ix.

Bîrzéa, César (2000). *Project on "Education for Democratic Citizenship" – Education for Democratic Citizenship: A Lifelong Learning Perspective. Council of Europe*. Retrieved from: www.bpb.de/system/files/pdf/F0R5Q8.pdf (23/06/21).

Byram, Michael (1997). *Teaching and Assessing Intercultural Communicative Competence*. Clevedon: Multilingual Matters.

Cart, Michael (2008). *The Value of Young Adult Literature*. Retrieved from: http://www.ala.org/yalsa/guidelines/whitepapers/yalit (23/06/21).

Corbett, Sue (2018). *YA Authors Respond to Teen Activism*. Retrieved from: https://www.publishersweekly.com/pw/by-topic/childrens/childrens-book-news/article/76774-ya-2018-booklist-the-revolution-will-be-anthologized.html (23/06/21).

Council of Europe (2008). *Whitepaper on Intercultural Dialogue – "Living together As Equals in Dignity*. Retrieved from: https://www.coe.int/t/dg4/ intercultural/source/white%20paper_final_revised_en.pdf (04/07/21).

Council of Europe (2001). Common European Framework of References for Languages: Learning, Teaching, Assessment. Retrieved from: https://rm.coe.int/1680459f97 (04/07/21).

Council of Europe (2010). Council of Europe Charter on Education for Democratic Citizenship and Human Rights Education. Retrieved from: https://rm.coe.int/CoERMPublicCommonSearchServices/DisplayDCTMContent?documentId=09000016803034e3 (04/07/21).

Council of Europe (2017). Citizenship and Participation. Retrieved from: https://www.coe.int/en/web/compass/citizenship-and-participation (04/07/21).

Council of Europe (2018). *Reference Framework of Competences for Democratic Culture. Volume 1: Contexts, Concepts and Model*. Retrieved from: https://rm.coe.int/prems-008318-gbr-2508-reference-framework-of-competences-vol-1-8573-co/16807bc66c (04/07/21).

Delanoy, Werner (2006). Transculturality and (Inter-)Cultural Learning in the EFL Classroom. In: Delanoy, Werner / Volkmann, Laurenz (eds.). *Cultural Studies in the EFL Classroom*. Heidelberg: Winter, 233–248.

Doff, Sabine / Schulze-Engler, Frank (eds.) (2011). *Beyond 'Other Cultures'. Transcultural Perspectives on Teaching the New Literatures in English*. Trier: WVT Wissenschaftlicher Verlag Trier.

Elis, Franziska / Von Blanckenburg, Max / Hack, Adrian (2016). In die dramapädagogische Arbeit ein- und aussteigen. In: *Der Fremdsprachliche Unterricht Englisch* (142), 4.

Freeman, Michael (2002). *Human Rights: An Interdisciplinary Approach*. Cambridge: Polity.

Freitag-Hild, Britta (2018). Teaching Culture: Intercultural Competence, Transcultural Learning, Global Education. In: Surkamp, Carola / Viebrock, Britta (eds.). *Teaching English as a Foreign Language: An Introduction*. Stuttgart: Metzler, 159-175

Gaudelli, William (2016). *Global Citizenship Education*. New York: Routledge.

Gollob, Rolf / Krapf, Peter / Weidinger, Wiltrud (eds.) (2010). *Educating for Democracy. Background Materials on Democratic Citizenship and Human Rights Education for Teachers. Vol. 1 of EDC/HRE Volumes I-VI*. Council of Europe Publishing. Retrieved from: https://www.living-democracy.com/pdf/en/V1/V01.pdf (04/07/21).

Hallet, Wolfgang (2011). *Lernen fördern – Englisch. Kompetenzorientierter Unterricht in der Sekundarstufe I*. Seelze: Klett/Kallmeyer.

Hallet, Wolfgang (2015). Die Performativität und Theatralität des Alltagshandelns: Performative Kompetenz und kulturelles Lernen. In: Hallet, Wolfgang / Surkamp, Carola (eds.). *Dramenpädagogik im Fremdsprachenunterricht*. Trier: WVT, 51-88.

Henseler, Roswita / Surkamp, Carola (2007). Leselust statt Lesefrust. In: *Der Fremdsprachliche Unterricht Englisch* 89, 2-11.

Hesse, Mechthild (2012). *Teenage Fiction in the Active English Classroom.* Stuttgart: Klett.

Jackson, Liz (2019). *Questioning Allegiance. Resituating Civic Education.* London: Routledge.

Knippertz, Daniel / Möller, Stefan (2015). 800 Years of the Magna Carta. Demokratielernen im Unterricht fördern. In: *Der Fremdsprachliche Unterricht Englisch* 137, 2-8.

Kramsch, Claire (2006). From Communicative to Symbolic Competence. *The Modern Language Journal*, 90, 249–252.

Kultusministerkonferenz (2004). *Bildungsstandards für die erste Fremdsprache (Englisch/Französisch) für den Mittleren Schulabschluss.* Beschluss von 04.12.2003. München: Wolters Kluwer. Retrieved from: https://www.kmk.org/fileadmin/Dateien/veroeffentlichungen_beschluesse/2003/2003_12_04-BS-erste-Fremdsprache.pdf (04/07/21).

Kultusministerkonferenz (2012). *Bildungsstandards für die fortgeführte Fremdsprache (Englisch/Französisch) für die Allgemeine Hochschulreife.* Retrieved from: https://www.kmk.org/fileadmin/Dateien/ veroeffentlichungen_beschluesse/2012/2012_10_18-Bildungsstandards-Fortgef-FS-Abi.pdf (04/07/21).

Lütge, Christiane (2015). Handlungs- und Produktionsorientierung im Dramenunterricht: Perspektiven für die fremdsprachliche Literatur- und Kulturdidaktik. In: Hallet, Wolfgang / Surkamp, Carola (eds.). *Dramenpädagogik im Fremdsprachenunterricht*. Trier: WVT, 189-202.

Matz, Frauke / Stieger, Anne (2015). Teaching Young Adult Fiction. In: Delanoy, Werner / Eisenmann, Maria / Matz, Frauke (eds.). *Learning with Literature in the EFL Classroom*. Frankfurt a.M.: Peter Lang, 121-140.

Matz, Frauke / Rumlich, Dominik (2020). Englischsprachige Jugendbücher im und außerhalb des Englischunterrichts: Young Adult Fiction als empirischer Gegenstand. In: Grünewald, Andreas / Hetehy, Meike / Struve, Karen (eds.). *KONTROVERS – Literaturdidaktik meets Literaturwissenschaft*. Trier: WVT, 159-175.

National Theatre (2019). *National Theatre Connections 2019*. Retrieved from: https://www.nationaltheatre.org.uk/learning/connections (04/07/2021).

New London Group (2000). A Pedagogy of Multiliteracies. Designing Social Futures. In: Cope, Bill / Kalantzis, Mary (eds.). *Multiliteracies. Literacy Learning and the Design of Social Futures*. London: Routledge, 9-37.

Nicholson, Helen (2009). *Theatre and Education*. New York: Palgrave Macmillian.

Osler, Audrey / Starkey, Hugh (2010). *Teachers and Human Rights Education*. London: UCL.

Schewe, Manfred (2011). Die Welt auch im fremdsprachlichen Unterricht immer wieder neu verzaubern – Plädoyer für eine neue performative Lehr- und

Lernkultur. In: Küppers, Almut / Schmidt, Torben / Walter, Maik (eds.). *Inszenierungen im Fremdsprachenunterricht. Grundlagen, Formen, Perspektiven*. Braunschweig: Diesterweg, 20-31.

Smith, Stef (2015). Remote. In: The National Theatre (ed.). *National Theatre Connections 2015 – New Plays for Young People*. London: Bloomsbury, 479-559.

Starkey, Hugh (2015). *Learning to Live Together. Struggles for Citizenship and Human Rights Education*. London: Institute of Education Press.

Surkamp, Carola (2015). Playful Learning with Short Plays. In: Delanoy, Werner / Eisenmann, Maria / Matz, Frauke (eds.). *Learning with Literature in the EFL Classroom*. Frankfurt a.M.: Peter Lang, 141-156.

Surkamp, Carola / Elis, Franziska (2016). Dramenpädagogik. Spielerisch Sprache lernen. In: *Der Fremdsprachliche Unterricht Englisch* (142), 2-8.

Volkmann, Laurenz (2015). Challenging the Paradigm of Cultural Difference and Diversity: Transcultural Learning and Global Education. In: Lütge, Christiane (ed.). *Global Education. Perspectives for English Language Teaching*. Zürich: Lit, 19-38.

Walter, Maik (2012). Theater in der Fremdsprachenvermittlung. In: Nix, Christoph / Sachser, Dietmar / Streisand, Marianne (eds.). *Theaterpädagogik*. Berlin: Theater der Zeit, 182-188.

UNESCO. *Global Citizenship Education*. Retrieved from: https://en.unesco.org/themes/gced/definition(04//07/21).

GRIT ALTER (REGENSBURG UNIVERSITY)

Theatricality of Visual Literature – EnACTing Picturebooks

This paper examines how visual literature, in particular picturebooks, can serve as a multisensory basis for dramatic approaches to learning English in the first two years of primary school. In order to do so, the paper synchronizes the design of picturebooks with drama and plays to analyze in how far the visual design of these texts entails theatricality and encourages performativity. This leads to a discussion of the potential of dramatic adaptations in primary school. Using the example of Yo! Yes! *(Raschka 2007), the paper suggests how students can engage in dramatic readings that lead to performances.*

1. Introduction

In 1934, educational philosopher Dewey proposed that 'learning by doing' is a most promising means for cognitive growth. In 1945, developmental psychologist Piaget argued that playing and pretending are among the first stages of a child's learning process and are a natural part of the development of human thought and language. In 1955, Poley was among the first to suggest the high potential of playing and pretending in the form of drama for language teaching, as he expressed firmly that "I won't stop to establish the importance of learning how to read plays for pleasure and for growth in understanding of human beings" (Poley 1955: 148). In 1962, Vygotsky's theory of social interaction supports prior ideas in that he also argues that play is one of children's primary learning activities. He sees a close connection of children's cognitive development to their engagement in interactive play and imagination that they themselves act in worlds slightly beyond their current cognitive stage. This long tradition of acknowledging the power of play, pretending, and performing can still be identified in constructivist theories of learning and mirror the line of argument of current advocates of drama pedagogy. Even in 2001, Winston and Tandy argue that

> Since we were very young children, we have learnt to distinguish between the convention of play and those of everyday life and exploring the boundaries between the two can be a great source of delight… it is from children's innate capacity for play, and upon the understandings they gain from participating in play, that dramatic activity can be constructed. (2001: vii-viii)

Hence, to this day, dramatic approaches are still central elements of a holistic pedagogy, be it L1 or foreign language learning. Wagner was among the first to reflect drama in education systematically. She differentiates between creative drama and drama in education to explore the potential both offer students from the elementary school level onwards. Her seminal publication *Educational Drama and Language Arts* (1998) offers insights to the close connection of dramatic performance and furthering language skills including speaking, writing, and reading, but also communicative competences such as participating and understanding dialogue. Wagner also addresses the potential of drama to enhance reflective and cognitive competences, the benefits of changing perspectives by changing a role, and comprehension through reader responses and engaging in stories. While young children engage in play and submerge themselves in fantasy worlds where narratives unfold and conflicts need to be solved, older children and young adults participate in role-plays and improvisations to reflect and solve (non)fictional situations and cultural encounters.

Despite the validity of the general line of argument for language learning in general, this article focusses on English language teaching (ELT). It carves out the special potential of drama for ELT in primary schools. More specifically, the argumentation considers dramatizing picturebooks as a beneficial means to design communicative and action-oriented ELT classrooms already on a pre-A1 and A1 level and thus prepare even very young students for dramatic approaches to language learning. The first part of this paper offers reflections on the connection of drama pedagogy and action-orientation and on drama's potential to integrate marginalized and partly neglected paralinguistic language competences. The second part introduces *Yo! Yes!* by Chris Raschka (2007) and offers a close reading and analysis of the picturebook that particularly focusses on its theatricality and its contribution to intercultural learning. Suggestions for how the picturebook can be used in primary ELT round up the argumentation.

2. Action-orientation: Focus on marginalized language competences

In the German tradition, Schewe and Hallet continually point out the benefits of drama in ELT. While Schewe, e.g., endorses performative teaching and learning of cultures (2011), Hallet defines performative competence as a central dimension of English language teaching (2010). This indicates that researchers and practitioners have acknowledged drama's potential for education and (foreign language) learning throughout past decades, highlighting its benefits for implementing communicative and action-oriented methodologies.

Scholars such as Vitz (1984) and Kao (1994) empirically researched drama's beneficial effect on language competences. Both were able to show that students made "notable progress in speaking English" (in Wagner 1998: 54) when drama activities were part of the lessons. Wagner summarizes that in view of drama and second language learning, students "use a wide range of registers and styles and for a much broader range of purposes than customary school dialogues" (ibid.).

A close link of drama and foreign language education is established by one of ELT's central principles: action-orientation (e.g., Weier 2008). In its Greek root, drama refers to 'dran' which means 'doing' or 'acting'. Hence, dramatic performance is, by its very term, engrained in action-orientation. For Schewe, both foreign language education and staging are therefore inherently connected (1993). This can be recognized by taking into consideration methods such as role-plays, acting out dialogues, or performing scenes from original plays, usually with intermediate and advanced learners. Here, students take on scripted roles, imitate or improvise given dialogues, e.g., in textbooks, or negotiate conflicts and/or meanings by playing themselves in acted dialogues that refer to daily situations in their own communities or target cultures.

Within this action-oriented paradigm of foreign language teaching, it becomes apparent that drama provides opportunities for multisensory and kinaesthetic responses to stories. Drama engages children in 'learning by doing' as it "involves children at many levels, through their bodies, minds, emotions, language, and social interaction" (Phillips 2003: 6). Performances can be visceral, intellectual and/or emotional experiences that make learning more meaningful and memorable as well as more transferable to the real world (Almond 2005: 10). Such an understanding of enactments as a "whole-person approach to language teaching" (ibid.) involves holistic communication that allows integrating reflections on senses and body language as well as conscious body movements into language teaching. Similar to language dimensions such as voice, intonation and prosody (see below), incentives for developing senses and body language are two aspects of language teaching that are often pushed to the margins. Yet, Volkmann (2008: 429, 433, 440) and Wessels (1987) particularly emphasize how important these features are for language use and how beneficial drama activities can be to foster dynamic intonation.

Numerous activities invite students to explore their senses and body movements (e.g., in Almond 2005). Students can, for example, be asked to imagine that they are given a balloon: they are to blow it up, close it, throw it into the air and catch it again (cf. Wickham 2013: 15-16). They can imagine eating different food that is very sweet, hot, or spicy and show their reactions, or be invited to react to listening to their favorite song through headphones. A more complex and challenging activity would be to have students imitate a dialogue without voices and speaking, but solely based on acting, i.e., using body language, mimics and gestures to express greetings, a suggestion, agreement or rejection, and a farewell.

The development of communicative competences needs to address paralinguistic features as well. These include voice, intonation, and prosody as well as facial expressions, gestures and body language. Whereas the range of realizing one's voice in terms of volume, pace, melody, and pitch significantly contributes to the message, the audible dimension in language acquisition is repeatedly reduced to pronunciation. However, the "more clearly and expressively we speak, the more effectively we convey our messages. What we say is often less important than the way we say it" (Maley / Duff 2005: 69). Thus, it is essential that students have the option to develop these dimensions of language use in language teaching scenarios. Scholars such as Almond and Maley have suggested numerous methods to consider these. For example, students could stand in a line and have one student stand on the opposite side of the room. While the students standing in line talk to each other, this single student functions as the volume control. He or she moves forwards and backwards indicating the volume with which the students speak. The closer he or she gets to the group, the quieter they have to speak; the further away he or she steps, the louder they become (Almond 2005: 69). Another means would be to find different ways of saying 'yes' and 'no'. Students read selected scenarios and decide how they would say either 'yes' or 'no' as a reply, e.g., a) Your favorite team has just scored a goal. b) Your friend has told you that his dog is sick. c) You don't believe a story someone is telling you. d) You are telling someone not to do something dangerous. e) Someone asks you whether you ate all the cookies. You answer but want to hide the truth (Almond 2005: 74-75). One last example is the activity "Changing voices" (Maley / Duff 2005: 81-82) in which students select a pair of opposites, e.g., young and old, friendly and unfriendly, interesting and boring. They get a few sentences (e.g., It's time to go. Let's hurry. / How much farther is it?) and pay attention to the way in which the message changes according to the mood in which they say these. Here, stress, intonation, mime, and bodies to express meaning extend leaning language in context (Phillips 2003: 13).

Students can benefit from such activities in preparation of their drama performances because these offer incentives to feel their bodies and to gain conscious access to their voices, movements, and emotions. Especially the activities that refer to the voice can additionally enhance their awareness of aspects that influence communication and transmitting a message. As these activities do not demand language production on a high level, teachers can already implement these at primary school level and thus allow students to develop this holistic language competence from an early age on.

The fact that drama and action-oriented methods rely on body language and facial expressions also benefits learners who may have difficulty speaking English. As Volkmann argues, drama can motivate shy and reserved students because they do not need to create language creatively when they can rely on scripted text. Additionally, students do not play themselves but take on different roles which offers them the opportunity to transcend their own limitations and to temporarily experiment with different identities (cf. Volkmann 2008: 428).

Thus, it is worthwhile to use literary-dramatic content and methods already in primary school and with beginning learners and not reserve it for intermediate or advanced learners (Hallet 2008: 399). As the discussion of picturebooks and theatricality and the example *Yo! Yes!* in the following part show, drama pedagogy can contribute to developing competences needed to engage in social encounters and solve communicative conflicts. The analysis and classroom implementation of *Yo! Yes!* offers incentives to combine drama and language work with fostering further competences such as intercultural communicative competence and visual literacy.

3. EnACTing picturebooks

Drama activities with beginning learners of English as a foreign language (EFL) need to be adapted to a pre-A1 level. At this age, their language skills are only approaching the ability to produce short phrases about themselves, to give personal information, e.g., name, address, family, nationality (cf. CEFR 2018: 69) and to ask and answer questions about daily routines in short formulaic language (ibid.: 83). Remarkably, the Companion Volume to the *Common European Framework of References* (CEFR 2018) acknowledges the importance of body language and gestures at this leaner level. It describes overall spoken interaction on a pre-A1 level as making oneself understood by "relying on gestures to reinforce the information" (ibid.: 83), by saying how you feel by "using simple words like 'happy', 'tired', accompanied by body language" (ibid.: 70) and by managing "very short, isolated, rehearsed, utterances using gesture and signaled requests for help when necessary" (ibid.: 144).

Accordingly, the text base on which language and performative competences are developed needs to be selected carefully. It would not be possible for pre-A1 learners to read and understand a script for a play. At the pre-A1 level, reading is limited to "simplest information material that consists of familiar words [...] or an illustrated story formulated in very simple, everyday words" (ibid.: 63); the scale for reading as a leisure activity does not include descriptors for pre-A1.

Thus, simple picturebooks could be a promising foundation for critical literary reading experiences and performances. The interplay of verbal and visual text supports the students in understanding the text, especially when both modes are symmetrical to each other (Nikolajeva/Scott 2000: 226). As literary texts, picturebooks are beneficial for primary ELT because the narrative structure in tune with illustrations involves learners on a personal level. Similarly to other literary texts, picturebooks "allow for emotional and individual reactions", "provide protective spaces for learner's imagination and personal response", and offer incentives for creative follow-up activities (Lütge 2018: 180). In view of communicative competences, picturebooks support the development of reading comprehension as the pictures not only illustrate the text but also support understanding the plot. When verbal and visual text are contradicting each other, this may also increase learner's critical reading and engagement with the text. Thus, picturebooks could also "support the development of general text and media competence" (ibid.). In *Yo! Yes!* (Raschka 1993), the picturebook discussed below, this is e.g., prevalent when learners search the visual texts for clues for the protagonists' feelings (cf. discussion of visual literacy below). Here, even young learners encounter the interplay of verbal and visual text and can interpret their relationship. Such an experience may broaden their understanding of formal features in a text and their meaning, a relationship that is not coincidental. It can be assumed that learners are sensitized to these features when they read other picturebooks in the future. For example, it is likely that they are able to identify the specific meaning of the font of Priscilla's name in *It's a George Thing!* (Bedford/Julian 2008), which is as delicate as the giraffe herself. After all, reading a picturebook is also an aesthetic experience and thus opens students to incentives for aesthetic learning (Lütge 2018: 180). As such, picturebooks engage "Multiple Intelligences" (Read 2008: 6) as they engage learners emotionally, aesthetically, and cognitively. When picturebooks offer insights to Anglophone cultures and lifestyles or deal with common norms and values, they also address cultural learning. This invites learners to change and coordinate different perspectives (Lütge 2018: 180, Volkmann 2008: 429) which may enhance empathy.

"Dramatizing a story is a complex project" (Serrurier-Zucker / Gobbé-Mévellec 2014: 16). Yet, with picturebooks, visuals offer clues on how to stage the body, emotions, and the general atmosphere in a scene, and thus support learners' performances. In prose texts, students often need to derive these aspects from the context and their staging depends on interpretation. In order to gain this information from the visual text in picturebooks, learners have to engage with the visuals in detail and read these critically. Hence, and additionally to the potential of picturebooks in primary ELT, dramatizations of picturebooks foster visual literacy. Visual literacy refers to the critical perception, analysis, and interpretation of visual images (Avgerinou 2009). While reading picturebooks, visual literacy is paramount, because, as indicated above, verbal and visual text can interact in very specific ways. Both modes can tell the same story. Yet, whereas the verbal text in picturebooks can be rather straight forward, the visual text often offers additional information, i.e., both modes can enhance but also contradict each other (Nikolajeva/Scott 2000). In order to enjoy picturebooks fully, readers need to engage with the verbal and the visual mode to understand the richness of the plot. Similarly, also engaging in a dramatic adaptation of a picturebook is a complex task as students need to read and understand both modes, interpret the text and develop their performance based on their reader responses.

Theatricality in picturebooks

The following section offers an analysis of Chris Raschka's *Yo! Yes!* (1993). I argue that this picturebook can be used as a foundation for dramatic performances with very young learners in primary school. *Yo! Yes!* is a book about two nameless boys who at the beginning of the text do not know each other but become friends in the course of the story. Both boys do not seem to have much in common. The first boy to appear in the peritext of the book – the parts that surround the core text of the picturebook and thus extend it, e.g., illustrations in the opening pages (Genette 1997: 1) – has dark skin color, is wearing untied sneakers, baggy shorts, and a loose white T-shirt with a large red dot on the front. He is folding his arms in front of his body, is leaning back, his head and face turned down, eyes closed as if he was sleeping while standing there. The second boy appears on the right half of this opening. Readers can see him from the side, taking a large step exiting the page. His skin is much lighter that the other boy's, he is wearing long brown pants, a green jacket, and brown and black shoes. His eyes are closed as well, but compared to the other boy he is not smiling so that he appears sad while the first boy's posture indicates that he is content with himself and more self-confident. In the following pages, each opening is divided so that the boys occupy their own space: the boy in the white T-shirt on the left and the boy in the jacket on the right. As such, the picture-book appears as an authentic scenic-dialogical text which can be differentiated from Hallet's didactic scenic-dialogical texts that can often be found in students' textbooks (2008: 407).

Within the book itself, a dialogue between boys develops which carries the plot. The dialogue between both boys is limited to very few words and phrases. In the first opening, the boy on the left is putting his hands on his hips, bending his left knee slightly forward, turning is head a little downwards and says "Yo!" He is placed on the very edge of the page, his shadow placed in the middle of the left side of this opening. The boy on the right is placed in the corner of the right page, his body turned away from the other boy. He is turning his head downward, looking at the other boy from below. His reply is a simple "Yes?" The background is mainly light blue, whereas the space directly behind the boys is white, imitating the general shape of the two protagonists. The verbal text is written on top of both boys. While "Yo!" is printed in large black letters using up a lot of space, the "Yes?" is much smaller, yet printed in the same color and font.

In the next opening, both boys appear on their sides again, but now the boy on the left is taking one step forward, raising his head and stretching his left arm to point into the direction of the other boy. He exclaims "Hey!" to which the boy on the right answers "Who?" While he is also moving one step toward the boy on the left, his legs are closed, his head still slightly turned to the ground. He uses both arms to point at himself. Thumbing through the remaining pages reveals that both boys further approach each other. One can see that the boy on the right is sad because he does not have any friends. He is then taken aback when the boy on the left offers to be his friend. In the end, they both embrace each other and celebrate their newly formed friendship with a loud "YOW!", jumping into the air while holding hands.

Throughout the book, the dramatic development and climax are based on whether and how the boys become friends. Because the verbal text is limited to simple and single words and phrases, the boys' body language, mimics, and gestures create the tension in the book.

Body language, mimics and gestures reveal each boy's character. The boy on the left takes up much more space in the opening pages than the boy on the right. He is extensively using his arms to support his words, moving them up and down, to the front and back, pointing at the other boy. He is leaning for- and backwards to move toward the boy on the right when he asks questions and is leaning back when he gets surprising or unexpected answers. The boy on the right is usually keeping his arms close to this body and is taking only small steps. It is only when he recognizes that the other boy offers his friendship that he opens up and allows his body to take more space and become more visible; only then does he raise his head and really look at the boy on the left. While the boy on the left side of each opening appears self-confident and cool, the other is rather shy, insecure, and self-conscious.

In addition, the very design of the verbal text and its changes from one opening to the next indicate how the relationship between both boys develops. From one opening to the next, the design of the verbal text changes according to the message it conveys. Size, shape, and colour of the font and its placement on the page lend intensity and emotion to the speech (Van der Linden 2005 in Serrurier-Zucker / Gobbé-Mévellec 21). This is particularly visible when the sadness of the boy on the right is attributed to him not having any friends. The dialogue until then consists of:

L: Yo!

R: Yes?

L: Hey!

R: Who?

L: You!

R: Me?

L: Yes, you!

R: Oh.

L: What's up?

R: Not much.

L: Why?

R: NO fun.

L: Oh?

R: **No friends**.

Until here, the verbal text was printed in black and only varied in size, with the speech of the boy on the left usually printed slightly bigger than the boy's on the right. "No friends", however, is much smaller than all prior expressions and printed in bright red, thus contributing to the dramatization of the issue.

This change in color emphasizes the story's conflict and signals an emotional turn in the book. In the following pages, the print returns to black. It is only when the boy on the left moves his body forward and exclaims, "**Look!**", thus offering his friendship, that the red print appears again, indicating the climax of the plot. The boy on the right is unsure and surprised, increases his distance to the other boy and ponders what to do. Now the boy on the left is uncertain as well. Although he moved to the very right edge of this side of the opening being as close to the other as his space allows, he only has a question mark above his head which is, for the first time in the book, smaller than the "Yes!" that the boy on the right exclaims as a delayed answer. While the verbal text on the right is printed in large letters, seemingly expressing a loud and self-confident voice, the respective boy himself is still focussed on himself, holding his arms close to his body and seemingly giggling to himself. Thus, the verbal text codes this characterization of the boys.

While so far the boys have been placed on the lower third of each page and the verbal text in the upper part, this is reversed when both are friends and jump into the air while holding hands. Now a big "Yow!" printed in red is at the bottom of the page, metaphorically establishing the foundation of their friendship. Here, and also in the second last opening, the boy on the right left his space and moved to join the boy on the left. Both boys share the left side of the opening, while their exclamations "Yo!" (the boy on the left) and "Yes!" (the boy formerly on the right), still remain in their original spaces.

Interestingly, also the color-coding of the background changes. The more the distance between both decreases, bodily as well as emotionally, the warmer the color in the background becomes. While it was light blue at the beginning, it turns pink when the boy on the left offers his friendship and bright yellow when the boy on the right accepts it.

The visual indication of the boys becoming friends could also be critically scrutinized. The boy on the right joins the boy on the left, and one could ask why they move in this direction rather than having the boy on the left join his friend on the right. An answer could be that the boy on the left offered his friendship in the first place and thus made the first move. Now that the boy on the right accepts it, he makes the next literal move and joins him. A power-critical reading could also interpret this as an act of establishing the self-confident boy as the one who is leading and higher up on the hierarchal ladder of the boys' newly formed relationship. Another aspect readers could see critically is the characterization of both boys using skin color. It seems stereotypical to identify the boy with dark skin color as the cool and relaxed one, who swaggers toward the shy boy, sporting an outfit that reminds of hip-hop and basketball culture. However, the different skin colors contribute to the effect of establishing a friendship across an ethnic border, which the strict separation of each opening creates. Furthermore, readers could imagine whether and how the meaning and message of the book changes if the protagonists where female. If one was male and one was female, they could also investigate who would occupy which side of the opening and play around with this characterization, i.e., the self-confident protagonist on the right being female, and the shy one male and the other way around.

A detailed reading and interpretation of the plot, illustrations, and print of the verbal text can be transformed into a dramatization of the picturebook. As discussed above, the verbal text of *Yo! Yes!* mainly consists of single words and phrases. What carries the dialogue, though, are body language, mimics, gestures, and the design of the printed text. The different sizes and colors of the verbal text could verbally be interpreted and realized using varying volumes, intonations, stress, and adapted voices in a reader's theatre or performance. In addition, body movements, mimics and gestures can be imitated and adapted during a performance. Thus, students have the opportunity to engage with aspects that are often neglected in language teaching.

Quality markers of picturebooks for drama adaptations

Some aspects of Burke and O'Sullivan's argumentation of what makes a good play (2002: 67ff.) apply to evaluating the features of a picturebook that can be used for dramatic adaptations. First and foremost, it needs to be about a topic young learners can identify with, it should not be too serious, but funny and humorous, whereas this does not mean that it could not present a conflict or deeper meaning, e.g., (lack of) friendship, respect, and openness to others as in *Yo! Yes!* It should offer space for interpretation and engagement with the story or characters and thus offer incentives for repeated readings during which readers can discover something new and exciting, e.g., the meaningful change of the background color in the picturebook discussed above. The illustrations should at least hint at facial expressions and body language so that especially young learners can still perceive the plot development, particularly when the verbal text becomes more complex. For young learners it is paramount to present the dialogues, the narration, and plot development clearly. As mentioned above, their receptive and productive communicative competences are rather limited. They only approach the A1 level and will not be able to understand authentic books with too much and complex verbal text. Hence, the picturebook and the narration within should not be too long but manageable for young readers, who potentially become performers in the dramatic adaptation or reader's theatre. Compared to an actual dramatic adaptation, a reader's theatre allows students to hold the text or script in their hands and asks them to read with expression and emphasis.

While Burke and O'Sullivan (2002) include colors, action, and the amount and quality of direct speech as markers of good plays for language learning, these need to be qualified in view of picturebooks. *Yo! Yes!* only entails direct speech that is not even identified as such. That the phrases above the protagonists' heads can be read as direct speech only becomes visible through their positioning and the matching body language the boys display. The action of the picturebooks is reduced to both boys decreasing the distance between each other and becoming friends. This is very limited action, even for a picturebook for young readers. Apart from the changing color scheme and the white spotlights for the protagonists, there is no background design. One could claim that the book could offer more colors and design elements. Yet, this reduction also contributes to focussing on the conflict and establishment of the friendship as presented verbally and especially visually.

This reading of a picturebook suggests that it entails a certain level of orality which can be beneficially applied to readers' theatres and performances. The images and printing of the verbal text open up avenues for the imagination to give shape to, voice, and act out the story. According to the design of the words in the page, students give voice to these words and thus construct meaning. On top of the construction of the openings, the onomatopoeia, repetitions, rhythm, and sonorities structure and organize the reading and subsequent dramatic adaptation. The boys' gesticulation, their facial expressions and eye movements and how these change from one opening to the next, their posture, movement, and proximity can be transferred to dramatic readings and performances that examine and practice these broader aspects of communication. This lively design of the picturebook itself appears as a spectacularization of the printed page that young learners can explore with their own bodies and voices. This, in turn, is promising to increase their communicative competences.

A performance of this picturebook also offers the opportunity to foster cultural competences. Learners are likely to encounter the situation depicted in the book, two people who do not know each other meet and, after some hesitation, become friends, in real life as well. In the book, both boys happen to be from different ethnic backgrounds which does not hinder them from getting to know each other. Imitating real life situations such as in *Yo! Yes!* "accurately targets the requirements of a communicative approach to language teaching" (Almond

2005: 9), namely preparing students for real life communication in meaningful ways.

Changing perspectives is one of the central elements of intercultural communicative competence (ICC). Using this story, learners can do exactly this. By performing a dramatic adaptation of the picturebook, they imitate the dialogue, move into boys' roles and change from their own perspective into the boys'. Embodying one of the boys and potentially feeling what they feel increases their empathy. Their affective response to the narrative becomes manifest in the performed reading of the verbal text in direct interplay with the visual text. As Küppers argues, drama pedagogy and intercultural learning share central principles especially in view of action-orientation (2015: 146), which is likewise a central aim of ICC. By applying drama-based methods in contexts of intercultural learning, students can establish and maintain relationships with others and communicate with and mediate between people from different cultural backgrounds and speakers of different languages (ibid.: 147). Using *Yo! Yes!* as a text base illustrates how both approaches, intercultural learning and action-orientation, can already be integrated in primary school and on a pre-A1 level.

Cultural learning is also closely linked to body language, and both need to be approached more directly. As Sarter observes, it is particularly in the communication between partners with different cultural backgrounds that the role of verbal language is subordinate to the role of the body language (Sarter 1997: 121). Yet, body language and the use of voice carry essential meaning in (intercultural) communication. Hallet argues similarly and states that understanding and the cognitive acquisition of dramatic structures is primarily not a literary competence, but primarily a social competence that comes into effect in all situational-social interactions (Hallet 2008: 393). Thus, *Yo! Yes!* can also be beneficial in context of inter- and transcultural learning and understanding otherness.

Yo! Yes! in the primary EFL classroom

In order to realize a dramatization of *Yo! Yes!* in the primary EFL classroom, it is necessary to read the text carefully. Learners should get to know the two protagonists, e.g., by describing their clothes and maybe giving them names. They should take a detailed look at their body language, mimics, and gestures, and draw conclusions about the way both boys feel and learn the words to label these emotions. They could also speculate why the verbal text is printed in different sizes and colors. Such a detailed consideration of the different elements that form the picturebook not only prepares a dramatic reading and eventually the enactment, but also develops visual literacy at this young learner level. Certainly, not all of the vocabulary and structures to express their discoveries are available in English. Teachers may need to provide scaffolding in order to allow students to express their discoveries in the foreign language. Yet, this provides an opportunity to introduce and learn these in a meaningful context, even if the retention rate of the new language could be rather low and the new language might not be available productively in other contexts. Retention and availability could, however, be supported by enacting the feelings and dramatizing the dialogue (Keehn / Harmon / Shoho 2008).

As a warm-up, exploring and experimenting with facial expressions and body movements prepares learners for their own active readings. Apart from a detailed reading of the picturebooks and its different modes, teachers can apply straightforward total physical response (TPR) activities to invite learners to show different facial expressions. The teacher would name an expression, perform it and have learners imitate it, e.g., frowning, raising both eyebrows, twisting the mouth, pursing lips, opening the eyes widely, smiling out of the side of the mouth, winking or wrinkling the nose (Burke / O'Sullivan 2002: 33). Learners can then connect these movements to the emotions the visual clues transfer and can find matching phrases. They can also read sentences and show the content with their bodies, e.g., 'A cold day in winter.' – 'A hot day in summer.' – 'There is a yummy fruit salad in front of you.' – 'A ride on a bumpy bus.' The other students watch the performance and say what the student is performing. In case they may not know the English phrases yet, these can be given on the board, with a choice of four of which only one is correct.

When teachers introduces the book, they could only present the first two openings and ask the learners to describe both boys. Again, if the language is available, teachers can collect the ideas on the board. If not, options of which students need to select the appropriate ones could be offered in the board, i.e., words and phrases for both boys which the learners need to match to the respective protagonist. As to engage with the story, the teacher could only read the book until the boy on the left offers his friendship and then ask the learners how they think the story continues.

Once the learners have a general understanding of both protagonists, the conflict and the solution that develops between them, they are asked to read the story themselves. Eventually, they can add performance to their reading aloud. This could first be done while still sitting at their desks and reading the book aloud with expression. Here, they have to express the different feelings with their voices, using intonation, stress, and volume. They may also add facial expressions that match these feelings while they read. In a second step, the learners stand up and impersonate the emotions that they identified while reading the book together, i.e., to show with their bodies that they are self-confident and happy or sad and insecure. Finally, the learners perform the dialogue, putting together the text, facial expressions and respective body language. As the verbal text is reduced to a minimum, it should not be problematic to remember the text by heart. The learners could also be invited to improvise the text, as long as they pay attention to the phonologic, facial, and bodily features of their performances. When the students' language competences reach the A2-level, they could also get the task to extend the reduced dialogue to complete sentences and come up with a conversation that includes more phrases.

In terms of ICC, the situation depicted in the picturebook invites learners to ponder whom they consider a friend. How do they make friends and how do they approach someone they do not know (yet)? In this case, *Yo! Yes!* can function "as an interactive support, which permits the channelling of the young learners' physical energy and its transformation into intellectual energy" (Perrot 1999: 117). This guides even young learners in developing openness to people who at first seem a little different but who eventually have similar needs, such as being friends.

4. Conclusion and outlook: Drama beyond primary school

The discussion above argued that drama activities can be beneficial for ELT because they make use of play, which is characteristic in children's approaches to discovering the world around them. For younger learners at the pre-A1 and A1 level, drama activities may even appear as play when they are to transfer themselves into different situations or use their imagination to create action. It is essential, however, that furthering language competences takes centre stage; implementing drama in ELT is not about teaching drama, but using drama to teach English. While the verbal language material is reduced to a minimum at the pre-A1 level, it can be focussed more strongly when drama activities continue to be used in their intermediate and advanced ELT classrooms. Drama activities then also allow learners a smooth transition from primary school to middle school (cf. Volkmann 2008: 434).

The combination of drama and picturebooks is promising as learners can engage in drama performances despite a lack of extended language competences. As exemplified with *Yo! Yes!*, picturebooks lend themselves particularly well as a foundation to invite learners to explore the foreign language in action-oriented and meaningful contexts. The multimodal design of the text, the attention to detail in the illustrations, and the approachable storyline can be a useful basis upon which young learners build the development of holistic communicative competences. Yet, this does not necessarily have to be a one-to-one dramatization of the text, as gaps and stylistic devices such as the print design of the verbal text are also open to interpretation and different readings. Students can explore these with their voices and translate these into facial expressions, gestures, and body language.

When developing language competences, a focus on paralinguistic and phonologic features is essential as these play an important role in communication. Meaning is not only created by what is said, but also, and in certain situations even more decisively, by how something is said. Yet, language teaching often neglects these aspects. The theatricality of picturebooks and enacting the plot provides learners with an opportunity to engage with these elements to create meaning. Drama adaptations allow learners to really "experience[e] the text" (Lütge 2018: 178) and engage in "multiple perspectives provided through the narrative structure of the character constellation" (ibid.). As such, enactments of picturebooks are embodied literary experiences that can support learners in reading and understanding more complex texts in their career as language learners and avid readers. Looking for clues about a protagonist's character in the visual text can be seen as a foundation for learners' active engagement with the text. Learners can then apply this to looking for similar clues that help to understand the characterization of protagonists and the plot development in chapter books, short stories and novel appear. Hence, such action-oriented drama approaches to picturebooks not only develop visual, but also literary literacy (Alter / Ratheiser 2019).

Bibliography

Almond, Mark (2005). *Teaching English with Drama. How to Use Drama and Plays when Teaching – For the Professional English Language Teacher*. Chichester: Keyways Publishing.

Alter, Grit / Ratheiser, Ulla (2019). A new model of literary competences and the revised CEFR descriptors. *ELTJournal* 73(4), 377-386.

Avgerinou, Maria D. (2009). Re-Viewing Visual Literacy in the 'Bain d'Images' Era. *TechTrends. Linking Research and Practice to Improve Learning* 53(2), 28-34.

Bedford, David (2008). *It's a George Thing!* J. Russell (Illus.). London: Egmont.

Bonnet, Andreas / Küppers, Almut (2011). Wozu taugen kooperatives Lernen und Dramapädagogik? Vergleich zweier populärer Inszenierungsformen. In:

Küppers, Almut / Schmidt, Torben / Walter, Maik (eds.). *Inszenierungen im Fremdsprachenunterricht*. Braunschweig: Diesterweg/Klinkhardt, 32-52.

Burke, Ann F. / O'Sullivan, Julia C. (2002). *Stage by Stage. A Handbook for Using Drama in the Second Language Classroom*. Portsmouth: Heinemann.

Butzkamm, Wolfgang (2012*). Lust zum Lehren. Lust zum Lernen – Fremdsprachen von Anfang an anders unterrichten*. Tübingen: Franke Verlag.

Council of Europe (2018). *Common European Framework of References for Languages: Learning, Teaching, Assessment. Companion Volume with New Descriptors*. Straßbourg: Council of Europe.

Dewey, John (1934). *Art as Experience*. New York: G.P. Putnam's Sons.

Genette, G. (1997). *Paratexts: Thresholds of Interpretation.* Cambridge: Cambridge University Press.

Hallet, Wolfgang (2008). Staging Lives: die Entwicklung performativer Kompetenz im Englischunterricht. In: Ahrens, Rüdiger / Eisenmann, Maria / Merkl, Matthias (eds.). *Moderne Dramendidaktik für den Englischunterricht*. Heidelberg: Winter, 387-408.

Hallet, Wolfgang (2010). Performative Kompetenz und Fremdsprachenunterricht. In: *Scenario* 1/2010, 4-17.

Keehn, Susan / Harmon, Janis / Shoho, Alan (2008). A Study of Raders Theater in Eighth Grade: Issues of Fluency, Comprehension, and Vocabulary. In: *Reading & Writing Quarterly* 24(4), 335-362.

Küppers, Almut (2015). Interkulturelle Kompetenzen, Dramapädagogik und Theaterwissenschaften. In: Hallet, Wolfgang / Surkamp, Carola (eds.). *Dramendidaktik und Dramapädagogik im Fremdsprachenunterricht*. Trier: WVT, 145-164.

Lütge, Christiane (2018). Literature and Film. In: Surkamp, Carola / Viebrock, Britta (eds.). *Teaching English as a Foreign Language: An Introduction*. Stuttgart: Metzler.

Maley, Alan / Duff, Alan (2005). *Drama Techniques. A Resource Book of Communication Activities for Language Teachers*. Cambridge: Cambridge University Press.

Nikolajeva, Maria / Scott, Carol (2000). The Dynamics of Picturebook Communication. In: *Children's Literature in Education* 31(4), 225-239.

Phillips, Sarah (2003). *Drama with Children*. Oxford: Oxford University Press.

Piaget, Jean (1945). *Play, Dreams, and Imitation in Childhood*. New York: WW Norton and Company.

Poley, Irvin (1955). Drama in the Classroom. In: *The English Journal* 44(3), 148-151.

Raschka, Chris (2007). *Yo! Yes!* Scholastic Bookshelf.

Read, Carol (2008). Scaffolding Children's Learning through Story and Drama. In: *CATS: Children and Teenagers*, 2008, n.p.

Sarter, Heidemarie (1997). *Fremdsprachenarbeit in der Grundschule. Neue Wege, neue Ziele*. Darmstadt: Wissenschaftliche Buchgesellschaft.

Schewe, Manfred (2011). Die Welt auch im fremdsprachlichen Unterricht immer wieder neu verzaubern – Plädoyer für eine performative Lehr- und Lernkultur. In: Küppers, Almut/Schmidt, Torben/Walter, Maik (eds.). *Inszenierungen im Fremdsprachenunterricht. Braunschweig*: Diesterweg / Klinkhardt, 20-31.

Schewe, Manfred (1993). *Fremdsprache inszenieren. Zur Fundierung einer dramapädagogischen Lehr- und Lernpraxis*. Oldenburg: BIS Verlag.

Serrurier-Zucker, Carol / Gobbé-Mévellec, Euriell (2014). The Page IS the Stage: From Picturebooks to Drama with Young Learners. In: *CLELEjournal* 2(2), 13-30.

Volkmann, Laurenz (2008). Acting out: Möglichkeiten des darstellenden Spiels mit englischen Texten von der Unter- bis zur Oberstufe. In: Ahrens, Rüdiger / Eisenmann, Maria / Merkl, Matthias (2008) (eds.). *Moderne Dramendidaktik für den Englischunterricht*. Heidelberg: Winter, 424-449.

Vygotsky, Lev (1962). *Thought and Language*. Cambridge: MIT Press.

Wagner, Betty (1998). *Educational Drama and Language Arts: What Research Shows*. Portsmouth: Heinemann.

Wickham, Ruth (2013). *Plays and Drama for Young Learners*. Institute Pendidikan Guru Kampus Dato' Razali Ismail. Retrieved from: http://ktf2013.weebly.com/uploads/8/7/6/1/8761106/lga3104_module.pdf (23/07/21).

Weier, Ursula (2008). Grundformen dramatischer Interaktion im Englischunterricht der Grundschule. In: Ahrens, Rüdiger / Eisenmann, Maria / Merkl, Matthias (eds.). *Moderne Dramendidaktik für den Englischunterricht*. Heidelberg: Winter, 522-542.

Wessels, Carolyn (1987). *Drama*. Oxford: Oxford University Press.

CHRISTIANE LÜTGE & MAX VON BLANCKENBURG (LUDWIG-MAXIMILIANS-UNIVERSITÄT MÜNCHEN)

Drama and Performance in Digital Spaces

This contribution will discuss the changing role of drama and performance with a view to its impact on new formats in increasingly digitalised educational contexts. We argue that digitality and performance in various media products need to be understood more thoroughly in their interdependence, their reciprocity and their creative potential that is likely to transform the notion of drama and how we perceive it. Processes of self-staging in social media and other performative acts offer new options for learner-oriented approaches and they will lead to different modes of perception as well as new facets of aesthetic re-enactments. Dramatic and performative dimensions of digital literature, digital political performances and digital sociocultural performances will be related to what might eventually develop into an increasingly performative gaze *– fostered by various digital spaces.*

1. Introduction

In many educational discourses drama and performance seem to be diametrically opposed to all kinds of digital practices. This traditionally not only applies to their alleged goals and purposes, ethics and aesthetics, degrees of (human) interaction but also to assumptions of identity formation and educational values. Underlying notions of a superiority of performative and drama-related practices over digital applications and routines might be responsible for a stereotypical image wavering between highly acclaimed amateur school theatre productions and conspicuously observed digital games marathons. However, digitality per se is not a natural enemy to drama and performance, to theatre activities, acting out or improv games in a (foreign language) classroom. Drama and performance in digital spaces can develop in various ways and come in different shapes and facets. It needs to be pointed out, though, that the performative and the digital spheres are not necessarily in opposition but may even complement each other. In fact, networking capabilities of digital technology can enable textual interactivity to be coupled with interaction between users. Identity in online and offline contexts may shift much more easily in the future with readers and authors treating dramatic play as a bridge between their online and offline experiences.

While there might be no reason for one-sided cybertopian enthusiasm, one may well come to terms with the educational potential of collaborative interaction and plot development in digital spaces. However, a departure from merely textually oriented studies of drama is not a new development and foreign language education might considerably profit from methods and approaches that take into account new ideas for communicative and intercultural intersections with digital tools and in digital spaces.

2. Dramatic and performative dimensions in digital literature

In the digital age, new media formats such as mobile apps are gradually working their way into the foreign language classroom. This process requires sound pedagogic and purposeful reasoning and is still often selective and unsystematic. It also calls for a deep understanding and typologisation of frequently emerging digital media in view of their learning and teaching potential (cf. Lütge / Merse / Owczarek / Stannard 2019). Apart from this more pragmatic and instrumental view, larger questions evolve concerning e.g. how whole phenomena and fields of inquiry – such as literature and literature didactics – are affected on a broader level that might call into question and renegotiate their disciplinary and material self-conception (cf. Hammond 2016; Zimmermann 2015).

With a view to the special features of dramatic texts, their depiction of characters and setting and differences concerning narrative stance in epic texts, the potential of digital spaces is of special interest.

Furthermore, a focus on digitally (re-)designed dramatic texts might add another facet to the phenomenon of crossing boundaries between genres, both important for the production and reception of literary texts. Digital games are interesting examples here, especially as interactive as-if worlds (cf. O'Mara 2012) and when they appear in the form of ludonarratives (cf. Stannard / von Blanckenburg 2018), which meander between text and game.

O'Mara refers to Beavis (2012: 130), who in a similar vein points out:

> A particular quality of games, as digital forms, is that they come into existence only when played – the narrative literally comes into being only through the physical interaction between one and more players, the game and the machine. Game play is therefore quintessentially situated and depends entirely on an ongoing interaction between player and the unfolding iteration on the screen.

It is this aspect of gaming that O'Mara sees as most similar to process drama. As she points out, without the event of the drama the text does not exist, "and often it exists only within the action or playing out of the game or the drama" (O'Mara 2012: 523).

While O'Mara is not advocating that digital gaming might be a replacement for drama, she points out that the "in-action" aspects of process drama might be described as literacy practices (O'Mara 2012: 531) and it seems that these show relatively close connections to digital gaming and literacy. Digital games as interactive *as-if worlds* (ibid.) in all their theatricality might in fact sometimes serve as showcases that stage conflicts and passions traditionally developed in dramatic texts.

Considering the selection of authors and texts, drama and performance in EFL contexts is inextricably linked to Shakespeare and the reception and re-readings of his plays. Digital spaces have meanwhile entered the bard's universe and provide various digitised versions of plays.

The tablet app *The Tempest* by Heuristic Shakespeare (2016) adopts many established functionalities from e-books and digital informational environments for making Shakespeare's work easier to navigate and understand, including pop-up vocabulary glosses, the ability to highlight, copy and take notes, as well as providing hyper-links to paratexts and informational articles. Moreover, the app includes an eloquent design for layering modal forms (e.g. videos of performers speaking lines are synchronised to the playtext scrolling below) and allows for multiple, novel ways for reconfiguring and re-visualizing the play-text.

Within *The Tempest*, the reconfigurability of the app can facilitate novel readings of the play (e.g. multi-modal readings at the intersection of play text, video performances, and the expressive illustrations provided in the app). Similarly, a learner-oriented approach to drama is possible here through readings that engage with the language of one character. For instance, the app offers a scene map where users can select scenes and watch as the character icons rearrange themselves to illustrate who is in which setting and with which players at different points in the play. Users may additionally see the line density of a particular character's role, along with a full list of that character's lines linking back to the core text. While engaging with the core play text, users can tap on the right margin to pull up a timeline of the play, concise summaries, illustrations and curated lines of text that are especially iconic or significant to the play. Those very specific options would be prohibitively complex and time consuming within a language learning context relying on analogue media alone and offer insights into the features of dramatic texts (cf. Lütge / Merse / Stannard 2021).

Countless re-arrangements and re-readings of Shakespeare's dramas have given rise to approaches that only loosely relate to the original text but highlight notorious text passages or dialogues. *Srsly Hamlet* by Courtney Carbone (2015) draws on this desire to expand freely from a Shakespearean text. Hamlet turned into a chat conversation might inspire creative re-enactments. What if Hamlet and Ophelia had had smartphones: this is the underlying question that Carbone transferred into a novel for young adult readers – in a book version. The element of digital culture here, i.e. the assumption of a dramatically different course of action (in the real sense of the word) can be acted out in a creative endeavour to actually sense how communication works in the digital age. Still, especially in light of constantly changing conventions of digital interaction (e.g. concerning popular emojis and acronyms in chat conversations), adaptations such as *Srsly Hamlet* need to be seen as snapshots of a particular (or perhaps even assumed) youth language in digital spaces that may well develop further within a short time. Thus, such texts can be starting points for a reflection on how certain performative acts may be expressed by learners themselves – through the tools, genres and the language they use in everyday digital communication.

When trying to understand key characteristics of drama and performance in digital spaces, creativity, in our view, plays a vital role. As counter-intuitive as this integration of digital and creative dimensions might sound at first, this assumption becomes more plausible when we have a look at Cameron et al.'s four domains of a drama framework for exploring digital arts cultures (cf. Cameron et al. 2017: 13) that we would like to introduce at this point. The authors point out creativity, playfulness, performance and digital liveness as important elements in this context.

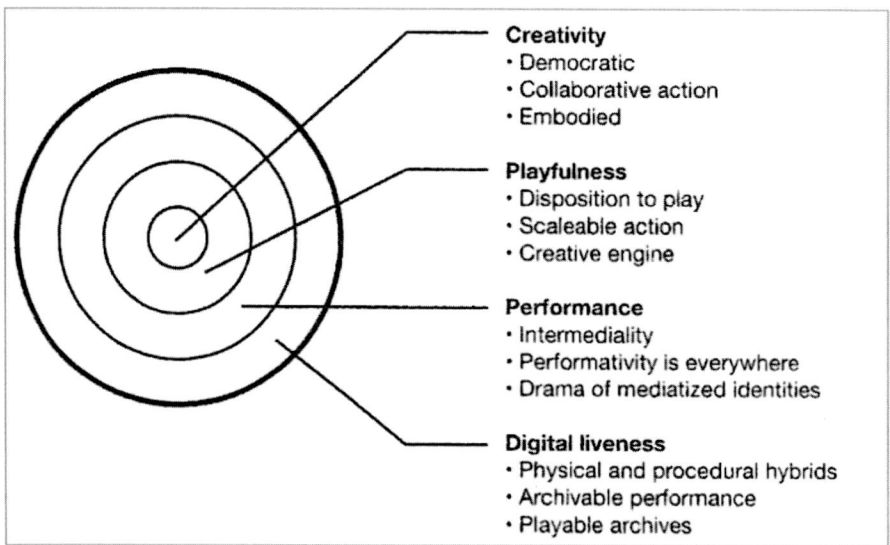

Figure 1: Drama framework for exploring digital arts cultures
(Cameron et al. 2017: 13)

- Creativity is defined as a disciplined and structured process, which is central to theatre, gaming, and other forms of cultural production, both in education and the creative industries. More counter-intuitive insights can be traced in their deconstruction of the "myth about creativity" as an individual striving disconnected from others, often idealised in the cliché of "a loner artist starving in the attic" (2017:17). In fact, interaction and commonly shared sets of experience are vital here and creativity as collaborative action is possible in both analogue, digital as well as hybrid formats.

- Playfulness is closely connected to creativity and also refers to processes of human motivations behind learning, of socialisation and individual development. As part of identity formation and exploration the use of technology to support play "as a transformative and creative platform" (ibid.) is not at all a contradiction but rather a next possible step, as we would like to argue.

- Performance encompasses the role and identity play which we can also encounter in digital cultures. According to Cameron et al., "the ergodic literacies apparent in the collaborative engagement with interactive art forms, and the transmedia nature of production and content" (ibid.: 14) must be mentioned here. We would like to point out that an awareness for this more complex notion of performance is often not adequately developed, while in fact performativity can be considered as omnipresent, and is especially found in various digital media products.

- Digital liveness addresses questions about participation and audience and the future possibilities of digital arts and creativity based on intermediality and hypermedia (ibid.).

This drama framework for digital arts cultures serves as a helpful starting point for a more in-depth exploration of drama and performance in educational settings, extending far beyond drama group activities. Yet, we should take more into account aspects of identity formation in this context, especially with a focus on young adults' and learners' practices of self-expression in digital spaces.

3. Self-staging and autobiographical narration in digital spaces

While students may or may not be prone to acting out dialogues and scenes in a classroom situation, they arguably do engage in drama and performance nonetheless as part of their own social and communicative practices. Notions of performative societies (cf. Nicholson 2009: 44f) and the theatricality of everyday life (cf. Hallet 2015a) draw attention to the fact that young adults enter into and navigate through social contexts in which they continuously practise and play with roles and role expectations.

From an observer's perspective, it is curious to think about when forms of behaviour begin to classify as performative. In a broad sense, this may include ways of dressing, being a member of social groups and societies, following artists on social media or attending cultural events. All of these contribute to the creation of an image that holds meaning for oneself or others. It therefore becomes obvious that performative practices can but do not need to be based around the use of language. Rather, it is the case that all meaning-making modes described in the multiliteracies framework (cf. Kalantzis et al. 2016: 3) can be drawn on to stage oneself in a particular fashion and within a certain social situation.

Likewise, self-staging is not only a matter of acting out a public role but also relates to creating textual representations and interpretations of one's self-image and identity. That is, by means of written and multimodal autobiographical narratives, young adults creatively explore and reflect on who they are, want to be, or would like to be seen as. Such texts tend to take generic shapes and range from self-portraits over diary entries to multimodal social media or blog posts (cf. Hallet 2015b). They allow for experimentation with realistic, wishful or aesthetically crafted versions of one's self and hence can be understood in a performative sense. Taking into consideration that these performative artefacts can be self-addressed or reaching out to private as well as public audiences, they have to be seen as individually meaningful and culturally embedded discursive practices, which are often created and shared via digital tools and platforms. As a result, when identity is textually and visually formed and communicated along these lines, it becomes a collage of digital forms of self-expression, which may be preliminary, not necessarily coherent but often eclectic and fragmented.

In bringing such forms of drama and performance into language classrooms, learners are given an opportunity to engage in multimodal meaning-making practices in a playful, yet serious fashion. Thereby, teachers can draw on "students' real-world experience with digital and mobile media to generate classroom-based drama" (Anderson et al. 2009: 64) and hence include various text types and genres that students are familiar with. As such, learners are regarded as cultural agents, entitled to their communicative preferences and styles but likewise challenged to reflect on the texts they create and performances they act out through these texts.

The following two activities illustrate how digital self-staging and autobiographical narration can be implemented in a classroom scenario on a smaller or larger scale. The thematic context is that students reflect on either the past year or the year ahead and make up their mind as to what was or will be important to them.

Activity 1:

Students choose a picture on their phone showing a moment from last year that they like to think back to. They present it to the person next to them and explain why they chose it. The viewer is then also asked to comment on the picture and describe their associations as well as the impression they get of the scene through the way the image was taken.

Activity 2:

In this activity, students create a series of social media posts in which they are asked to either reflect on moments and learning points from their past year or describe expectations, resolutions or wishes for the coming year. They can choose from freely available tools that allow to create 'fake' Instagram, Snapchat, Twitter or Facebook posts. That way, the genre of a particular social media platform may be drawn on without necessarily having to actually post and publish texts online. These products are subsequently presented in small groups and serve as a speech incentive, supported by a set of guiding questions, such the following:

As a viewer,

- what are the central points raised in the social media posts and how are they conveyed through text and images?

- what impression would you get of the person/people in the posts as someone who doesn't know them?

As an author,

- why did you select these exact moments and how are you trying to describe them in the posts?

- what parts of your own person and what experiences are you foregrounding / emphasising with these posts?

Such activities open up avenues for "creative learning spaces infused with technology" (Anderson et al. 2009: 14). Students can create and play with versions of themselves, reflect on role expectations that they accept, thwart or struggle with, and articulate their observations in the foreign language as well as through multimodal designs. Moreover, especially when it comes to teaching and learning in digital spaces, the stages on which students can explore drama and negotiate meaning are often already there and ready to be used: In a videoconference during distance learning, students could, for instance, create digital images as virtual background screens for their class. It is also possible to ask learners to bring something from their room to the camera, e.g. an object that they have had for a long time / couldn't live without / want to get rid of – to start a discussion. Likewise, when using dialogic tasks in remote learning scenarios, it can be promising to have students go to their wardrobes and put on a piece of clothing that fits to the role they are adapting in the activity. In addition, teachers can also harness the software options that videoconferencing holds available, such as switching on and off cameras for students to enter or exit a stage, creating screenshots as still images that capture a certain scene from a play, or using breakout rooms as different stages/locations where characters can be approached and talked to. These teaching ideas illustrate that the ways in which teachers and learners communicate through technology are often inherently dramatic and performative, to start with, and can hence be expanded through didactic reflection in order to create room for playfulness, spontaneity, and serious engagement with role-based communication in the foreign language.

4. Digital political performances

The observation that communication in digital spaces can often be characterised as performative extends from the individual to a larger political sphere. Metaphors such as 'the political stage' have long been established and years before social media gained the status and relevance it has today, Silverstone notes: "Politics is inconceivable and unsustainable without its appearance and its performance on the screens and through the speakers of the world's media" (Silverstone 2007: 25). Such medialised performance typically involves self-stagings, i.e. constructions of a particular ethos and political message, as well as deliberate and evaluative stagings of 'other' political figures and themes. Against this background, it becomes possible to read "the social drama of Brexit as a multi-actor cultural performance" (Sommer 2019: 294) or to understand presidential debates as "an exercise in political theatre" (Roe-Crines 2020: online). What follows from this is that drama gains further relevance also for EFL learning as it provides a heuristic to identify role constellations and trace the dramaturgy of political developments broadcasted digitally and on screen for global audiences.

As emblematic examples of self-staging, two images that could be harnessed in a language classroom are the 2017 portrait of Queen Elizabeth II and Prince Philip on the one hand, and a family photo shoot commissioned in 2010 by the Trump family (see online links below). In both images, the respective protagonist sits in a golden chair, whereas other than that the pictures could hardly be more unlike each other. The former is characterised by muted colours and a grey minimalistic background, arguably communicating modesty and tradition. The latter, in turn, was taken in an all-golden luxurious room high up in a New York City skyscraper and clearly signals pomp and opulence. Bringing these images into a classroom, it would be promising to investigate the composition of the pictures with a particular focus on their theatricality (i.e. analysing the stage / setting, character constellation and positions, facial expressions and body language, clothing and props). Thereby, learners can develop an understanding of how theatrical design elements contribute to creating a particular public image of political figures. The language of drama and theatre, hence, becomes a meaning-making tool that raises awareness for the – often latent – persuasiveness inherent in visual texts.

Exploring the visual design of political images and their rhetorical functions can, in turn, serve as a pathway into a more content- and discourse-based analysis of political performances. These performances often revolve around visual or filmic texts, published through media channels, which subsequently become part of discourses in digital spaces. In 2020, a photo op that became internationally known showed the then-US president holding up a bible in front of a Washington church after having streets with peaceful protesters cleared by the military using tear gas and rubber bullets. This appeal to conservative followers of the president was in the following termed as a symbolic "culture war" by some and as "completely appropriate" by others (Coppins 2020: online). Such reactions to political theatrical images may be a starting point for an investigation of underlying beliefs and attitudes held by different groups across the political landscape. Hence, analysing the picture as well as its reception in digital spaces can provide valuable insights into both meaning-making practices in political communication as well as into current discourses, e.g. surrounding elections in the US. Moreover, similar performances can be perceived on all sides of the political spectrum which allows for establishing multi-perspectivity in the classroom and helps resist potential hasty judgments about the use of self-staging by politicians.[1] On the contrary, engaging learners with such 'dramatic texts' can raise awareness for the ubiquity and even necessity of the performative in the public political sphere. That is to say, digital performance may be explored by EFL learners as a fundamental mechanism in political communication and as symbolic rhetorical acts which serve to subtly or overtly bring messages across to both targeted and non-targeted audiences.

Furthermore, it is vital to note that political performances in digital spaces are inevitably influenced by the platforms on which discourses take place. It is therefore vital to approach digital environments as hierarchically structured spaces that have an impact on agency, outreach and subsequently on the promotion or marginalisation of certain actors and voices (cf. von Blanckenburg 2021: 228 ff.). In recent years, especially social media has evolved even more strongly into a prominent digital stage where political communication occurs according to the systemic affordances and conventionalised genres of a respective platform. The interactional design of Twitter, for instance, has given rise to a form of political discourse which, according to Colley (2019: 34), favours bluntness and brevity over a differentiated and multifaceted negotiation of meaning. These developments, in turn, need to be taken into account when fostering discourse competence in the classroom and call for analytical approaches focusing on questions, such as:

- How does a digital space allow for self-staging and the staging of others?
- How are political performances received, commented on, redesigned (and potentially subverted) in a particular digital environment?
- Who is capable of and successful in communicating their political message by means of a particular digital genre?

---

[1] Another example would be a picture of leading Democratic lawmakers such as Nancy Pelosi, Chuck Schumer and Kamala Harris kneeling down in the US capitol to honour victims of police brutality, all wearing Ghanaian kente-cloth stoles. Whether such symbolism successfully communicates solidarity or rather marks an example of cultural appropriation could be discussed with language learners. Similarly, this performance has sparked varying responses from appraisal to strong criticism, e.g. in the New Yorker: "The theatrics from Democratic lawmakers […] felt not just misguided but like an outright mockery" (St. Félix 2020: online).

- How are communicative roles distributed in a digital space? Whose messages manage to gain momentum, and for what reasons?[2]

Thus, learners can investigate, for instance, how well-known political figures harness digital platforms to communicate messages, often through symbolic performative action. That is, when Boris Johnson presents himself on Instagram 'Getting breakfast done' or delivering milk to conservative voters (see online references), such posts contain less political content than they mark an attempt to, somewhat half-jokingly, create the ethos of a man of action who will subsequently also deliver Brexit to those wishing for it. More recently, the US-democrat Alexandria Ocasio-Cortez appeared on the gaming platform Twitch in the run-up to the US elections of 2020. In doing so, she reached more than 5.2 million viewers by playing a video game and, notably, was perceived as "acting normal" (Rivera 2020: online). What can be learned from these examples is that fostering an understanding of political communication in digital spaces requires a careful analysis and reflection of how social media platforms are used to connect to audiences in a (supposedly) personal manner by emphasizing specific role aspects of somebody's desired public persona.

Furthermore, the rise of social media has notably enabled also less well-known social actors to enter the political stage, create considerable outreach, and make their voices heard. Digital communication has therefore contributed to a democratisation of political performance, which particularly rewards those who are able to cater to the genre conventions and viewing preferences of recipients in a specific digital environment. More precisely, one can argue that the rhetorical effects of digital performative action depend on individual behaviour, on recipients who engage with digital content as well as on an opportune moment and systemic factors of a digital space. A social media network that has recently seen a strong surge in the staging and negotiation of political themes is the online video platform TikTok, where users create and share short videos, typically underlined by music. While TikTok did not intend to become a political platform, it has indeed turned out to be widely used by young adults taking a stance on current social and political issues and harnessing the characteristic genre formats of this social media service (cf. Literat & Kligler-Vilenchik 2019; Jebens 2020). In doing so, users create individual and performative political expressions that result in a unique, platform-specific form of political meaning-making.

---

[2] For a systematic and more comprehensive overview of analytical questions for rhetorical analysis of 'texts' in digital spaces, see the taxonomy in Von Blanckenburg (2021).

TikTok users do not just merely circulate content and comment it; they *become* the content. […] Since every user seeks increased popularity to disseminate their messages more widely, they create short political spectacles resulting in the realization of *politics as entertainment*. (Medina Serrano et al. 2020; emphasis in original)

At the same time, it is crucial to understand that not everyone can and will be widely received when sharing their political views on TikTok. Instead, it is mostly those – rather few – users who are very active content creators and who benefit from the platform's own algorithmic recommender systems, hence managing for their videos to appear in other users' news feeds (cf. Papakyriakopoulos et al. 2019). Whether a contribution turns out to be a successful (even viral) political performance is therefore also subject to the digital infrastructure and underlying mechanisms inherent in the platform's design. Users with large follower bases, in turn, have the power to put topics on the agenda, become opinion leaders and thereby considerably change the political discourse in a digital space.[3]

This becomes evident when considering the case of teenage influencer Charlie D'Amelio, who became famous for her dance performances and, by July 2021, had collected more than 120 million followers on TikTok. As many others, she has spoken in support of the Black Lives Matter movement, thus addressing audiences on a scale beyond any politician's media outreach. Likewise, the network features many more contributions under the hashtag *#blacklivesmatter*, which range from supportive or critical statements to a plethora of documentations as well as deliberate stagings of political protests in the US. The social media service has hence become a political medium showcasing and fuelling discourses on racial discrimination and violence and, as such, lends itself to being explored with language learners from a global and citizenship education perspective. Here, it can be especially fruitful to have learners investigate the theatricality of political content on TikTok. In the list of online sources below, we have collected five examples that stage the BLM protests in different ways through an interplay of images, music and video editing. For instance, they underline the relevance of protests through dramatic music, show peaceful or violent encounters between the police and protesters and hence each create their own political message.

Such videos can be approached as both multimodal texts as well as performative acts and, in our view, require a functional analysis as well as ethical reflection. That is to say, by using split-viewing tasks, teachers can in a first

---

[3] This effect is even more noteworthy when opinion leaders hold opinions that deviate from majority views on a topic, as Papakyriakopoulos et al. (2019) could show.

step draw attention to dramatic or cinematic aspects and their functions in expressing a particular political view. In a second step, it would also be important to spark a discussion around the question whether the respective way of showcasing this issue can be considered as appropriate and fair. When, for example, riots are shown in a positive light, it can be debated in class whether this may be considered as a statement of empowerment or as an action that runs the risk of romanticising or even inciting violence. In any case, such engagement with political communication in digital spaces serves to sensitise learners to the inherent performativity rooted in the aesthetic and expressive multimodal design of digital texts and mediated through specific platforms with their idiosyncratic communicative genres and their underlying software architecture.

5. Digital sociocultural performances

Digital texts are much more than bits and bytes – sometimes artistically composed – in order to be read on different digital tools and gadgets. They are sociocultural expressions and very often, as we would like to argue, in fact performances allowing readers/viewers/consumers or even "prodUsers" (Lütge / Merse / Owczarek / Stannard 2019) to learn about the self-presentation of groups and communities as discursive practices through which cultural self-images are constructed, mediated and subverted. This can be seen, for instance, in the music video "Stadium Pow Wow" by the Canadian First Nation electronic music group *A Tribe Called Red* (see online reference).[4] On a musical level, this song is characterised by a strong electronic beat layered with samples of traditional vocal chants. The characters appearing in the video, in turn, are portrayed in rural or urban surroundings, embracing both modern city life and Aboriginal cultural heritage. With their music and videos, the band also engage in activism and aim to showcase and support Aboriginal culture. Exploring such a music video with language learners can hence foster an understanding of the performative dimensions of cultural self-expressions which are created through multimodal design and become part of digital discourses.

Furthermore, satirical alienation is a common characteristic of posing and staging, also drawing on the self-staging of groups or individuals. One such example can be seen in a satire of hipster culture on Instagram with a barbie doll hat playfully stages commonly shared experiences in Instagram situations (cf. Cameron et al. 2017: 77). Another example can be found in the Instagram

---

[4] In 2021, the music group changed their name into *The Halluci Nation*.

account of the Dead Millenials (see online references for both sources), which pushes satire even further into a sardonic grin involving some memento mori elements in its self-staging of death and decay. In both cases the stories told in these accounts are carefully designed examples of parodies on self-staging without one element we usually encounter in these situations: an individual subject that attracts the audience's attention and gets objectified by the 'gaze' of thousands or millions of viewers. In fact, many digital performances are carefully scripted and, in turn, require what we would like to call a *performative gaze* to be decoded. For educators, this performative gaze is vital as it allows identifying elements of drama and performance in (often digital) cultural texts and acts, and, in that, serves as a prerequisite for helping learners to actively, creatively and critically respond to such elements. That is, a performative gaze establishes a particular perspective on digital autobiographical genres, political images or sociocultural performances, as described above.

Digital texts thus have the potential to change our awareness of well-established settings or culturally scripted clichés. They can help establish an awareness for the constructedness of performances – regardless of whether those are analogue theatre productions or digital formats. The changing role of the reader/user/viewer in reception theory is taken even further in times when swift re-readings of media products and a constant negotiation of meaning in seemingly unauthored and widely shared digital artefacts pose new challenges to learners and educators. Adopting a performative gaze in language education can lead to a reflection of questions, such as the following:

- Who is supposed to be the addressee of an Instagram post or a music video, such as the ones discussed above? Is there even a clearly identified target audience? Does it matter to answer this question unambiguously? What is the role of ambiguity in this context after all?

- What are the real-life references of these performances? What situations do they echo, quote, mirror, criticise, satirise? Which one of the aforementioned might be the most fitting verb in this context? Can we find other verbs that describe the reception process of these posts? How are emotions created, how are reactions provoked?

- What is happening in aesthetic terms? How is the context visualised? Why are we watching and might feel interested, puzzled, irritated, amused? How is our reception process influenced by the chosen scenario?

Sociocultural performances in digital spaces are not unidirectional and predetermined processes in clearly delineated steps. Rather, we would like to suggest a continuous flow and interdependence (see Figure 2). Digital arts cultures reflect on (digital) performances while simultaneously performative practices characterise today´s approach to digital arts cultures.

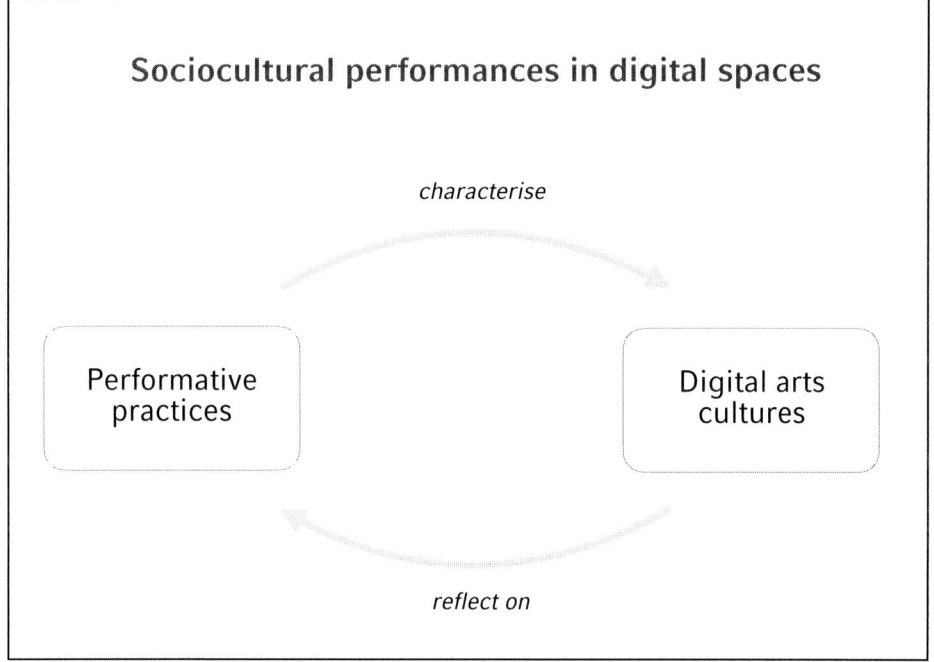

Figure 2: Sociocultural performances in digital spaces

In close connection with this line of argumentation, we would like to point out that drama and performance in digital spaces have many more connections that will impact on educational processes in the future. We summarise them according to the following criteria:

- **Fluidity**: performative dimensions become increasingly more fluid and flexible blurring the borders between textual features and reader/viewer roles. No longer are they limited to drama as written text but – maybe paradoxically – via the digital medium their original script character reaches a new dimension.

- **Reciprocity**: reception processes can become more swift and immediate in digital scenarios, sometimes not only passively addressing an anonymous audience but even requiring their active contribution. Reciprocal activity might be part of self-staging activities.

- **Diversity**: a large variety of diverse dramatic forms and processes are possible in increasingly digitalised classrooms. The breadth of accessible material offers dialogic responses, invites the exploration of culturally diverse scenarios and allows engagement with new and interactive forms of digital dramatic literatures.

6. Conclusion

Digital spaces offer new challenges but even more options for drama and performance, and may open up avenues for various forms of production- and action-oriented as well as reflective teaching and learning. The concept of digital arts cultures, encompassing creativity, playfulness, performance and digital liveness (cf. Cameron et al. 2017), might thus be helpful in crossing boundaries between genres of digitally (re-)designed dramatic texts. Encounters with self-staging in social media and with digital political performances are far more than some kind of exotic add-on, rather we consider them to be a vital interface of language, media and cultural learning in a broader sense. Digital practices and their performative dimensions hence need to be scrutinised much more thoroughly in the context of media literacy. On the one hand, this requires an understanding of the constructedness of (self-)staging through various textual and generic expressions with a view to both functional and aesthetic design elements. On the other hand, we want to point that there is a need to develop a *performative gaze* that allows us and our learners to not only passively consume but to actively, creatively and critically respond to various forms of drama and performance in digital spaces.

Bibliography

Anderson, Michael / Cameron, David / Caroll, John (eds.) (2009). *Drama Education with Digital Technology.* New York: Bloomsbury.

Beavis, Catherine (2012). Digital Games, New Literacies and English. In: Green, Bill / Beavis, Catherine (eds.). *Literacy in 3D: A Multi-Dimensional Framework for Rethinking Literacy Education.* Melbourne: Australian Council for Educational Research, 127-141.

Blanckenburg, Max von (2021). *Rhetorische Perspektiven auf fremdsprachliche Bildung im Fach Englisch. Theorie – Empirie – Unterricht.* Elektronische Hochschulschriften LMU München. Retrieved from: https://edoc.ub.uni-muenchen.de/27689/ (16/07/21).

Cameron, David / Anderson, Michael / Wotzko, Rebecca (2017). *Drama and Digital Arts Cultures.* New York: Bloomsbury.

Carbone, Courtney (2015). *Srsly Hamlet.* New York: Random House Books

Colley, Dawn F. (2019). Of Twit-storms and Demagogues. Trump, Illosury Truths of Patriotism, and the Language of the Twittersphere. In: Lockhart, Michele (ed.). *President Donald Trump and His Political Discourse. Ramifications of Rhetoric via Zwitter.* New York & London: Routledge, 33-51.

Coppins, McKay (2020). The Christians Who Loved Trump's Stunt. *The Atlantic.* Retrieved from: https://www.theatlantic.com/politics/archive/2020/06/trumps-biblical-spectacle-outside-st-johns-church/612529/ (16/07/21).

Hallet, Wolfgang (2015a). Die Performativität und Theatralität des Alltagshandelns. Performative Kompetenz und kulturelles Lernen. In: Hallet, Wolfgang / Surkamp, Carola (eds.). *Dramendidaktik und Dramapädagogik im Fremdsprachenunterricht.* Trier: WVT, 51-68

Hallet, Wolfgang (2015b). Autobiographies. *Der fremdsprachliche Unterricht Englisch* 136, 2-7.

Hammond, Adam (2016). *Literature in a Digital Age: A Critical Introduction.* Cambridge: Cambridge University Press.

Jebens, Caroline (2020). App als Protestplattform: Was Tiktok zeigt – und was nicht. *Frankfurter Allgemeine.* Retrieved from: https://www.faz.net/aktuell/feuilleton/medien/tiktok-als-medium-der-blacklivesmatter-proteste-16824851.html (16/07/21).

Kalantzis, Mary / Cope, Bill / Chan, Eveline / Dalley-Trim, Leanne (2016). *Literacies.* 2nd edition. Cambridge: Cambridge University Press.

Literat, Ioana / Kligler-Vilenchik, Neta (2019). Youth Collective Political Expression on Social Media: The Role of Affordances and Memetic Dimensions for Voicing Political Views. *New Media & Society* 21(9), 1988–2009. Retrieved from: https://doi.org/10.1177/1461444819837571 (16/07/21).

Lütge, Christiane (2015). Handlungs- und Produktionsorientierung im Dramenunterricht: Perspektiven für die fremdsprachliche Literatur- und Kulturdidaktik. In: Hallet, Wolfgang / Surkamp, Carola (eds.). *Dramendidaktik und Dramapädagogik im Fremdsprachenunterricht.* Trier: Wissenschaftlicher Verlag, 189-201.

Lütge, Christiane / Merse, Thorsten / Stannard, Michelle (2021). Digital Textualities: Innovative Practices with Social Media, Digital Literatures and Virtual Realities. In: Lütge, Christiane / Merse, Thorsten (eds.). *Digital Teaching and Learning: Perspectives for English Language Education.* Tübingen: Narr, 231-254.

Lütge, Christiane / Merse, Thorsten / Owczarek, Claudia / Stannard, Michelle (2019). Crossovers: Digitalization and Literature in Foreign Language Education. *Studies in Second Language Learning and Teaching* 3/2019, 519-540.

Medina Serrano, Juan Carlos / Papakyriakopoulos, Orestis, / Hegelich, Simon (2020). Dancing to the Partisan Beat: A First Analysis of Political Communication on TikTok. *Southampton '20: 12th ACM Conference on Web Science, July 07–10, 2020.* Retrieved from: https://arxiv.org/pdf/2004.05478.pdf (16/07/21).

O'Mara, Joanne (2012). Process Drama and Digital Games as Text and Action in Virtual Worlds: Developing New Literacies in School. *The Journal of Applied Theatre and Performance* 17/4, 517-534.

Papakyriakopoulos, Orestis / Medina Serrano, Juan Carlos / Hegelich, Simon (2019). Political Communication on Social Media: A Tale of Hyperactive Users and Bias in Recommender Systems. *Online Social Networks and Media 15.* Retrieved from: https://doi.org/10.1016/j.osnem.2019.100058 (16/07/21).

Rivera, Joshua (2020). AOC played Among Us and Achieved What Most Politicians Fail at: Acting Normal. *The Guardian.* Retrieved from: https://www.theguardian.com/games/2020/oct/22/alexandria-ocasio-cortez-ilhan-omar-among-us-twitch-stream-aoc (16/07/21).

Roe-Crines, Andrew (2020). Trump vs Biden: An Exercise in Political Theatre. *Political Studies Association.* Retrieved from: https://www.psa.ac.uk/psa/news/trump-vs-biden-exercise-political-theatre (16/07/21).

Silverstone, Roger (2007). *Media and Morality. On the Rise of the Mediapolis.* Cambridge: Polity Press.

Sommer, Roy (2019). Brexit as Cultural Performance. Towards a Narratology of Social Drama. In: Erll, Astrid / Sommer, Roy (eds.). *Narrative in Culture.* Berlin/Boston: De Gruyter, 293-320.

St. Félix, Dorren (2020). The Embarrassment of Democrats Wearing Kente-Cloth Stoles. *The New Yorker.* Retrieved from: https://www.newyorker.com/culture/on-and-off-the-avenue/the-embarrassment-of-democrats-wearing-kente-cloth-stoles (16/07/21).

Zimmermann, Heiko (2015). *Autorschaft und digitale Literatur. Geschichte, Medienpraxis und Theoriebildung.* Trier: Wissenschaftlicher Verlag Trier.

Online References

A Tribe Called Red – Stadium Pow Wow: https://vimeo.com/170704652 (04/07/21)

Instagram – Dead Millenials: https://www.instagram.com/deadmillennials/ (04/07/21)

Instagram – Socality Barbie: https://www.instagram.com/socalitybarbie/ (04/07/21)

Instagram – Boris Johnson: https://www.instagram.com/p/B57cbxOA1NJ/?utm_source=ig_web_copy_link (04/07/21)

Portrait of Queen Elizabeth and Prince Philipp: https://bit.ly/2F906ST (04/07/21)

Portrait of Trump Family in New York: https://bit.ly/3rXN12T (04/07/21)

Online references of political protests on TikTok: (04/07/21)

https://www.tiktok.com/@segyrella/video/6831635119669873925
https://www.tiktok.com/@supremeking14/video/6834575774356425989
https://www.tiktok.com/@complex/video/6833759604237798662
https://www.tiktok.com/@glossyzen/video/6835877701920836870
https://www.tiktok.com/@alex.stemp/video/6833470882963279110

Part II – Drama Pedagogy, Language Learner and Teacher Performance

LAURENZ VOLKMANN (FRIEDRICH-SCHILLER-UNIVERSITY OF JENA)

Taking Literature off the Page: Drama, Drama Techniques and the Performative Turn in EFL

This contribution provides a brief survey of how the recent EFL trend to view communication as performance is rooted in a long tradition of incorporating the use of drama and drama-related activities. It characterises four interrelated, though historically subsequent paradigms of using drama in EFL and discusses the activities prevalent under each paradigm. (1) Desk-bound approaches to teaching drama. (2) Learning about "communication as discourse" with the help of drama. (3) Using drama activities to develop and practice aesthetic and communication competences. (4) Highlighting the significance of "communication as performance" beyond the use of dramatic texts. It is suggested that teachers pick and choose wisely from the traditions, models and activities outlined here.

Introduction

Let me begin this article with observations on an apparent paradox: undoubtedly, advocating drama and drama techniques is a long-standing tradition in German and international EFL discourse (see, e.g., Amtmann 1967, Wagner 1976, Stern 1980, Holden 1982, Maley / Duff 1984, Byron 1986, Dougill 1987, Wessels 1987, Schewe 1993, Nünning 1998, Rau 1999). Yet many recent publications at one point or another lament the lack of drama and drama techniques or even the lack of literature on drama in EFL (see, e.g., Scherer 2005, Peters et al. 2006, Hentschel et al. 2007, Ahrens et al. 2008, Volkmann 2008a,b, Küppers et al. 2011, Hallet / Surkamp 2015). Why this apparent paradox? I suggest that this is, to a lesser degree, due to the absence of academic discourse on drama or a discursive gambit to propagate one's own contribution as the ultimate guide to teaching drama. Instead, it may be related to the semantic ambivalences inherent in the world fields of drama, theatre and performance. In other words, these semantic fields carry so many different and even obfuscatory meanings, specifically in EFL discourse, that "new" suggestions for teaching and learning are constantly proposed.

In this contribution, I intend to single out four different, though also intertwined strands of discourse regarding the issue at hand. Interestingly, they have evolved historically, with newer approaches frequently shifting older ones to the back, yet never completely eclipsing them *in toto*. As indicated above, the four different strands are rooted in the semantic ambiguity of "drama" (see Elam 2002: 190) which may have caused irritation about the combination of drama and language learning/teaching as "awkward bedfellows" (Byron 1986: 19). For drama can, first, be regarded as a textual component and as such as one of the three literary genres (besides fiction and poetry). As a text, drama is traditionally taught within literary departments and at schools with a focus on its compositional aspects. When studying the script of a play, students respond to it orally or in writing, in an analytical or productive and creative manner. Second, drama can refer to the staging of a written text, but also to practices of performance and, ultimately, to questions of how actors and spectators interact. The broad spectrum of this semantic field – from focus on the text to focus on performance – is reflected in the historic evolution of drama in EFL, harking back to its genesis in the eighteenth and nineteenth centuries. In a nutshell, the four strands can be characterized as follows:

The philological paradigm, where students are meant to study a literary text to analyse and interpret its meaning. The standard German publication here is Manfred Pfister's handbook on drama analysis, first published in 1977 and arguably still the crucial academic study for close readings.

The discourse paradigm, where students regard the playscript as a close-to-life and paradigmatic example of language in action and study it with the aim of understanding how language works in context. A typical example would be Rüdiger Ahrens' suggestion for teaching *Waiting for Godot*, first published in 1973.

The literature off the page paradigm, where the written playtext, often in excerpts, is used to hone language and interactive skills and to gain insights into the routines and peculiarities of real-life communication. A good introduction is offered in acting-out approaches to teaching Shakespeare as propounded by Rex Gibson (1998) or in the surveys of dramatic activities for the foreign language classroom published by Maley and Duff (1984).

The communication as performance paradigm, where there is a decisive shift away from the text to actual or fictional examples of human interaction, with communication exchanges basically understood as a performative act, where individuals adhere to or modify culture-inflected communicative scripts (see for example Appel 2000, Reisener 2005 and Hallet 2015).

The following four parts of this article will elaborate on the four perspectives. While they have gained momentum and significance in the chronological order outlined here, it should become clear that they remain interrelated.

They continue to be historically indebted to one another, with multiple intersections and cross-influences.

1. The philological paradigm: Focus on the written and/or multimodal text

As part of a long-standing tradition of teaching and learning literature both at university and in school, here the textual component takes the centre stage when it comes to dealing with drama. A wide array of text-focused methods are standard procedure, including interpretation and analysis, a focus on compositional and generic aspects or even more recent forms of reacting to a play in a productive and creative manner. Without giving much thought to its staging, this literary appreciation of the theatre, rather than of practices and the world of the stage or performance, is characteristic of the philological paradigm. Reasons for the disregard of theatrical aspects may be seen as relating back to Plato and notably the early modern age. The questionable, if not amoral and disreputable image of the theatre world was established from early times of history (see Kohansky 1984). In the world of academia and education, the dubious reputation was historically linked to the misconception that theatre productions or stage presentations were merely an inessential adjunct to the printed play. This focus on the "text" and its intrinsic composition continued even when films – in this case film adaptations of plays – started to replace literature as the preferred medium.

In post-World War II Germany, the so-called "deskbound approach" became established as the norm, indebted to theories and practices of "close reading" (New Criticism) or text-intrinsic approaches. At schools, notably the *Gymnasium* with its elitist agenda, textual analysis, frequently conducted in German even in English lessons, was closely linked to the tradition of the grammar-translation method. Both aimed at honing the students' intellectual and analytical skills, providing model examples of "great literature". Moreover, canonical texts from the target cultures Great Britain and the United States were meant to offer moral and ethical guidance (for details, see Volkmann 2016). One of the most influential academic publications of the 1970s and 1980s and still regarded as the standard study of the genre, Manfred Pfister's 1977 *Dramenanalyse* (*Drama analysis*), fixed the norms and practices of interpreting drama both at university and in advanced EFL classes. While defining drama as a "plurimedial text" (Pfister 1994: 41) and integrating sociological factors and semiotic approaches, Pfister's study, which had numerous reprints and was translated into

English, clearly showcases the strict protocols of close reading in the text-intrinsic manner. This focus on the text continued, even though in the 1980s and 1990s drama and theatre became increasingly seen as a multimodal and multi-genre form of art, employing fine art, architecture, music, dance, film footage etc. in its creation and performance.

In EFL publications, this approach was closely mirrored. Projecting the goal of the appreciation of great literature, plays were scrutinized, in an attempt to acquaint students with various aspects of the cultural background from which a play originated. Moreover, intertextual references could be taken into account to create an awareness of literary traditions and specific elements of the literary genre drama, such as the famous "drama triangle" of classical tragedy by Gustav Freytag or characteristics of drama according to Aristotle. In the case of Shakespeare as the undisputed champion of the genre in the German EFL classroom, various aspects came under consideration such as the playhouse, the age of Shakespeare and England under Queen Elizabeth I, the language of Shakespeare, the history of staging his plays and the classics of film adaptations. A look into manuals dealing with film adaptations – which were often interpreted with regard to how "close" they were to the original – quickly reveals how practices of close reading were adapted to film analysis. Considering a classroom-oriented publication on Roman Polanski's 1971 film version of *Macbeth*, one is amazed at the highly exacting suggestions for a thorough analysis of the opening scene of the film. There are detailed analyses concerning setting and atmosphere, action, soundtrack and sound effects, visual symbols, camera use, characterization of dramatis personae – all discussed with regard to the question of how all these elements contribute to the function of the scene by itself and how this opening scene relates to the whole drama (Blume 2003: 31).

The concept of Literature with a capital L, numerous teaching manuals and the often bemoaned inertia of classroom practices led to a fossilized tradition of a time-honored fare of canonical literature in German EFL classes (often dubbed the "secret canon"). Even before the new millennium, an array of EFL publications (see, e.g., Nünning 1998) lamented the perpetuation of teaching the same well-established dramas (notably the favourite *Macbeth* and a few other Shakespearean dramas; plays by Wilde, Beckett, Osborne, Pinter and American playwrights such as Wilder, Miller, Albee). It was (and still is) strongly suggested that alternatives be considered. More recent playwrights and more contemporary topics have been recommended along the lines of gender and ethnicity as well as with regard to minorities and English language countries different from the UK and the United States of America.

It may be worth noting that the new interest in "alternative" methodological questions – how to approach a text in a motivating, student-oriented manner – when it first surfaced in the 1980s and 1990s was first and foremost concerned with the question of how to deal with a specific text. Ironically, the demand for "alternative" activities concerning literary texts was from the beginning on embedded in or at least indebted to the philological paradigm. The three-phases-approach to teaching literature ("pre-, while-, post-reading") which now has become the norm, of course, goes beyond the analytical and cerebral reception of a text, incorporating productive and creative activities such as textual or genre transformations (e.g., rewriting a play or scenes from a play in the mode of a short story, a letter or a poem). Ultimately, as critics argue, this could lead towards using the literary text merely as a stepping stone or launching pad for any sort of creative activity, which might – as in the case of drawing pictures based on a play – be far removed from the traditional goals of foreign language learning altogether (for a more detailed discussion see Grimm et al. 2015: 173-196).

There is, to my knowledge, no large scale study on how practices of close reading as described above continue to be part and parcel of EFL classrooms for advanced learners. Yet, from the teacher manuals galore which are apparently still in demand – as a short amazon.de research reveals – it may be assumed that, to a certain degree, actual classroom practices remain moored in the stasis of time-honored traditions. While the delusion may disappear that a play is primarily intended for reading and interpreting, it seems that the idea that watching it or acting it out, even in parts, can be a more holistic experience has not yet completely sunk in. Is the philological approach utterly antiquated, then? An easy answer is "no" if the following additional approaches are integrated as well. They are in line with Nissen's 1994 exhortation that in the EFL classroom "the text should be staged, not analysed" (as the title of his contribution stresses, i.e. "Den Text inszenieren statt analysieren").

2. The discourse paradigm: Analysing and acting out dialogues

What is referred to as the discourse paradigm here differs from the philological perspective in as far as literary texts are not seen as self-enclosed entities, carrying timeless meanings and being representative of supreme art. Rather, the discourse paradigm construes literary texts as examples of language and culture "in action", offering perspectives on mechanisms and procedures of meaning creation in socio-cultural and linguistic contexts. Drama is hereby seen as an outstanding source material of language use, and specifically spoken dialogue is viewed as exemplary of sociocultural negotiations of meaning. The approach to drama is still analytical and cerebral; however, depending on the angle, aspects of staging and performance as well as non-verbal elements tend to gain attention as well.

The discourse paradigm needs to be seen against the background of the Communicative Turn of the 1970s with its focus on authentic language use. Theories of communicative competence embraced insights of discourse analysis and linguistic pragmatism. In Germany, the communicative turn was highly influenced by Habermas' notion of "hierarchy-free communication" which in turn led to an awareness of how social asymmetries and imbalances are created through language use. In line with concepts of critical discourse analysis, which "draws attention to systematic organizational properties of dialogue and provides ways of describing them" (Fairclough 1992: 15), literature teaching became interested in the structural units of texts or utterances. Literary texts began to be analysed with regard to their communicative functions. Concerning drama, issues came into focus such as how does topic control or turn taking occur, or what functions do idiomatic expressions or sociolects fulfill, or how are social relations constructed in and constituted through discourses as social practice. Apart from the goal of furthering students' critical skills with regard to language use, on a more practical level drama texts were seen as providing models of discourse organization. Since certain practices – from using chunks to idiomatic language to formulaic expressions – are internalized, dialogues in dramas offer examples of "speech acts" (see Searle 1969), of register, accent, allusion and connotation, both as material for study and for skill development. Obviously, this entails not only written playtexts, but notably issues of how performance creates additional or different layers of meaning through non-verbal clues, different intonation, etc. Typical speech acts, patterns and their artistic rendition in literature can be studied, performed and worked with creatively in role plays or simulations of real-life scenarios.

> Structural ambivalences of literary texts and their openness to different ways of making sense are meant to create space for discussions, interpretations and activities, in connection with differing individual backgrounds, experiences and perspectives regarding reading. Texts from foreign language literature through their fictional nature, language creation and real life connection demand per se an integrative form of foreign language didactics. (Hellwig 1990: 28f., transl. LV)

Accordingly, using drama and dramatic texts can be regarded as a first step towards an interactive mode accommodating the live experience. Here working with a text incorporates the performatory angle at most steps, focussing on alternative possibilities of significance in or interpretation of dialogue when the same words are delivered in different ways or in a different physical positioning of the characters (which is called blocking in theatrical parlance). For example, students can experience how the same scene can have radically divergent readings. Literature is fixed, a performance is fluid and evanescent: passages from the original text may be dropped, intentionally or inadvertently, gestures can add meaning to words and can and will never be repeated in the same manner; performers vary their acting, and responses by audiences are never the same. Thus, focusing on texts in performance can create a motivating learning environment and a laboratory of meaning creation.

An additional aspect of the drama as discourse paradigm consists of aspects that link language use with its cultural context. Increasingly, with the wane of the text-intrinsic perspective, literary texts have come to be seen as deeply integrated in culture, thus offering perspectives on their cultural context.

> Each literary or area studies text is as an English text always also a stimulus for foreign language learning. Every literary text, because it is embedded in its cultural context, always has significance for area studies. And every text that is used in language learning is also always the carrier of some sort of content, possibly in the field of area studies or literary studies. (Freese 1980: 29, transl. LV)

Depending on the theoretical angle and the drama under discussion, different facets of discourse are foregrounded in EFL publications recommending certain dramas for classroom use. To single out a few paradigmatic examples, the initial critical impulse of the discourse paradigm is mirrored in Rüdiger Ahrens' (1973 / 2004) recommendation to use Samuel Beckett's *Waiting for Godot* to gain insights into the mechanisms of meaning creation through linguistic gambits; Maria Eisenmann suggests ways of learning about the American Dream and its critique through an analysis of *Death of a Salesman* (2008); the issue of gender discourse is highlighted in a contribution to Susan Glaspell's feminist short play *Trifles* (Decke-Cornill 1993). Focusing on discursive practices can also entail experiencing sites of performance such as during a visit to the theatre, a tour of the Globe Theatre in London as part of a school trip or discussing performance practices in the context of a visit of a travelling English theatre company (see contributions in Hallet / Surkamp 2015).

Again, there is a thin and occasionally non-existent line between regarding plays as discursive models and practices on the one hand and focusing on elements of acting out a play or parts of it on the other. The link is suggested in the teaching and learning trajectory proposed by Nünning in the motto of "from playtext to blueprint for acting out" (Nünning 1998: 4, transl. LV).

3. The literature off the page paradigm and the acting out or workshop approach

As described above, the discourse paradigm still focuses on analytical skills and aims at getting insights into the communicative and sociocultural functions of literary texts. There is a shift of focus in the paradigm sketched out in this part. Literary elements receive less, little or no attention here when the students act out a text, be it in close adherence to it, be it moving far beyond the printed words in improvisation and role play. The spectrum of performative engagement with a text can include a fully-fledged public staging of a whole play or an in-class reading with various roles, involving gesture, different voices etc. as with the less-known Readers Theatre method (Curry 1985). On the other side of the spectrum, it can mean working with passages, even only short lines from a text, which can also be written by the students themselves, following the textual model of a dialogue for scenarios which are close to the students' interests. In this contribution, I can only outline some characteristics of approaches which share the idea that texts are meant to be performed and that performance has a central place in developing aesthetic and language competences.

The best of all instructive methods with regard to teaching drama and performance may be the participation of students in the complete enactment of a text, from warming up activities to practical design projects on sets, costumes or music. This includes endless rehearsals for honing the students' thespian talents, tackling questions of editing and engaging in pronunciation training; it raises challenges with regard to the logistics of organising the show; and finally there is the actual performance in front of an audience. However, as is well-known, a full-length production, even of a short play, is laborious and time-consuming – though satisfying pedagogically since it involves every single aspect of theatre in a hands-on manner (see Scherer 2005).

Educators have therefore recommended using short and very short plays (playlets) or encouraging students to write their own play or sketch (e.g., Scherer 2005, Hermes 2008). This involves "step by step" skill building, where short literary texts (anecdotes, fables, fairy tales, etc.) or textbook scenes could serve as models. It can include practices of story-telling as a performative art and technique in its own right (Baker / Greene 1987). Mainly, non-dramatic texts are transformed into a dramatic script. Alternatively, students could choose an interesting topic or issue as the core of a play which they later dramatize, rehearse and perform in class or at a special event at school.

Crucially, when texts are taken off the page, the classroom is turned into a stage, where the teacher does not teach as the leading actor or as the stage-manager, with the students as the audience. Rather, gradually educators withdraw to take on the part of the organiser and facilitator "behind the scenes", who is also responsible for the class's full involvement (see Volkmann 2010). This "taking literature off the page" is indebted to many traditions and forms of drama pedagogy and is known by various terminologies such as the dramatic approach or the workshop or acting out approach. To single out one very influential tradition, the dramatic approach has been very prominent in British education projects, which in turn have influenced German classrooms – students visiting the Globe Theatre in London traditionally can participate in workshop activities organised and conducted by professional actors there, in line with concepts devised by educators such as Rex Gibson (1998), Peter Reynolds (Hahlo / Reynolds 2000) and James Stredder (2004). They were instrumental in promoting projects such as "Shakespeare in School" or "Active Shakespeare" aimed at native-speaker audiences, but also at learners of English on an international scale. Stredder lists the advantages of finding access to Shakespeare by focusing on acting-out activities as follows:

> [I]t offers every individual personal contact with the plays, in the context of the pleasure and support of social, creative activity. It also requires learners to be, and assumes they will be, responsible for the work that goes on in the classroom or workshop, and to become involved with it. Practical work is especially effective in motivating, 'empowering', and developing confidence. (Stredder 2004: 6)

The *dramatic approach* places special importance on the methodology of dealing intensively with single scenes of a play. Instead of looking at longer passages first, students work with single lines, short dialogues or parts of monologues. These should be worked with in a conscious manner in order to achieve learning goals step by step: students are encouraged to speak actively and consciously, which, in turn, promotes active, focused and intensive reading. Thus, very short passages are learned by heart and are performed by using language, emphasis, gestures, facial expressions etc. in an experimental manner. Thereby, an incipient step is taken towards a deeper, more holistic understanding of the drama, a role or only a single passage. Undoubtedly, the dramatic approach does not only allow for alternative and creative forms of access to a play, incorporating all of the senses. It does not only offer the possibility of social interaction and of letting the texts of dramas come alive, but it also enables students to directly experience the world of the respective play and to gain deeper insights into its structures and textual potential. Three typical activities are listed below:

- *Micro-drama*: a very short section of a sometimes slightly re-organized text is played over a number of times, engaging students to use the personalities and dynamics of a group of learners to create a collective moment of performance.

- *Tableaux* or *freeze-frames*: they represent specific moments in the action and the relationship of the characters at those moments where, for example, a student "sculptor" forms the image of character constellation with the help of various members of the group, while the other members comment on the image created by the actors.

- *One word* or *one line reductions*: here students choose or are given snippets from a play; they work on their own, in pairs or groups or dispersed through the room, using different areas of the classroom, using different pitch, voices, mimics, movements and thus experiment with the text.

All workshop activities share the idea that if students work in an active way with the text they will be more motivated to search and study the text and follow up with their own questions regarding the text, similar to professional actors who often display an astonishing knowledge of everything about the character they are playing.

The concept of working only with parts of a drama is summed up in the following statement by drama experts Dalziel and Pennacchi:

> Workshop, improvisation and story-telling activities can help students to acquire in-depth knowledge of and important insights into the text and, by means of various distancing techniques [i.e., discussing various approaches to acting out passages of a text], to focus on *story* and *emotion*. (Dalziel, Pennacchi 2012: 14)

To situate such approaches historically, in Germany they can clearly be linked to traditions of *Darstellendes Spiel*, which has recently seen a pedagogic revival (see Hentschel et al. 2007, Küppers et al. 2011). In the Anglophone world they can be anchored in the "speech and drama tradition", dating back to the early twentieth century and the New Education Movement in England. Both traditions aim to elicit self-expression from students and suggest activities for learner-centered, holistic formats of education. Interestingly, these traditions hark back to the world of the theatre since they are influenced by drama techniques as used in theatres and by actors and actresses. A second tradition, dating back to the 1950s and 1960s, stresses the playful and child-like components of plays and aims at what would be called "gamification" of language learning today. In the 1980s, educators and scholars such as Betty Jane Wagner and Dorothy Heathcote changed the perception of drama as less a fun activity than a teaching tool and an instrument that combined social, intellectual and linguistic education (see Dougill 1987: 2-5, Schewe 1993: 1-19). The arguments in favour of acting out or role playing in class still hold today: rather than engaging in tedious pattern and language drills or the long-winded scrutinizing and over-interpretation of literary texts, learning should focus on acting out dialogues as an imitation of real life situations. "[It] enables learners to shift the focus of their attention beyond the more mechanical aspects of the foreign language system" (Collie / Slater 1990: 5). With no more just "learning time as sitting time" ("Lernzeiten [...] als Sitzzeiten", Reisener 2005: 20), it potentially motivates less confident students, supports autonomous learning and learning with all senses – specifically role playing is thus seen as the ideal form of learner engagement (Ladousse 1987).

There is an almost invisible line between using dramatic texts for practicing drama techniques to "dramatic activities" without a literary script to work with. This approach will be elaborated on in the next section.

4. The communication as performance paradigm: All the world's a stage

Drama activities or performance activities such as role play, to name an obvious example, differ from the activities under discussion so far in that they are not linked to a literary text; they can even be without any reference to a text selected or produced by the instructor or learners. These "dramatic activities" – as they were dubbed by Maley and Duff (1984), for instance – do not primarily serve the purpose of establishing or probing the connection between a text on the page and its use as acting out material off the page. Rather, first and foremost, they serve educational purposes. In the case of EFL classes, pedagogues and scholars advocating them have described them as more than just adding spice and lively, multisensory elements to the alleged dreariness of teacher and textbook centred classes. As a multi-methodological method they can be integrated in everyday foreign language classes in an effort to create a learning environment which creates real-life situations, incorporating humour, movement, improvisation and learning with all senses – specifically as a move away from the artificial mode of *teacherese* input and textbook activities. The full gamut of dramatic activities has been defined as follows:

> They are activities which give the student an opportunity to use his or her own personality in creating the material on which *part* of the language class is to be based. These activities draw on the natural ability of every person to imitate, mimic and express himself or herself through gesture. They draw, too, on the student's imagination and memory, and natural capacity to bring to life parts of his or her past experience that might never otherwise emerge. They are dramatic because

> they arouse our interest, which they do by drawing no the unpredictable power generated when one person is brought together with others. Each student brings a different life, a different background into the class. We would like students to be able to use this when working with others. (Maley / Duff 1984: 5)

Here, many multisensory, interactive, creative and general education goals are taken under one umbrella: breathing, body control and concentration exercises, voice and pronunciation activities, perception and imagination activities, body movement and body language, gesture, mime, engaging in activities with sound and rhythm, language games, use of puppets and masks, chanting, singing, storytelling, story reading, improvisation and role play (see Scheller 1980).

As becomes clear when looking at publications on dramatic activities, the world of make-believe, of imitating real life as it happens outside the classroom, ideally leads to fleeting moments where there is a "suspension of disbelief". These are moments where participants forget that they are merely playing or play-acting, where using the foreign language becomes a natural part of performing the role one has been allotted to or chosen. Both the teacher or teachers and the students become enmeshed in the world of performance.

In recent publications on drama in EFL classroom – be they about staging plays or dramatic activities – this "holistic" angle of performance activities has been widened and given a whole new and much larger dimension. In accordance with what in cultural theory has been described as the "performative turn" (Bachmann-Medick 2006: 104-143), there is a clear tendency to go beyond the traditional comparison of the classroom and classroom interaction with the world of the theatre and role play, with both teachers and students as performers, each meant to play their allotted roles. Rather, human interaction as a whole has increasingly been defined as being a performance. In other words, human interaction takes place according to certain definable and teachable cognitive, affective, linguistic and para-linguistic codes which are encoded by the speaker or sender in a manner to create a certain meaning with an audience or recipient(s). The insight that all communication is basically performance is not a new and very original one, yet seems to be culturally ever more significant in the postmodern age of fluid and malleable identities (see Auslander 1999), of (digital) self-fashioning and of what Germans – using a linguistic false friend – call the urge to "inscene oneself". Indeed it was over half a century ago that Erving Goffman, a highly influential Canadian-American social anthropologist, developed a theoretical model with a focus on humans as performative beings and life as a stage. As Goffman described in sometimes dry sociological prose, "[t]he general notion that we make a presentation of ourselves to others is hardly novel" (1984 [first 1959]: 244). One may go back to the Shakespearean motto that "all the world's a stage and we are merely actors on it" (see *Henry V*) to understand how different contexts demand different selves and different performances. Goffman elaborates on how we are all actors in communication, playing out social roles and particular scripts depending on our respective environment and our audience. In the seminal study *The Presentation of Self in Everyday Life* (1959) he sums up his main idea:

> In this report, the individual was divided by implication into two basic parts: he was viewed as a *performer*, a harried fabricator of impressions involved in the all-too-human task of staging a performance; he was viewed as a *character,* a figure, typically a fine one, whose spirit, strength, and other sterling qualities the performance was designed to evoke. (Goffman 1984: 244)

In other words, Goffman defined two modes: first, the expressions we give (without thinking about their consequences) and, second, the expressions we give off (to make people think in a certain way). Later, Goffman expanded on his theories by suggesting that humans in interaction basically engage in "face work" (Goffman 1967), that is either avoiding threatening an interlocutor's self-image (negative face-work) or attempting to reinforce the self-image of the other person in communication (positive face-work). These anthropological concepts were the root theories for linguistic areas of pragmatics, mainly the study of conversational routines, politeness strategies, etc.

What, then, for the foreign language classroom are the consequences of the assumption that all human interaction is performative? In EFL publications, the concept of communication as based on certain mental schemata, scripts or frames which translate into formulaic or structured language use (see Ventola 1979) has been highly influential. Basically, the concept of mental schemata which have become habitualized and are culturally conditioned and therefore express themselves in prototypical language use (idioms, chunks, speech acts) can be closely linked to the idea of communication as performance, as becomes clear in a paradigmatic quote by Nila Banton Smith: "If we go to a restaurant we store the experience in our restaurant schema, if we attend a party, our party schema, and so on" (quoted in Grimm et al. 2015: 120). Be it the "scripts" of a telephone conversation, political speeches or the schemata of certain text genres, ranging from a post card to a novel of a certain genre, communication and texts follow certain patterns which call for activities emulating "archetypal" communicative situations – yet without returning to the patterned, stilted and artificial role plays of the heydays of behaviourist audio-visual language learning.

To mention just two prominent and interrelated areas of learning, the idea of communication as performance can be reflected in activities fostering intercultural awareness and nonverbal communication (see Oomen-Welke 2004). As to intercultural learning, using so-called "critical incidents" in class can allow insights into the hidden norms, values and assumptions which can lead to culture clash or intercultural misunderstandings (see Bredella 2010, Busse 2017). Using film clips or text examples as learning material, students can act out scenes of intercultural *faux pas*, discuss them and their underlying causes and engage in performative activities aimed at avoiding such misunderstandings. Part of such intercultural training could be calling students' attention to the importance of paralinguistic elements in communication, a significant factor which is often disregarded in traditional language teaching. Apart from differences in tone of voice, stress, prosody etc. it seems important to stress the function of nonverbal cues. In communication, these include finger pointing, staring, smiling, frowning, looking away or sideways, head movement, folding arms, leaning forward or leaning back, proximity etc. Both intercultural critical incidents and para- and non-verbal communication activities can be designed for students to experience the importance of differences with regard to ethnicity, culture, society, region, environment, age and gender – concerning the issue of how these factors inflect interpersonal exchanges.

5. Conclusion

Given the call for a performative turn in recent EFL publications, it comes as no surprise that scholars have devised scales and descriptors covering multifarious aspects of "communication as performance" (Hallet 2015) and suggested ways of assessing and evaluating "performative competences" (Hallet 2015, Bosenius 2017). The recent spate of publications on performative competences in EFL is a clear indication of how far EFL discourse has moved from traditional assumptions about drama and dramatic activities in the classroom. As outlined above, there is a clear trajectory from a focus on the printed drama to dramatic activities to the recent objective of teaching a foreign language as a versatile tool to engage in real-life activities which are all marked by the idea of communication as performance. The approaches and activities sketched out above therefore range from working with a literary text to working just on the assumption that language learning must be seen as "performance training". Clearly, with the wide spectrum of activities in the area of theatre, drama and performance at offer, teachers are invited to use activities in this area eclectically and, most importantly, according to their own preferences and needs and those of their students.

Bibliography

Ahrens, Rüdiger (2004). Kompositionsprinzipien in S. Becketts *Waiting for Godot* und *Endgame*. 1st published: 1973/1982. In: Merkl, Matthias / Volkmann, Laurenz (eds.). *Anglophone Kulturwissenschaft und Englische Fachdidaktik. Gesammelte Aufsätze von Rüdiger Ahrens*. Heidelberg: Winter, 55-60.

Ahrens, Rüdiger / Eisenmann, Maria / Merkl, Matthias (eds.) (2008). *Moderne Dramendidaktik für den Englischunterricht*. Heidelberg: Winter.

Appel, Joachim (2000). Sprechen als performance. In: *Der Fremdsprachliche Unterricht Englisch* 34, 28-31.

Amtmann, Paul (1967). *Darstellendes Spiel im neusprachlichen Unterricht. Ein Handbuch für Volksschulen, Realschulen und Gymnasien*. München: Manz.

Auslander, Philip (1999). *Liveness: Performance in a Mediatized Culture*. London: Routledge.

Bachmann-Medick, Doris (2006). *Cultural Turns. Neuorientierungen in den Kulturwissenschaften*. Reinbeck bei Hamburg: Rowohlt.

Baker, Augusta / Greene, Ellin (1987). *Storytelling: Art and Technique*. 2nd ed. New York: R.R: Bowker.

Blume, Antje (2003). *EinFach Englisch. Roman Polanski's Macbeth: Filmanalyse*. Paderborn: Schöningh.

Bolton, Gavin (1979). *Towards a Theory of Drama in Education*. London: Longman.

Bosenius, Petra (2017). Assessing Performative Competence in German ELF-Classrooms – The Task of Teachers and Learners. In: *Scenario* 2, 50-65.

Bredella, Lothar (2010). Überlegungen zur Lehre interkultureller Kompetenz. In: Weidemann, Arne / Straub, Jürgen / Nothnagel, Steffi (eds.). *Wie lehrt man interkulturelle Kompetenz? Theorie und Praxis von Lehrmethoden in der Universitäts- und Hochschulausbildung*. Bielefeld: transcript, 99-120.

Busse, Vera (2017). Critical Incidents: Zwischen Cultural Awareness und kultureller Reduktion. In: *Praxis Fremdsprachenunterricht* 2, 13-15.

Byron, Ken (1986). *Drama in the English Classroom*. London, New York: Methuen.

Collie, Joanne / Slater, Stephen (1990). *Literature in the Language Classroom. A Resource Book of Ideas and Activities*. Cambridge: Cambridge University Press.

Curry, Dean (1985). *Plays for Reading: Using Readers Theatre in EFL*. Washington, D.C.: English Language Programs Division. Bureau of Educational and Cultural Affairs.

Dalziel, Fiona, Andrea Pennacchi (2012). Looking for Henry: Improvisation and Storytelling in Foreign-Language Theatre. In: *Scenario* 2: 6-17.

Decke-Cornill, Helene (1993). Den eigenen Augen nicht trauen. Literaturunterricht mit Susan Glaspells Einakter *Trifles* (1916). In: Decke-Cornill, Helene (ed.). *Begegnung mit Texten.* Pfaffenweiler: Centaurus, 57-71.
Dougill, John (1987). *Drama Activities for Language Learning.* London: McMillan.
Eisenmann, Maria (2007). Shakespeares Hamlet im Englischunterricht der gymnasialen Oberstufe. In: *Scenario* 1, 1-15.
Eisenmann, Maria (2008). *Teaching Classics of American Drama.* Göttingen: Vandenhoeck & Ruprecht.
Elam, Keir (2002). *The Semiotics of Theatre and Drama.* Second ed. London: Routledge.
Fairclough, Norman (1992). *Discourse and Social Change.* London: Polity.
Freese, Peter (1980). Zur Erstellung von Textsequenzen für den Englischunterricht der reformierten Sekundarstufe II. In: *Praxis des neusprachlichen Unterrichts* 27, 22-34.
Gibson, Rex (1998). *Teaching Shakespeare: A Handbook for Teachers.* Cambridge: CUP.
Goffman, Erving (1967). *Interaction Ritual: Essays on Face-To-Face Behavior.* New York: Pantheon Books.
Goffman, Erving (1984). *The Presentation of Self in Everyday Life.* 1st ed. 1959. Harmondsworth: Penguin.
Grimm, Nancy, Michael Meyer, Laurenz Volkmann (2015). *Teaching English.* Tübingen: Narr.
Hahlo, Richard / Reynolds, Peter (2000). *Dramatic Events: How to Run a Workshop for Theater, Education or Business.* London: Faber & Faber.
Hallet, Wolfgang (2015). Die Performativität und Theatralik des Alltagshandelns: Performative Kompetenz und kulturelles Lernen. In: Hallet, Wolfgang / Surkamp, Carola (eds.). *Dramendidaktik und Dramenpädagogik im Fremdsprachenunterricht.* Trier: WVT, 51-67.
Hallet, Wolfgang / Surkamp, Carola (eds.) (2015). *Dramendidaktik und Dramenpädagogik im Fremdsprachenunterricht.* Trier: WVT.
Hellwig, Karlheinz (ed.) (1990). *Textdidaktik für den Fremdsprachenunterricht – isoliert oder integrativ?* Tübingen: Narr.
Hentschel, Ulrike et al. (2007). Thematic issue "Theater in der Schule." In: *Zeitschrift für Theaterpädagogik.* 23.51.
Hermes, Liesel (2008). Vom Lehrwerkdialog zur szenischen Gestaltung: Dramendidaktik am Beginn der Sekundarstufe I. In: Ahrens, Rüdiger / Eisenmann, Maria / Merkl, Matthias (eds.). *Moderne Dramendidaktik für den Englischunterricht.* Heidelberg: Winter, 509-522.
Holden, Susan (1982). *Drama in Language Teaching.* Harlow: Longman.
Kohansky, Mendel (1984). *The Disreputable Profession: The Actor in Society.* New York: Praeger.

Küppers, Almut / Schmidt, Torben / Walter, Maik (eds.) (2011). *Inszenierungen im Fremdsprachenunterricht. Grundlagen, Formen, Perspektiven.* Braunschweig: Diesterweg.

Ladousse, Gillian Porter (1987). *Role Play.* Oxford: OUP.

Maley, Alan / Duff, Alan (1984). *Drama Techniques in Language Learning: A Resource Book of Communication Activities for Language Teachers.* 7th edition. 1st edition 1978. Cambridge: Cambridge University Press.

Nissen, Peter (1994). Den Text inszenieren – statt analysieren. In: *Der Fremdsprachliche Unterricht Englisch* 28(3), 36-39.

Nünning, Ansgar (1998). Von 'Teaching Drama' zu 'Teaching Plays': Spielend Lernen durch dramatische Formen und mit dramatischen Texten. In: *Der fremdsprachliche Unterricht Englisch* 32(1), 4-15.

Oomen-Welke, Ingelore (2004). Körpersprachen und Extrasprachliches verschiedener Kulturen in Welt, Schule und Unterricht. In: Rosenbusch, Heinz S. / Schober, Otto (eds.). *Körpersprache und Pädagogik: Das Handbuch.* Baltmannsweiler: Schneider Verlag Hohengehren, 68-98.

Peters, Susanne / Klaus Stierstorfer / Laurenz Volkmann (eds.) (2006). *Teaching Contemporary Literature and Culture: Drama.* Vols. 1 & 2. Trier: WVT.

Petersohn, Roland / Volkmann, Laurenz (eds.) (2006). *Shakespeare didaktisch I. Neue Perspektiven für den Unterricht.* Tübingen: Stauffenburg.

Pfister, Manfred (1994). *Das Drama. Theorie und Analyse.* 5th ed. 1st ed. 1977. München: Fink.

Rau, Albert (1999). Short texts in action – more than action in the classroom. In: *Der Fremdsprachliche Unterricht Englisch* 33, 4-10.

Reisener, Helmut (2005). Das Klassenzimmer als Bühne. In: *Der Fremdsprachliche Unterricht Englisch* 39, 20-22.

Scheller, Ingo (1998). *Szenisches Spiel. Handbuch für die pädagogische Praxis.* Berlin: Cornelsen.

Scherer, Thomas (2005). Drama in the Classroom: Writing and Staging Plays. In: *Neusprachliche Mitteilungen* 58(4), 22-26.

Schewe, Manfred (1993). *Fremdsprache inszenieren: Zur Fundierung einer dramapädagogischen Lehr- und Lernpraxis.* Oldenburg: Carl von Ossietzky Universität.

Searle, John R. (1969). *Speech Acts: An Essay in the Philosophy of Language.* Cambridge: CUP.

Stern, Susan L. (1980). Drama in Second Language Learning from a Psycholinguistic Perspective. In: *Language Learning* 30(1), 77-97.

Stredder, James (2004). *The North Face of Shakespeare: Activities for Teaching the Plays.* Stratford-upon-Avon: Wincot Press.

Ventola, Eija (1979). The Structure of Casual Conversation. In: *Journal of Pragmatics* 3, 267-298.

Volkmann, Laurenz (2008a). Drama und Kultur im Englischunterricht. In: *Fremdsprachen Lehren und Lernen.* 37, 184-196.

Volkmann, Laurenz (2008b). Acting out: Möglichkeiten des darstellenden Spiels mit englischen Texten von der Unter- bis zur Oberstufe. In: Ahrens, Rüdiger / Eisenmann, Maria / Merkl, Matthias (eds.). *Moderne Dramendidaktik für den Englischunterricht.* Heidelberg: Winter, 425-450.

Volkmann, Laurenz (2010). Literature off the Page: Integrating Acting-Out Approaches in Literature Courses. In: *Literatur in Wissenschaft und Unterricht.* Ed. Michael Meyer, 131-143.

Volkmann, Laurenz (2016). Functions of Literary Texts in the Tradition of German EFL Teaching. In: Schaff, Barbara / Schlegel, Johannes / Surkamp, Carola (eds.). *The Institution of English Literature: Formation and Mediation.* Göttingen: V & R, 179-206.

Volkmann, Laurenz / Petersohn, Roland (2006). Teaching William Shakespeare: New Approaches to the Bard in the EFL Classroom. In: Delanoy, Werner / Volkmann, Laurenz (eds.). *Cultural Studies in the EFL Classroom.* Heidelberg: Winter, 251-268.

Wagner, Betty Jane (1976). *Drama as a Learning Medium.* Washington: National Education Association.

Wessels, Charlyn (1987). *Drama. Resource Book for Teachers.* Oxford: OUP.

Zitzelsperger, Helga (1993). *Kinder spielen Märchen.* Basel: Beltz.

CHRISTIANE KLEMPIN (FREIE UNIVERSITÄT BERLIN)

German English Teacher Trainees' Drama-Based Instructions: Exploring the Status Quo

This paper outlines current research on the impact of drama-based teaching approaches on learners of English as a foreign or second language (EFL or ESL). Review of past research studies revealed an urgent need for systematic quasi- or experimental studies in order to better gauge the effects of drama-based instruction for foreign language learning. A first exploratory study will thus investigate to what extent EFL teacher trainees employ drama-based instruction during their school internships at primary and secondary schools in Berlin. Preliminary results of a first cohort of trainees from summer term 2019 (N = 17) indicate differences for primary and secondary school teacher trainees, both in terms of quantity and quality of drama-based instruction in the English language classroom.

1. Effects of drama-based instruction on English language learning

Having synthesized research literature from 1990 until 2012 on potential effects of drama methods[1] on learning English as a second (ESL) or as a foreign language (EFL), Belliveau and Kim (2013: 1) conclude that:

> despite a wide-spread pedagogical interest and scholarly conviction in the possibilities of educational drama in creating a more contextually-situated, engaging, multi-modal, and empowering L2 learning experience, there is still little empirical evidence concerning what is actually taking place in L2 classrooms and how students perceive and react to their learning experiences when drama is introduced. More systematic, long-term research studies are needed to deepen our understanding of the impact of using drama in L2 classrooms on a range of aspects of teaching and learning.

Belliveau and Kim (2013) proceed to argue that transmissive instruction styles such as primarily teacher-driven discourses (Kramsch 1996; Wagner 1998; Paran 2006; Gilmore 2007; Cummins 2009; 2011) still largely prevail in todays' EFL classrooms. In line with this finding, drama appears to be either used in a decontextualized manner, solely for extra-curricular purposes, or not at all (Belliveau & Kim 2013: 10). Thus, drama is not used to hone learners' L2

---

[1] In line with Miladinović (2019: 11-12, translation C.K.) drama-based instruction – in this paper – is conceptualized as "all forms of foreign language teaching that [are] derived from the Arts or from associated (culture-specific) types of drama-/theatre-pedagogical practices".

speaking over the entire spectrum of language related sub-skills (e.g. reading or writing skills), even though many language teachers claim to be fervent advocates of drama-based teaching (Kao & O'Neill 1998; Liu 2000; Even 2008; Dinapoli 2009).

The popularity of using drama for learning can probably also be attributed to its often-claimed impact on the following three purposes of the L2 learning process. Drama may help EFL teachers to create holistic (e.g. Rieg & Paquette 2009; Evatt 2010), alternative (e.g. Wagner 1998; Donnery 2009; Even 2011), and authentic learning experiences (e.g. Song 2000; Cumico 2005; Even 2008) whilst further stimulating learners' (Belliveau & Kim 2013: 11-13):

- intercultural communicative competence (ICC) (e.g. Byram 1997; Boudreault 2010),
- imagination (e.g. Liu 2000; Even 2008; Donnery 2009; Boudreault 2010), and
- student interaction and communication (e.g. Byram 1997; Butt 1998; Burke & O'Sullivan 2002; Cumico 2005),
- speaking confidence and motivation (e.g. Ralph 1997; Athiemoolam 2006; Aita 2009).

Drama and intercultural communicative competence

With regard to raising intercultural awareness and empathy, McGowan-Rick (1994), Isbell (1999), Dodson (2002), Donnery (2009), and Dinapoli (2009) report positive impacts of drama-based approaches on many types and different age groups of L2 learners. Adult foreign language learners (Dinapoli 2009), Japanese EFL college students (Isbell 1999; Donnery 2009), university ESL students (Dodson 2002), or migrant American EFL learners (McGowan-Rick 1994) were all found to benefit in their cultural understanding from engaging in drama-based activities. However, all of the aforementioned studies are flawed by scholarly subjectivity. These studies mostly rely on descriptive data and were selected and eventually interpreted by the researchers themselves. Two exceptions include a controlled mixed-methods research design investigating potential effects of process drama on the learning outcomes of elementary French learners in Canada by Bournot-Trites and colleagues (2007) as well as the large-scale research project DICE (2010; Küppers 2011).

Bournot-Trites (2007; cited in Belliveau & Kim 2013: 16) deployed data triangulation yielding the observation that the:

experimental (drama) group demonstrated higher achievement in overall composition abilities in French, and a more positive attitude and higher motivation towards learning both language and content.

Findings of the DICE project (2010; Küppers 2011) – a representative mixed methods study carried out in twelve European countries on 5.000 learners – contribute to the corpus of positive links between drama-based approaches and development of intercultural communicative competencies in foreign language learners.

Drama and student interaction

Drama-based instruction also appears to be conducive to classroom interactions. Kao and O'Neill (1998) found that Taiwanese university EFL students' participation in classroom discourses improved as soon as drama was involved. Wilburn (1992) further observed a shift from teacher-oriented communication to student-driven classroom discourse in an elementary Spanish lesson when drama was embedded.

Liu (2000) employed *Action Research* and multiple data sources such as researcher and student journals, writing assignments and surveys to elicit students' drama-based reading attitudes. It was found that learner "engagement with language [...], peer collaborations, and [...] class atmosphere" (Belliveau & Kim 2013: 15) improved as students were involved in a dramatic reading project.

Drama and speaking confidence and motivation

Several non-European studies revealed desirable interplays between learners' engagement with drama activities and their confidence and motivation to communicate in a foreign or second language (L2; El-Nady 2000; Cheng & Winston 2001; Louis 2002; 2005; Janudom & Wasanasomsithi 2009). Miccoli's (2003) case study on 37 Brazilian EFL learners' self-reported use of drama for L2 learning suggests "that learners experienced an improvement of oral skills, and an increased confidence in speaking in the target language" (Belliveau & Kim 2013: 14).

Elgar (2002), as part of an *Action Research* project, further evidenced that EFL learners experience "rich opportunities for intensive language learning practice" (ibid.) when being engaged in playwriting. Further, playwriting appeared to be motivating for these learners and seemed to provide them with a sense of agency and responsibility of their own writing.

2. Research gap on drama effectiveness for L2 learning

What we can take away from this research review is that drama-based instruction assumedly improves various domains closely linked to EFL or ESL learning. Drama-based approaches not only appear to boost speaking confidence and motivation, they also seem to increase student engagement in classroom discourse, foster imagination, and even raise intercultural awareness. Yet only a limited number of the aforementioned studies occurred under experimental or quasi-experimental research conditions confining reliability and generalizability of most of the generated findings (Belliveau & Kim 2013: 17). A predominant amount of data was additionally collected in non-European school contexts further limiting scope and transferability of their results to the educational context in which this very present study is situated.

I therefore want to support Belliveau's and Kim's (2013: 17) reasoning that "there is still need for more [systematic] empirical evidence in the literature on this topic" based on their comprehensive review of twenty decades of drama effectiveness research. The research study presented in this paper taps right into this research gap. It provides a quasi-experimental research design to systematically collect, analyze, and eventually interpret various data sources in order to yield valid and reliable insights into the effectiveness of **drama-based teaching approaches (DTA)** for language learning.

3. A systematic and representative research proposal

The research study I want to detail further with regard to its participants (teacher trainees as subjects), drama-based training environment (a theory-practice university class as intervention), methods of measurement (rating manuals), and analysis (descriptive statistics) can be identified as quasi-experimental in nature. It describes a type of research conducted in the actual field, similar to action research studies (e.g. Liu 2000; Elgar 2002). One crucial difference, however, being that in quasi-experiments an intervention – a training unit based off of a specific theory (e.g. **DTA theory**) – is first developed, then implemented in the field and eventually assayed in terms of its training impact on the respective participants (e.g. EFL teacher trainees).

In the present study, EFL student teachers are exposed to a drama-based training within a regular university class to guarantee authentic field conditions (Klempin forthcoming). The effect of drama-based training, then, is contrasted with comparable subject groups who were similarly exposed to a drama intervention. This way, the impact of single "structural elements" of drama-based instruction can be investigated almost in isolation from other factors (Wirag in review: 17, translation C.K.).

In teaching contexts, simulation of experimental or even quasi-experimental conditions is, however, especially challenging. Contexts of teaching are intricate, many different agents – oftentimes with opposing agendas and needs – are involved (e.g. students versus teachers) (Helsper 2004: 56). Actions further occur simultaneously and classroom interactions often call for on the fly teacher responses. Under such complex circumstances, standardized research as in randomized, controlled experiments at first sight seems to be an impossible undertaking. One potential solution, though, might be the so-called *"Teaching and Learning Lab Seminar English (TLLSE) [German: Lehr-Lern-Labor Seminar Englisch (LLLSE)]"*. The TLLSE describes a university-based seminar combining phases of theory with repeated field practice elements through iterative reflective sessions (Klempin 2019).

Whole research study

Due to its cyclical seven-step structure, the TLLSE appears to be well-suited for conducting semi-controlled research on teacher students and EFL learners likewise. The TLLSE comprises seven consecutive steps, whereby theory informs practice and reflection of practice is informed by subject-matter theories. To achieve this kind of intersection of theory and practice, student participants of the TLLSE pass through the following consecutive, yet cyclical phases:

- Subject-matter theory input (e.g. on DTA)
- Theory-based planning of instructions (e.g. based on DTA theory)
- First acting out of drama-based instructions with EFL learners
- First theory-based reflections of instructional experiences (e.g. based on DTA theory)
- Theory- and reflection-based modification of instructions
- Second acting out of instructions with EFL learners
- Second theory-based reflections of instructional experiences

In this cycle, teacher students' attitudes may become subject to investigation at several points in time over the course of the TLLSE. Repeated phases, such as theory exposure, and repeated reflections succeeding iterative field explorations are ideal for tracing the longitudinal but also cross-sectional effects of particular phases of the TLLSE-intervention. Additionally, several agents are involved in the format: a teacher trainer (author C.K.), teacher students as well as experienced teachers and also EFL learners. This multi-agent setup enables the researcher to systematically dig deeper into questions such as: *Do EFL learners indeed benefit from the instructions of teacher trainees who were previously engaged with and exposed to drama-based teaching theories?*

Alongside this question, many other research hypotheses are of interest with regard to investigating the effectiveness of the TLLSE-intervention with a new theory focus on *drama-based teaching approaches (DTA)* since 2019 (see all hypotheses, except 3 & 6):

I. *DTAs* are rarely employed by teacher trainees during their school internships in German *EFL* classrooms.

II. *DTA* can be taught to *EFL* trainees through an on-campus intervention emphasizing phases of extensive performative theory, practice, and reflection: the *Drama Lab*.

III. *Lab*-participants acquire professional knowledge on *DTAs* over the course of the *Drama Lab*.
   1. *Drama Lab*-participants employ *DTA* while instructing EFL learners.
   2. *Drama Lab*-participants employ *DTA* stronger when being exposed to relevant DTA theories beforehand in the *Drama Lab*.
   3. *EFL* learners visiting the *Drama Lab* show improved English communicative skills when being instructed based on *DTA*.
   4. *EFL* learners who visited the *Drama Lab* will eventually achieve better grades in an English oral exam (*"Mittlere Schulabschlussprüfung" im Fach Englisch*) than *EFL* learners who did not attend the *Drama Lab*.

This paper focuses specifically on hypothesis I (highlighted in bold) as well as the theses which have emerged as a result of exploratory data collection and analysis. Hypotheses II and III will be discussed as part of the outlook of this contribution, as these are part of future inquiries.

Exploratory sub-study

As discussed in the first paragraph, one sobering observation from research is that drama-based instruction has still not reached mainstream EFL teaching practice despite its widespread popularity amongst educators (Kao & O'Neill 1998; Liu 2000; Even 2008; Dinapoli 2009). Evidence even more so indicates that transmissive, rather teacher-oriented instruction prevails in EFL classrooms worldwide (Kramsch 1996; Wagner 1998; Paran 2006; Gilmore 2007; Cummins 2009; 2011). As a first response to this, an exploration into whether this observation still holds true in German EFL classrooms is conducted. Insights from this exploratory study then serve to empirically secure the design of an intervention pursuing to impart on German EFL teacher trainees the knowledge and skills necessary for incorporating drama-based teaching approaches (DTA) into their own teaching.

In order to best encounter **hypothesis I,** the status quo of English teacher students' use of DTA in actual EFL classrooms in Berlin (n = 17) was assessed. This field exploration occurred during summer term 2019 as part of the obligatory field practicum (German: "Praxissemester") in the Master's program of English teacher education at a German university. Assessment will proceed until winter term 2020 even though this report will for now only focus on the initial findings yielded from the observations of the first cohort of summer term 2019. In total, 17 EFL teacher students' (f = 11 , m = 6) 45-minute lessons were examined with a rating manual covering various aspects of drama-based instruction.[2] During trainees' 45-minute instructions, assessment focused on the following 12 dimensions[3]:

    a. Student gender (e.g. male (m), female (f), etc.)
    b. Study program (e.g. English as first and Biology as second subject)
    c. School location
    d. School type (*Gymnasium (GYM)*, *Integrierte Sekundarschule (ISS)*, or *Grundschule (GS)*)
    e. Grade level (e.g. grades from 1-12)
    f. Lesson objective (speaking, listening, writing, reading, mediation, grammar, or none at all)
    g. DTA category[4]

---

[2] The observation manual is based on latest drama theory (Schewe & Crutchfield 2018). Further, several experts in the field of drama pedagogy in FLT were consulted, amongst them Prof. M. Sambanis (Freie Universität Berlin), Maik Walter (representative of the department of German philology, Universität Potsdam) as well as long-time drama practitioner (Jenifer Pötzsche, Wilhelm von Siemens Gymnasium Berlin).

[3] The observation manual can be provided by the author per request.

[4] Nine drama categories are differentiated: 1. Improvisation (no to little didactic scaffolding), 2. "Stegreifspiel" (didactic scaffolding provided), 3. role-play, 4. freeze frame, 5. dialogue (elaboration on dramatic texts), 6. presentation e.g. in the role of an expert, 7. Exploring and reflecting e.g. learners' text reception experience with roles cards, 8. interpretation and performance of daily situations, and 9. pantomime.

h. Instruction phase in which the DTA occurred (e.g. OFA-, GO-, TBA-, or PR-phase[5])
i. Game master (yes or no decision)
j. Teacher as game master (yes or no decision)
k. Duration of DTA (maximum: 45 minutes)
l. Alignment of DTA with lesson objective (s. dimension f; yes or no decision)

Variables a-e either describe the sample, or will be used as covariates in order to later statistically track whether some observations – for instance, a student teachers' (non)-application of DTA – can be explained by learners' grade level (s. e). As an illustration, EFL *primary* school teacher students might be more inclined towards DTA than *secondary* school trainees (e.g. ISS and GYM), simply because a preference for ludic learning is frequently attributed to better serve the needs of younger learners. Drama-based instruction makes use of exactly such kinesthetic learning experiences as it provides learners with action-orientation and *as-if-scenarios* (e.g. Baldwin 2008, Sambanis 2013).

Data on variable f ('lesson objective') is derived from class observations but also from trainees' lesson drafts available to the researcher before visitation. Ideally, trainees not only state their objectives clearly but also carry these out during their respective lessons. However, sometimes the objective stated (e.g. planned focus on speaking skills) noticeably departs from what happens during the actual lesson (e.g. instead the lesson focuses on listening skills). Combining information on variable f and g it now becomes possible to determine whether skill-oriented preferences on certain DTAs were made by student teachers: Role-plays, for example, might have been chosen for deliberate training of EFL learners' speaking fluency. Testing these kind of relationships potential breaches in current teacher training might surface from the data. These insights can then be used to tailor a university training for the specific needs of EFL teacher trainees (s. perspectives).

Along with variable g ('DTA category'), variable h ('lesson phase') can also provide clarification of the particular lesson phases in which DTA is most frequent. One hypothesis here might be that drama-based instruction dominates in such lesson phases in which EFL group members are asked to designate one expert to present team findings in plenum (e.g. acted-out *TED-talk* during PR-phase). Again, such interplays – between DTA type and lesson phase – would

---

[5] Abbreviations used here stand for: OFA = Opening a field of awareness, GO = Getting organized, TBA = Task-based learning, and PR = Presenting results.

point towards shortcomings of university-based teacher education, for example with respect to clarifying differences between a process- and product-oriented drama instruction (e.g. Schewe & Scott 2003).

Further, the mere existence of a game master (variable i & j) was of interest as well as to whether that role is assumed by the teacher or filled out by one of the EFL learners. The assumption here being that a game master is one of many characteristic features of drama-based instruction (e.g. Baldwin 2008). Assigning this role to neither teacher nor students might indicate student teachers' lack of familiarity with the theoretical frameworks of DTA. Also, assigning the role exclusively to the teacher might be indicative of a teacher-centered style of instruction (e.g. Kramsch 1996; Cumming 2009; 2011).

Eventually, the duration of DTA in minutes, relative to a regular 45-minute lesson, was of specific interest in order to determine the significance of drama-based instruction to boost EFL learning. Based on the above-mentioned 12 variables the following research questions were formulated:

Research questions (RQ) for exploratory study

RQ1: Does the frequency of DTA use vary for different school types?

RQ2: Which DTA types are used by EFL trainees for different school types?

RQ3: Is there an increased DTA-frequency in EFL lessons with focus on 'mediation skills' or 'speaking skills'?

RQ4: Is DTA more frequent in lower school grades (primary schools from grades 1-6) than in higher grades (secondary schools ISS and GYM combined: grades 7-12)?

RQ5: Are some DTA types more frequently used (e.g. expert presentations) than others (e.g. role-plays and "Stegreifspiele")?

RQ6: Is DTA more frequent in lesson phases such as PR and TBA as compared to less frequent use in GO- and OFA-phases?

RQ7 & 8: For DTA, was the role of the game leader explicitly assigned to someone? And if it was assigned, who took on the role of game leader?

RQ9: Did the DTA employed align with the lesson objectives stated in the instruction plan?

RQ10: How much of the total lesson time was dedicated to DTA?

4. Results for the exploratory study

In the following paragraphs preliminary results of the exploratory study on 17 observed lessons of EFL teacher students will be presented along the ten research questions mentioned above (s. RQ1-RQ10). Analyses occurred based on descriptive statistics but will later be extended to inferential statistical methods once sample sizes meet the methodological prerequisites to do so.

RQ1: Does the frequency of DTA-use in different lesson phases vary for various school types?

Indeed, the frequency of DTA use varies with respect to the type of school the English lesson was observed in (s. fig. 1). Surprisingly, DTAs were not deployed by trainees of the ISS-program at all. Primary school GSP-trainees, in contrast, used drama instruction across all lesson phases, whereby secondary school students missed out entirely on the chance of utilizing performative strategies for purposes of organizing language learning lessons. Secondary school trainees referred to DTA in 58,3% of the total amount of lessons observed (N = 12). Simultaneously, in only two lessons in primary schools (N = 2), six DTA instances were counted adding up to a 300% (!) employment of DTA.

Fig. 1: DTA frequency in five different lesson phases (OFA, GO, TBA, and PR) in three types of schools: secondary high school (GYM = light grey), secondary school (ISS = red), and primary school (GSP = dark grey).

RQ2: Which DTA-types are used by English teacher trainees for different school types?

First and foremost, only four (out of nine) DTA types were utilized by such students training to teach EFL at the *Gymnasium* level (see fig. 2). Primary school trainees resorted to a total of two DTA strategies in both lessons in which these student teachers used DTA. Since ISS student teachers' instructions did not rely on DTA at all, no DTA events were documented.

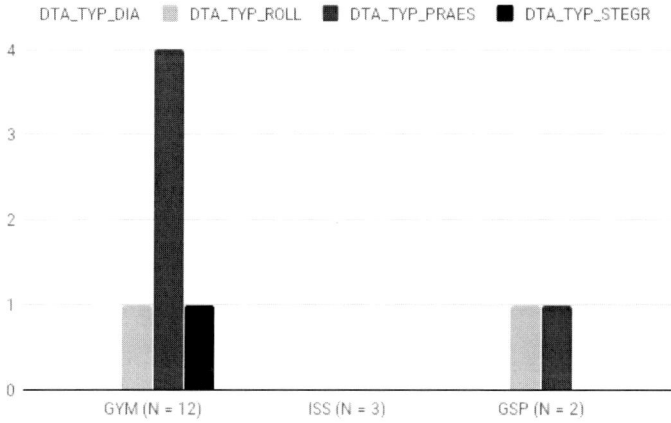

Fig. 2: DTA type frequency (only those four employed at all: DIA=dialogue, ROLL=roleplay, PRAES=presentation, STEGR=Stegreifspiel) in three types of schools: secondary high school (GYM), secondary school (ISS), and primary school (GSP).

RQ3: Is there an increased DTA-frequency in English lessons with focus on 'mediation skill' or 'speaking skills'?

In fact, only reading (42,9%) and speaking skills (57,1%) were targeted by students teachers in the overall lessons observed (s. fig. 3):

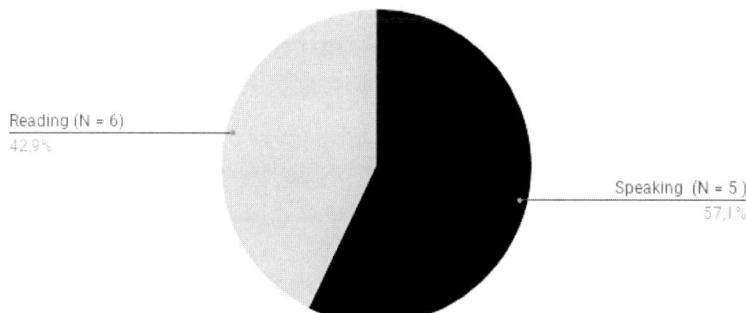

Fig. 3: DTA frequency in lessons with five different skill objectives (speaking, writing, mediation, reading, and listening).

RQ4: Is DTA more frequent in lower school grades (primary schools from grades 1-6) than in higher grades (secondary schools ISS and GYM combined: grades 7-12)?

Apparently, DTA is relatively more frequent (100%) in grades 1-6, and hence, in primary schools as compared to grades 7-12 in secondary schools (33%), ISS and GYM combined (s. fig. 4):

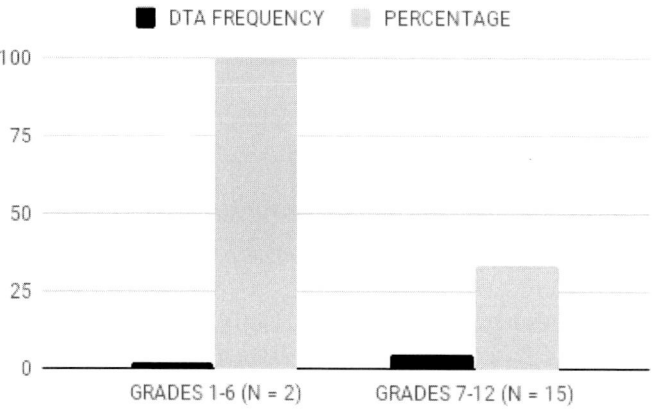

Fig. 4: Relative (dark grey) and absolute (light grey) DTA frequencies in lower school grades (primary schools: grades 1-6) and in higher grades (secondary schools ISS and GYM combined: grades 7-12).

RQ5: Are some DTA-types more frequent (e.g. presentations in *role of expert*) than others (e.g. 'Stegreifspiele', improvisation)?

First and foremost, only four out of nine DTA-types could be documented for the overall lessons observed: 'dialogues', 'role-plays', 'presentations', and 'Stegreifspiele'. These four DTAs were deployed, yet with a pronounced preference for strategies such as 'presentation' (55,6%) and 'dialogue' (22,2%) over 'role-play' (11%) and 'Stegreifspiele' (11%).

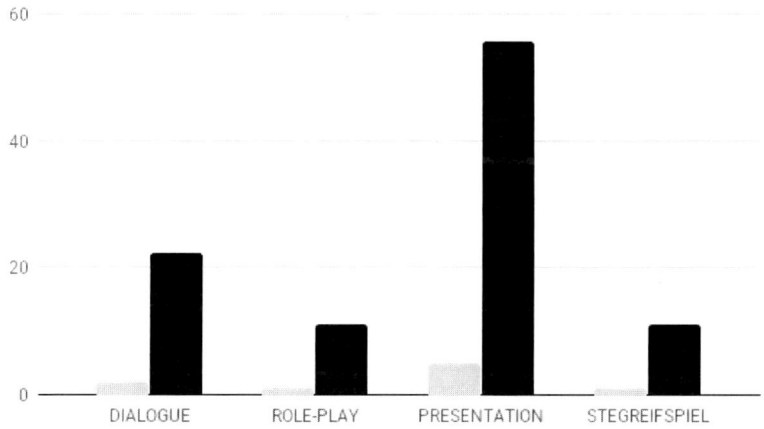

Fig. 5: Relative (light grey) and absolute (dark grey) frequency of five DTA types (DIALOGUE, ROLE-PLAY, PRESENTATION, STEGREIFSPIEL).

RQ6: Is DTA more frequent in lesson phases such as PR and TBA as compared to less frequent use in GO- and OFA-phases?

Indeed, DTA appears to prevail in such phases with a focus on task elaboration (e.g. TBA) and the presentation of products (e.g. PR) and was rather neglected in the introductory (OFA) or organizational lesson parts (GO, s. fig. 6):

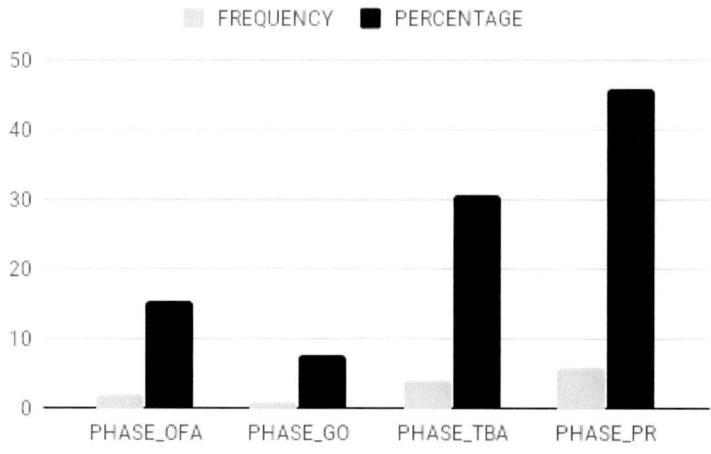

Fig. 6: Relative (light grey) and absolute (dark grey) frequency of DTA in four lesson phases (OFA, GO, TBA, and PR).

RQ7 & 8: For DTA, was the role of the game leader explicitly assigned to someone? And if it was assigned, who took the role of the game leader?

In less than one-third (29,4%) of the observed lessons (N = 17) student teachers visibly assigned a game leader, which was without exception the teacher students themselves.

RQ9: Did the DTA employed align with the lesson objectives stated in the lesson plan?

In 23,5% of the lessons observed (N =17) the lesson objectives did indeed align with the DTA employed to support that skill. In 76,5% of the observed cases, though, skill objectives and drama-based instructions failed to inform one another.

RQ10: How much of the lesson time was dedicated to DTA?

In 17 lessons and a total of 765 minutes observed, 118 minutes were dedicated to DTA. This makes 15,42% out of the entire lesson time, meaning that every student teacher has dedicated approximately M = 6.9 minutes to drama-based instruction.

5. Summary

First and foremost, it needs to be stated that these preliminary results rely on descriptive statistics. Therefore, inferences cannot be drawn to whether these findings are indicative of a general trend. Subsequent and more elaborate statistical investigations (e.g. calculation of statistical regression models) will be required for deeper understanding of the complex relations between different variables at play here. Nonetheless, I would like to summarize some of the findings generated during this early field exploration in order to then draw some conclusions for EFL teacher training:

1. So far, ISS-secondary school trainees did not resort to DTA.
2. GYM-secondary school trainees displayed a rather narrow DTA instruction repertoire.
3. Contrary to initial expectations, mediation was not trained by any of the teacher students making use of DTA instruction.
4. Preliminary observations indicate higher frequency of DTA for primary than for secondary school trainees.

5. Overall, student teachers appear to possess a limited repertoire of DTA as they resort to less than half of the strategies the methodology has in store.
6. So far, it seems as though DTA is used primarily when EFL learners are engaged with tasks or present activities' outcomes. This might hint towards a neglect of DTA's full potential for lesson sequences in which – for instance – EFL learners' prior knowledge is activated or connections between teaching contents and learners are drawn.
7. The fact that trainees exclusively assign themselves as game leaders in such rather rare teaching events with a game leader might be a first indication of a teacher-driven approach to drama-based instruction (e.g. Kramsch 1996; Cumming 2009; 2011).
8. In less than 1/5th of the lesson time, DTA was documented.

6. Perspectives

As mentioned previously in this article, the data presented in this paper serves as a first indicator to potential deficits in current EFL teacher training. One conclusion which might be drawn from this still tenuous data basis is that student teachers might need systematic in-depth training in performative teaching strategies. In rather practice- and reflection-oriented teacher training formats student teachers could get first familiarized with the evidence-based benefits of performative instruction, for instance on EFL learners' oral fluency, comprehensibility, and accentedness (e.g. Galante & Thomson, 2017). Future English teachers also should get a chance to act out said performative teaching strategies, for instance by way of on- or off-campus internships, via in-class micro-teachings, or through analysis of case studies. Experimenting with DTA might also be effective to let students self-experience the benefits DTA. Through exploration and reflection on the effects and effectiveness of DTA on foreign language learning, teacher trainees' acceptance for this novel way of instruction might improve. A higher approval of drama-based instruction, in turn, might affect the likelihood that student teachers will eventually incorporate this way of teaching to their repertoire.[6]

---

[6] Improving teacher trainees' assumptions on performative instruction might also be a response to one of the findings of this study that ISS-teacher students did not resort to DTA at all. However, in order to track the actual reasons for neglect of DTA by such trainees one has to collect more data points. If more data should confirm these preliminary findings, one could conduct interviews with students in the ISS-teacher training program. My initial impulse is that they might attribute

As an explicit on-campus format to equip teacher trainees with the above-mentioned skill and belief sets, the *Teaching and Learning Lab Seminar in English (TLLSE)*, was designed and first realized at Freie Universität Berlin during winter term 2019/20. The *TLLSE* has long been used for teacher training purposes in Physics subject-matter education (Nordmeier et al. 2014). In 2015, the format was then taken up by the English subject-matter department at Freie Universität Berlin and transformed in such a way as to meet the specific needs of English teacher students. From 2015 until 2018, the TLLSE was systematically investigated in a *Mixed Methods* research design with respect to its impact on the participating English teacher students' reflective skills (Klempin 2019).

From 2019 until 2021, the TLLSE concept is yet again adapted with the overall objective to now mend the above stated (assumed) gaps in EFL teacher training (s. discussion). As the so-called *Drama Lab* it is now designed to instill drama instructional skills and pro-DTA attitudes in English student teachers. Beginning with winter term 2019/20, the *Drama Lab* will also be subject to systematic investigation, both, with respect to its teacher student and EFL learner participants.

Bibliography

Aita, S. (2009). The Theatre in Language Learning (TiLL) Model: Exploring Theatre as Pedagogy in the L2 Environment. *Scenario: Journal for Drama and Theatre in Foreign and Second Language Education*, *3*(1), 64-80.

Belliveau, G. (2013). Drama in L2 learning: A Research Synthesis. *Scenario: Journal for Drama and Theatre in Foreign and Second Language Education*, *7*(2), 6-26.

Boudreault, C. (2019). The Benefits of Using Drama in the ESL/EFL Classroom. *The Internet TESL Journal, 16(1)*, 1-6.

Bournot-Trites, M. / Belliveau, G. / Spiliotopoulos, V. / Séror, J. (2007). The Role of Drama on Cultural Sensitivity, Motivation and Literacy in a Second Language Context. *Journal for Learning through the Arts*, *3*(1), 1-37.

Burke, A. F. (2002). *Stage by Stage: A Handbook for Using Drama in the Second Language Classroom*. Portsmouth, NH: Heinemann.

Butt, R. (1998). Notes from the Classroom: Improvisation and Language Acquisition: Actor Training as a Tool to Enhance Fluency. *College ESL*, *8*(2), 58-63.

EFL learners at the ISS-level with characteristics that run counter to that of the (assumed) drama-based instruction program (e.g. playfulness and action-orientation of DTA).

Byram, M. (1997). *Teaching and Assessing Intercultural Communicative Competence*. Clevedon [et al.]: Multilingual Matters.
Cheng, A. Y.-M. / Winston, J. (2011). Shakespeare as a Second Language: Playfulness, Power and Pedagogy in the ESL classroom. *Research in Drama Education: The Journal of Applied Theatre and Performance, 16*(4), 541-556.
Crutchfield, J. / Schewe, M. (2017). *Going Performative in Intercultural Education: International Contexts, Theoretical Perspectives and Models of Practice.* Bristol, Blue Ridge Summit: Multilingual Matter.
Cummins, J. (2009). Transformative Multiliteracies Pedagogy: School-Based Strategies for Closing the Achievement Gap. *Multiple Voices for Ethnically Diverse Exceptional Learners, 11*, 38-56.
Cummins, J. (2012). The Intersection of Cognitive and Sociocultural Factors in the Development of Reading Comprehension among Immigrant Students. *Reading and Writing, 25*(8), 1973-1990.
Cunico, S. (2005). Teaching Language and Intercultural Competence through Drama: Some Suggestions for a Neglected Resource. *The Language Learning Journal, 31*(1), 21–29.
Dinapoli, R. (2009). Using Dramatic Role-Play to Develop Emotional Aptitude. *International Journal of English Studies, 9*(2), 97–110.
Dodson, S. (2002). The Educational Potential of Drama for ESL. *Body and Language: Intercultural Learning through Drama* (p. 161–181). Westport, CT & London: Ablex Publishing.
Donnery, E. (2009). Testing the Waters: Drama in the Japanese University EFL Classroom. *Scenario: Journal for Drama and Theatre in Foreign and Second Language Education, 3*(1), 17-33.
Elgar, A. G. (2002). Student Playwriting for Language Development. *ELT Journal, 56*(1), 22–28.
El-Nady, M. (2000). *Drama as a Teaching Technique in the Second Language Classroom. 14*(1-2), 41-48.
Evatt, S. (2010). Drama in the English Language Learning Classroom: A Holistic Approach to Language Acquisition. *Insight, 2*(1), 11-12.
Even, S. (2008). Moving in(to) Imaginary Worlds: Drama Pedagogy for Foreign Language Teaching and Learning. *Unterrichtspraxis / Teaching German, 41*(2), 161–170.
Even, S. (2011). Drama Grammar: Towards a Performative Postmethod Pedagogy. *The Language Learning Journal, 39*(3), 299-312.
Galante, A. / Thomson, I. R. (2017). The Effectiveness of Drama as an Instructional Approach for the Development of Second Language Oral Fluency, Comprehensibility, and Accentedness. *TESOL Quarterly, 51*(1), 115-142.
Gilmore, A. (2007). Authentic Materials and Authenticity in Foreign Language Learning. *Language Teaching, 40*(2), 97-118.
Helsper, W. (2004). Antinomien, Widersprüche, Pradoxien: Lehrerarbeit - ein unmögliches Geschäft? Eine strukturtheoretisch-rekosntruktive Perspektive

auf das Lehrerhandeln. In: Koch-Priewe, B. / Kolbe, F. U. / Wildt, L. (eds.). *Grundlagenforschung und mikrodidaktische Reformansätze.* Bad Heilbrunn: Klinkhardt, 49-98.

Janudom, R. / Wasanasomsithi, P. (2009). Drama and Questioning Techniques: Powerful Tools for the Enhancement of Students' Speaking Abilities and Positive Attitudes towards EFL Learning. *ESP World 5*(26), 1–19.

Kao, S.-M. / O'Neill, C. (1998). *Words into Worlds: Learning a Second Language through Process Drama.* Stamford, CT: Ablex Publishing.

Klempin, C. (2019). *Reflexionskompetenz von Englischlehramtsstudierenden im Lehr-Lern-Labor-Seminar: Eine Interventionsstudie zur Förderung und Messung.* Stuttgart: J.B. Metzler Verlag (Bd. 7).

Kramsch, C. (1996). Proficiency Plus: The Next Step. ERIC Digest. Retrieved from: https://de.scribd.com/document/244183846/KRAMSCH-Proficiency-Plus-pdf (07/04/21).

Küppers, A. (2011). Review: The DICE Consortium (2010), The DICE has been cast. *Scenario: Journal for Drama and Theatre in Foreign and Second Language Education*, 5(1), 69-74.

Liu, J. (2000). The Power of Readers Theater: From Reading To Writing. *ELT Journal*, 54(4), 354-361.

Louis, R. (2002). *Critical Performative Pedagogy: Augusto Boal's Theatre of the Oppressed in the English as a Second Language Classroom* (ProQuest Dissertations Publishing).

Louis, R. (2005). Performing English, Performing Bodies: A Case for Critical Performative Language Pedagogy. *Text and Performance Quarterly 25*(4), 334-353.

Miladinović, D. (2019). Prinzipien eines performativen Fremdsprachenunterrichts. In: Even, S. / Miladinović, D. / Schmenk, B. (eds.). *Lernbewegungen inszenieren: Performative Zugänge in der Sprach-, Literatur- und Kulturdidaktik.* Tübingen: Narr Francke Attempto, 7-22.

Rost, D. (2013). *Interpretation und Bewertung pädagogisch-psychologischer Studien. Eine Einführung.* Bad Heilbrunn: UTB.

Schewe, M. / Scott, T. (2003). Literatur verstehen und inszenieren – Foreign Language Literature through Drama. A Research Project. *GFL – German as a Foreign Language*, (3), 56-83.

Schumann, A. (2017). Kommunikativer Fremdsprachenunterricht. In: Surkamp, C. (ed.). *Metzler Lexikon Fremdsprachendidaktik*: *Ansätze, Methoden, Grundbegriffe.* Stuttgart: J. B. Metzler, 163-166.

Thaler, E. (2012). *Englisch unterrichten: Grundlagen - Kompetenzen - Methoden.* Berlin: Cornelsen.

Wirag, A. (in review). Experimentelle Studien zu Theaterarbeit und Persönlichkeitsentwicklung: Die aktuelle Befundlage. *Scenario: Journal for Drama and Theatre in Foreign and Second Language Education.*

ANNETTE DESCHNER (PÄDAGOGISCHE HOCHSCHULE KARLSRUHE)
LISA PETER (THE SHAKESPEARE BIRTHPLACE TRUST)

Exploring Shakespeare in the Multilingual Classroom

Multilingualism is not new to a Europe promoting its language variety, yet teaching and school systems have not fully adapted to the challenges of migration and its consequences. Exploring Shakespeare in the many – and new – voices of Europe was the aim of a three-year venture of the Erasmus+ project CultureShake, where a transnational team of schools, universities and Shakespeare educators from different European countries designed teaching materials for multilingual classes. This article shares some of the developed and tested methods that employed drama techniques to include multilingual students in the language classroom. After some introductory remarks on the advantages of including the wealth of languages in the student body in the class and on why this can be successfully connected to the study and exploration of Shakespeare, we will introduce a number of activities. These teaching materials were created to bring together multilingual speakers and speakers of only one language or a dialect in a learning environment which opens up spaces of participation and social inclusion through drama techniques.

Linguistically and culturally diverse classrooms are becoming increasingly more common but in many cases teacher training does not include ways of dealing with or indeed making the most of the linguistic and cultural heterogeneity prevalent in the student body. Unfortunately, this multilingualism is often perceived as a drawback rather than an asset for the students. However, as amongst others Gogolin et al. (2005) have shown, including the students' home languages into the classroom can significantly raise self-esteem and support inclusion. Particularly since the arrival of refugees after 2015 teachers are also trying to integrate these newly arrived students in their new environments to foster inclusion. In order to offer materials and support, the transnational learning project *CultureShake*[1] used drama approaches to two of Shakespeare's plays among other methods in order to develop and test classroom activities that increase the inclusion of multilingual and multicultural students. We would like to share some of these activities as well as the underlying principles and ideas of the *CultureShake* project in order to showcase how drama methods can be used to increase language awareness in the entire class and to build confidence about the students' multilingualism while exploring classical literature together.

---

[1] The CultureShake project has been co-funded by Erasmus+ of the European Union.

1. Advantages of including multilingualism in the classroom

Why is it important to include student languages in the classroom? In the field of multilingual studies the positive implications for students and society have been widely demonstrated (cf. Tracy 2011). Amongst these are the importance of language diversity as cultural heritage and the valuing of language as appreciation of the individual and their cultures. Furthermore, the promotion of language awareness contributes to metalinguistic development. Therefore, EU policies on education and society such as *Rethinking Education* (European Parliament 2018: online) or the *Report on the role of intercultural dialogue, cultural diversity and education in promoting EU fundamental values* (Julie Ward 2015: online) recommend the promotion and appreciation of multilingualism. In these EU documents among others, inclusion is the paramount aim for successful education and societies. Integrating the home languages across the curriculum is one way of contributing to social inclusion.

A re-design of the *Common European Framework of Reference (CEFR)* became necessary in 2017 in order to adapt to this new situation of multilingual classrooms at schools. The *CEFR-Companion Volume with New Descriptors (CEFR-CV2017)* (Council of Europe 2018: online) puts no longer the native speaker but the plurilingual speaker as the reference point (Camerer/ Mader 2019: 42f.). In addition to the need to educate students for a globalised world and multilingual workspace, including the home languages, mother tongues or – as they have been referred to recently – the own languages (Hall 2019: 46f.) in the classroom, the integration of the mother tongues supports students´ linguistic and cognitive development (Cummins 1980; Butzkamm 2000). Code-switching between languages, for example, is no longer regarded as linguistic deficiency, but considered an asset, because students are capable to connect the languages to each other and add deeper meaning to their utterances by using the different connotation of the words (Baetens Beardsmore 2010).

These research results and new developments confront education systems with the tasks to implement EU strategies into national curricula and to find new approaches in TEFL. Intertwining TEFL and multilingual didactics may give a new twist, e.g. to teaching Shakespeare´s plays in a multilingual classroom.

How does Shakespeare fit into this, or better, why did the *CultureShake* project choose a classical writer most native speakers consider 'difficult' as the shared topic for their intercultural exchange between the German and Swedish students that took part in the project? The fact that Shakespeare wrote for performance rather than reading played a major factor in this decision, as this opened up much more varied ways of exploring topics that did not exclusively focus on language performance, for example by exploring non-verbal ways of expression like body language. In addition, Shakespeare's position as a writer whose works enjoy ever-increasing popularity around the globe made it comparatively easy to find access points for students from various cultural and linguistic backgrounds to the stories. Most of the plays are available in translation into most of the major languages and are performed the world over, often in 'localised' versions that establish connections between Shakespeare's works and local performance traditions, for example, Kabuki theatre in Japan or Indian popular theatre traditions (the MIT Global Shakespeare Video and Performance Archives are a great starting point if students would like to learn more about Shakespeare performances around the world: see online reference). This resonance of his writing made Shakespeare into a perfect example of cultural heritage that would allow for interrogation from an intercultural point of view as it highlights the commonalities as well as the differences between languages and cultures present in the classroom today. We therefore decided to use Shakespeare as a medium to develop teaching methods and activities that incorporate plurilingualism and multilingualism in their makeup.

2. The *CultureShake* project

In addition to the EU strategies that emphasise the value of and need for multilingual education a number of further EU documents have put forward the central importance of language learning and inclusive education for a Europe united in diversity in the last couple of years, for example, *Education and Training 2020* (European Commission 2013: online), the so called *Paris Declaration* (Eurydice 2018: online) or the Commission Staff Working Document on *Rethinking Education* (European Commission 2012: online). In alignment with these the *CultureShake* project set out to bridge the gap between theory and practice, i.e. between the research approaches discussed earlier and the school reality or teacher ability to cope with multilingual settings (cf. Gogolin 2005) by providing secondary level learning material for intercultural communication in multilingual educational settings. We tested a number of methods and activities that used Shakespeare as a tool and a shared topic for students to work on and that allowed for approaching literature from multilingual angles. The project consortium was made up of a range of organisations, spanning two universities (Karlsruhe University of Education in Germany and the University of Primorska in Slovenia), two secondary schools (the Friedrich-Woehler-

Gymnasium in Germany and the English School Gothenburg in Sweden), and an educational charity (the Shakespeare Birthplace Trust in the UK), who partnered up for three years between 2016 and 2019 in order to tackle these challenges together.

A selection of 26 students with 13 different languages between them met during three workshop weeks in 2017 and 2018 to explore their respective countries, but also to work together on the focus plays for the project, *A Midsummer Night's Dream* and *The Tempest*. Using an online dictionary platform, they compiled a glossary for the vocabulary in the 20-minute versions of the plays which formed the basis for much of the workshop work they did on the plays. In addition, the students themselves also developed a number of peer-teaching activities together, which are now available on the *CultureShake* website (see online reference).

On a more conceptual level and in order to develop and share teaching materials that were innovative and inclusive in terms of multilingual and multicultural classrooms, the project consortium decided to explore drama pedagogical approaches as well as other more creative and interactive methods of teaching. In the following we would like to showcase and share some of the activities that draw on drama methods and that can be used in the classroom to include multilingual students in Shakespeare lessons.[2] We will start with language biographies based on Brigitta Busch's ideas as a reflection on the participants' own multilingualism before we introduce the project geocaches that were not only used to familiarise the students' with the locations for their workshop weeks but that also asked for performative explorations of both *A Midsummer Night's Dream* and *The Tempest* and the participants' multilingualism. We will then move on to more play-specific activities that re-act to the language politics of both plays and that re-create the emotional landscape the plays, in particular *The Tempest*, inhabit.

---

[2] The majority of these activities were part of the project workshops in 2017 and 2018, and they have since been presented to conference audiences and the CultureShake stakeholders, whose comments and insights proved immensely useful for their final design. Any accompanying activity sheets or scripts are freely available for download on the CultureShake website as well as on the Shakespeare Birthplace Trust's pages (www.shakespeare.org.uk/education/teaching-resources). We hope the activities and exercises provide inspiration for including Shakespeare into the language learner classroom and that they prove useful in your teaching.

3. Reflecting on multilingualism: Language biographies

The language biography or language portrait according to Busch (2012) can be used as a tool to identify the languages of the speakers in a multilingual learning environment. The aim of the language biography is to become aware of the language diversity in the classroom. This method is not about just naming or listing the languages one has acquired as a home language or learned as a foreign language. Preparing the *CultureShake* project, students were asked to write down or report the languages they are familiar with to their teachers. Examples for foreign languages, official languages and home languages were given to make students confident to mention all languages, even tabooed ones. As it turned out, however, the students in the project did not mention all their languages in this preparatory step for the project: some students left some of the migrant and refugee languages initially out. Yet during the exercise of drawing their language biography, the students revealed further languages. We think that this may have been due to the meditative and narrative design of the method.

In the *CultureShake* project this activity was carried out with the students during the first workshop week, which was also the first face-to-face meeting of the students who before had only worked together online on various platforms.

When creating a language biography with students, the following steps may be helpful:

1) Students draw the outline of their bodies on a sheet of paper and choose different colours for their languages. They then write their languages in the chosen colours in a part of their body of their own choosing. It is crucial to mention to the students that it is not important to excel at this language but that it is a language they can connect with and have some basic knowledge. This "drawing" exercise can be seen as a kind of meditation.

2) Students are encouraged to write a short text about their usage of the language: when they use them, in which context, with whom, etc.

3) The students then share their individual language biographies with each other. Points for discussion could be the different parts of the body the languages were assigned to, or the different reasons for locating the language. For example, the home language can be written in the heart as something very dear to the student, or under their feet because it is the fundament they stand on.

Building on Busch (2012), we extended and altered how the language biography was carried out. For example, the body silhouette was not given as a template to the students, but instead, the students were asked to draw their bodies themselves in order to stronger identify with their body.

The language biography makes students and teachers aware of the diversity of languages within their class. After the revelation of this treasure of languages the students were then able to explore Shakespeare with their different languages.

4. Multilingual Shakespeare geocaches

Most of the times foreign language teachers are the ones responsible for school exchanges, so we asked ourselves how home languages could be integrated to a school exchange. In *CultureShake* the three workshop weeks were organised as school exchanges either at the partners' schools or at the Shakespeare Birthplace Trust in Stratford. Instead of predominantly visiting tourist attractions, students explored Singen in Germany, Stratford in the UK and Gothenburg in Sweden by solving a multilingual Shakespeare geocache for each town. We tailored this outdoor activity to school use in respect to time, locations, learning outcomes and group size. All the geocaches also promoted digital competence through using either a GPS device or the Maps.Me app on tablets or phones and all of them included elements of students' multilingual performances.

In Singen the traditional cache *Fairies Singen*[3] was performed. This geocache did not focus on famous sights in town, but instead on places with personal connections. The German students were asked to submit suggestions for places they liked or visited with their friends in advance, and which they also wanted their exchange partners to know about, for example, a favourite coffee place, sports ground or park. In contrast to a normal geocache for individuals, a geocache for a school class has to deal with a number of geocachers searching for the cache simultaneously rather than only one geocacher. We therefore designed five routes for five groups. This geocache could only be solved through the collaboration of the five multilingual teams because the final solutions of the five groups - arranged in the right order - form the "Fairies Song" from *A Midsummer Night's Dream*. At the final meeting point before heading out to

---

[3] The name of the geocache is a pun as the German school is located in the town Singen and `to sing' translates as `singen' into German, which refers to the "Fairies Song" in *A Midsummer Night's Dream*.

find the cache, students had to think about how they could perform their part of the "Fairies Song" in their languages. They were given some time to rehearse and this rehearsal time also served as a time buffer to wait for groups that had not arrived in time. One group created a rap version of the "Fairies Song" while another group collected natural materials to make flower wreaths as part of their costume. Performing this song in the many languages the group invoked Titania, the keeper of the cache, and thus the teams could find the container with the stash note.

In order to motivate and to challenge students, we built on each geocache during the three workshop weeks. For the second week at the Shakespeare Birthplace Trust, we designed a mystery cache that used the same groups as *Fairies Singen* but this time all the groups shared the same route. While for a traditional cache the coordinates are handed out at the beginning, for a mystery cache the geocachers have to complete an extra challenge: they need to solve a riddle first to find the coordinates that will lead them to the stations of the cache. The *Island Walk* was designed in such a way that the five groups ended up giving a tour of the whole focus play for that workshop week, i.e. *The Tempest*, while also tracing the steps of Shakespeare's life from his birthplace in Henley Street to his grave at Holy Trinity Church. The mystery of the *Island Walk*, i.e. the coordinates, could be unravelled in the archive of the Shakespeare Birthplace Trust, where translations of *A Midsummer Night's Dream* and *The Tempest* were provided in the students' home languages to help with solving the tasks each group had been set. Each of the tasks was related to one act of *The Tempest*, and the solutions revealed the coordinates for their group. The students were asked to choose their favourite line in their act of *The Tempest* and to prepare the tour they had to think of how to include this line into their performance of their act. Each group then performed a summary of one act of *The Tempest* at the correspondent coordinates.

The last geocache during the third workshop week in Gothenburg was designed as a virtual cache for three groups. In contrast to the two other geocache types, for the virtual cache the geocacher does not to have to collect information in order to discover a container with the stash – the reward in this case is to find the location itself. With the virtual cache *Our Heritage: Where the past meets the future*[4] the tasks for the geocaching were taken a step further by identifying a place in Gothenburg that was connected to Shakespeare. We decided to split

---

[4] The name of the geocache is a tribute to the European Year of Cultural Heritage 2018. The third workshop week in Gothenburg was awarded the EYCH 2018 label.

the students into three groups in Gothenburg, and we designed a virtual cache for each group. In preparation, we needed to choose locations that had some kind of connection to Shakespeare and his theatre. With the help of some of our project stakeholders, we were able to identify the site of the former Comedy House, where *Hamlet* was staged in 1787 as the first Shakespeare performance in Gothenburg, and at Lorensbergsteatern, where in the 1920s a range of Shakespeare plays where performed (see online reference). The replica ship from the times of the Swedish East India Company was chosen as a location to make students aware that a theatre is not the only place for Shakespeare, theatre and performance: there is evidence that on board of East India Company ships the crew performed Shakespeare plays to entertain themselves (see online reference).

Here's how this more abstract virtual cache worked out: the coordinates were given to the geocachers together with an introductory text that connects Shakespeare and his plays to the location in Gothenburg. The tasks they were given was to act parts of *The Tempest* in different languages at the location they had been given, and in order to log the virtual cache, the geocachers had to take photos and/or make videos of the performance to eventually share them on the project website after editing them back at school.

All the geocaches with detailed material are available on www.cultureshake.eu. We hope that the design of the multilingual Shakespeare geocaches contributes to innovative ways of teaching literature in a globalised world and digital era.

5. Play-related activities

Language politics in *A Midsummer Night's Dream*

Shakespeare shapes his characters as much by how they speak as through what they say and do. For example, Dogberry in *Much Ado About Nothing* is known for regularly using the wrong words, often ending up saying the opposite of what he intended without being aware of it. He wants to sound educated and tries to use sophisticated expressions like *apprehend* in the meaning of *arrest* but comes out with *comprehend* instead, which turns him into a figure of ridicule in the play:

One word, sir. Our watch, sir, have indeed comprehended two aspicious persons, and we would have them this morning examined before your worship.
(*Much Ado About Nothing*, Act III, Scene 5)

Dogberry does this so often throughout the play that cases like his malapropism used to be also called Dogberryism (*auspicious* (promising) instead of *suspicious* is another example of this from the quote above). On the other end of the linguistic spectrum, the pedant Holofernes in *Love's Labour's Lost*, is so uber-educated that his over-reliance on synonyms makes him come across like a thesaurus. Similarly, tragic characters like Othello are also shaped by their language: Othello is known to be a great orator at the beginning of the play, intensely lyrical in his choice of words, but after he has been convinced of his wife's unfaithfulness, his sentences become short and fragmented: towards the end of the play Othello has lost his way with words as he has lost his sense of self.

This way of characterising dramatic personnel reveals opportunities to explore the language politics of the plays in comparison and contrast to the language politics inherent in our societies today: is there a certain language (or a certain variant of the language) that is considered to be more prestigious than others? Are certain languages or dialects only used in certain contexts, for example at home, or to grandparents, or on special occasions?

In *A Midsummer Night's Dream* the four different groups of characters (lovers, fairies, the Court and the Mechanicals) are all as much characterised by their language as through their actions, so this play is perfect to explore how languages and dialects are associated with certain social constructs around education, class and social standing. For example, the Mechanicals' performance of *Pyramus and Thisbe* at the wedding is greeted with much derision from the Athenian court because of the Mechanicals' use of what is considered inappropriate language. Their way of public speaking is considered comic because it is 'wrong' and deficient, but at the same time the Mechanicals are probably the most authentic and upright characters in the whole play.[5] This scene is an excellent opportunity to raise awareness of how and when we employ language, and to discuss why we consider a certain language or a certain way of speaking and expressing oneself to be more prestigious than others. In order to take this further, it can be beneficial to your students discuss which language they would

---

[5] In fact, this play-within-the-play very often strikes a much more serious note in performance once Thisbe takes over from the overly dramatic Pyramus and kills herself, as she does not believe her life worth living without her lover. One wonders whether any of the other lovers in this play would go as far as her to die for their love.

allocate to which character group in the play, and then invite your multilingual students to roughly translate 'their' lines into their home language and perform the extract, thereby creating a performative response to the language politics inherent in the play. A worksheet that includes a shortened version of *Pyramus and Thisbe* with vocabulary is available open access (see online reference).

The Tempest: "Sounds and Sweet Airs"

Creating a soundscape can be a helpful exercise to get a sense of where the play is set and how these strange surroundings affect the characters. As the shipwrecked explore this unknown island, they are not only distraught by the loss they have just experienced in the storm but they also find themselves in alien and potentially very dangerous surroundings. The eerie sounds of the island are mentioned directly in the play, above all in the famous "this isle is full of noises" speech by Caliban in Act 3:

> Be not afeard; the isle is full of noises,
> Sounds and sweet airs, that give delight and hurt not.
> Sometimes a thousand twangling instruments
> Will hum about mine ears, and sometime voices
> That, if I then had waked after long sleep,
> Will make me sleep again: and then, in dreaming,
> The clouds methought would open and show riches
> Ready to drop upon me that, when I waked,
> I cried to dream again.
> (The Tempest, Act III, Scene 2)

This passage offers a number of approaches that are useful in the classroom, and we shall get back to some of them later for understanding the language politics of the play and the notions of home that can be gleaned from it. For now, let's focus on creating a soundscape of the island that might exemplify Caliban's love for his home or that might reflect the emotional state of the shipwrecked instead. A 'soundscape' is basically the sum of all the sounds and noises that are discernible in a certain landscape or space, for example, the soundscape of a busy pub would be made up of chatter, laughter, clinking glasses, perhaps some music in the background, the sound of the bell being rung for last orders, etc. A soundscape for The Tempest's island can be put together with very straightforward means in the classroom and without having to source musical instruments first: using the passage from above, the students can think about what the weather will sound like, whether we hear waves crashing at the shore, whether we hear insects (are there bees or crickets? mosquitoes?) or other animals, and what the other 'sounds and sweet airs' are. Which 'twangling instruments' can we imagine and imitate to add to the mix? A worksheet for this soundscape is available for free (see online reference). In order to include the heritage languages in the activity, it is possible to discuss different musical styles and instruments that would sound strange to ears that are not familiar with them. After all, what Caliban perceives as beautiful and soothing on the island might not sound the same to the ears of Stephano and Trinculo (or to any of the other shipwrecked on the island, for that matter), who are in an alien place where they have just met a 'monster' or 'mooncalf'. With the help of the internet, the soundscape can be extended to include musical instruments from around the world to create the "sounds and sweet airs" Caliban talks about. Another advantage of creating such a soundscape is that students also have the opportunity to deal with their feelings about the strange sounds of a different languages. Bebermeier (1994) describes how children encountering a foreign languages can also shy away from the eeriness of the other language. It might therefore be a good idea to foster language awareness in the classroom.

Ideas of home and exile in *The Tempest*

One of the interesting things about the island in the play is that apart from Caliban and the spirit Ariel none of the characters we get to know are native inhabitants of the island (although one could argue that Miranda cannot remember another home, as she was still a toddler when she and her father arrived). All the other characters probably think of other places as home: Prospero even after twelve years on the island is still angry enough about his brother's betrayal that he wants to carry out his revenge on those that exiled him, and the shipwrecked fear that they may never find their way back to Naples and Milan. During the second workshop week in Stratford-upon-Avon in 2017, we used this constellation of exiled characters and native characters to explore different ideas of home: whether it is the place where we were born, or the place we have spent most of our lives in, or whether home is related to the people one loves, no matter where you are. We gave out character cards to some of the students that briefly outlined the characters' back story and how they felt at the beginning of the play about their home. These students familiarised themselves with 'their' character and were then put in 'hot seats' in front of the rest of the group. It is possible to do this with each character individually, but we decided to lower the pressure for the individual students by having them answer questions about their characters while surrounded by the entire group, thereby creating a panel of characters being quizzed by their peers. In a second step, the students can then reflect on their own notions of what 'home' means to them. We created a worksheet for this activity that includes the character cards (see online reference).

"You taught me language"

The Tempest is nowadays very often read and performed with reference to post-colonial contexts, and there is a very good reason for this: the conflict between Prospero and Miranda on the one hand, and their slave Caliban on the other is fraught with discourses around colonising the island, taking over control of the land from the native inhabitant through the power of knowledge, in this case Prospero's magic. Wrapped up in this conflict are the language politics of the play: while Caliban, the "brute" and "devil", claims that the only profit he gained from learning Prospero and Miranda's language is that he now knows how to curse, he nevertheless utters the most sublime poetry of the play when he describes his feelings about his home in Act 3, Scene 2, as we have seen in the extract above.

Yet, for most of the play, Prospero's English in particular is the language of domination and oppression: all his relationships on the island – from his own daughter to his other servant Ariel and finally to the shipwrecked Ferdinand – are characterised by manipulation, threat and emotional blackmail, until Ariel teaches him forgiveness in Act 4. As problematic as this is within the play, it obviously opens up opportunities for discussion in the language classroom: how can language (and the teaching thereof) become embroiled in power politics and misused in order to dominate others? Are there ways to avoid this? Thinking about how language can enforce and sustain power, and how majorities and minorities influence language politics is an immensely important aspect of cross-cultural understanding, particularly in a European context where the representation and protection of smaller, more regional languages alongside the majority, mainstream ones is one of the pillars of the community.

"You taught me language, and my profit on't is I know how to curse" (Act I, Scene 2) is therefore one of the key moments in *The Tempest*, and makes for a perfect springboard for discussions around power and language. Some suggestions about how to guide the discussion and how to flip Caliban's negative example of language learning in the play into a positive one in your classroom can be found in a worksheet (see online reference).

5. Conclusion

The *CultureShake* project aimed at creating inclusive uses of drama techniques as well as other methods in linguistically and culturally diverse classrooms. Even though we were less interested in exploring individual scenes in the two focus plays the methods we developed and tested draw on interactive and creative approaches to Shakespeare. This kind of pedagogy may bring together fun and more serious language learning that allow for differentiated forms of learner performance. We wanted to create material that allowed for looking at classical literature from another perspective that is not wholly dependent on reading and individual study but that combined acting with an increase in knowledge of Shakespeare's work (contextual as well as textual understanding). In addition, the project consortium also wanted to open up different channels of expression, including non-verbal ones like gestures and body language, which are in most face-to-face contexts even more important for communication and understanding than the words we actually use.

We hope we have been able to showcase a number of activities that make it possible for students in multilingual and multicultural classrooms to discover Shakespeare's stories for themselves, no matter what their mother tongue or heritage culture. They offer opportunities for the students to bring their languages and cultures into the discussion of topics and themes prevalent in the two plays *CultureShake* set out to explore, *A Midsummer Night's Dream* and *The Tempest*.

Bibliography

Baetens Beardsmore, Hugo (2010). Le Problème de l'Unilinguism dans la Formation Bilingue. In: Erhart, Sabine / Hélot, Christine / Le Nevez, Adam (eds.). *Plurilinguisme et Formation des Einseignants. Plurilingualism and Teacher Education*. Frankfurt am Main: Peter Lang, 103-113.

Bebermeier, Hans (1994). Begegnung mit Sprache(n) in den Grundschulen Nordrhein-Westfalens. In: Hegele, Irmintraut et al. (ed.). *Kinder begegnen Fremdsprachen*. Braunschweig: Westermann, 33-50.

Busch, Brigitta (2012). The Linguistic Repertoire Revisited. *Applied Linguistics* 33 (5), 1–22.

Butzkamm, Wolfgang (2000). Über die planvolle Mitbenutzung der Muttersprache im bilingualen Sachfachunterricht. In: Bach, Gerhard / Niemeier, Susanne (eds.). *Bilingualer Unterricht: Grundlagen, Methoden, Praxis, Perspektiven*. Berlin/ Frankfurt am Main: Peter Lang, 97–113.

Camerer, Rudi / Mader, Judith (2019). Language-culture-identity: a paradigm for teaching English as a lingua franca. In: Pattison, Tania (ed.). *IATEFL: Brighton Conference Selections*. Kent: IATEFL, 42-45.

Cummins, James (1980). The Construct of Language Proficiency in Bilingual Education. In: Alatis, James E. (ed.). *Current Issues in Bilingual Education*. Washington: Georgetown University Press, 81-103.

Gogolin, Ingrid / Neumann, Ursula / Reuter, Lutz Rainer (2005). *Schulbildung für Kinder von Minderheiten in Deutschland 1989-1999. Schulrecht, Schulorganisation, curriculare Fragen, sprachliche Bildung.* Münster / New York: Waxmann.

Hall, Graham (2019). Own-Language Use in the Language Classroom: Why, When and How? In: Pattison, Tania (ed.). *IATEFL: Brighton Conference Selections.* Kent: IATEFL, 46-47.

Tracy, Rosemary (2011). Mehrsprachigkeit: Realität, Irrtümer, Visionen. In: Eichinger, Ludwig M. / Plewnia, Albrecht / Steinle Melanie (eds.). *Sprache und Integration. Über Mehrsprachigkeit und Migration.* Tübingen: Narr, 69–100.

Online References

http://cultureshake.eu/ (04/07/21)
https://ec.europa.eu/education/policies/european-policy-cooperation/et2020-framework_en (04/07/21)
https://ec.europa.eu/info/topics/education-and-training_en (December 2018)
https://globalshakespeares.mit.edu/ (04/07/21)
https://publications.europa.eu/en/publication-detail/-/publication/ebbab0bb-ef2f-11e5-8529-01aa75ed71a1 (04/07/21)
http://www.europarl.europa.eu/doceo/document/A-8-2015-0373_EN.html?redirect (04/07/21)
https://rm.coe.int/cefr-companion-volume-with-new-descriptors-2018/1680787989 (04/07/21)
https://www.rmg.co.uk/discover/explore/shakespeare-sea (04/07/21)
https://www.shakespeare.org.uk/education/teaching-resources (04/07/21)
Worksheet Soundscape: https://www.shakespeare.org.uk/education/teaching-resources/efl-tempest-soundscape/ (04/07/21)
Worksheet Home & Exile: https://www.shakespeare.org.uk/education/teaching-resources/home-and-exile-tempest/ (04/07/21)
Worksheet Pyramus & Thisbe:
https://www.shakespeare.org.uk/education/teaching-resources/language-politics-midsummer-nights-dream/ (04/07/21)
Worksheet You taught me language:
https://www.shakespeare.org.uk/education/teaching-resources/you-taught-me-language/ (04/07/21)

WERNER DELANOY (UNIVERSITY OF KLAGENFURT, AUSTRIA)

Dialogue, Drama Pedagogy and English Language Education

This article aims to bring together a certain notion of dialogue, current ELT perspectives, drama pedagogy, a case study and a new approach to educational research. This research approach is a dialogic variation on Manuel Delanda's (2016) assemblage theory. The case study is focussed on a drama project taught by the author. The project was inspired by Brian Friel's play Translations (1981).

1. Introduction

In the following reflections, a perspective for drama-based English language education will be discussed which is derived from a normative concept of dialogue. In the first part, this notion of dialogue will be introduced and linked to current ELT debates. What follows is a summary of how experts in the field have assessed the learning potential of drama for (English) language education. Thirdly, the focus is on a play, namely Brian Friel's Translations (1981), which served as the basis for a drama project. Before documenting this project, attention is drawn to a new perspective for researching educational practice. The approach in question is assemblage theory (cf. Delanda 2016), which is focussed on the interactions of the players involved in concrete projects and their joint creation of new meanings. In the remaining parts of this article, the Translations project will be discussed with the help of this research approach, plus in the light of dialogic, ELT- and drama-related educational aims.

2. Dialogue as a perspective for English language learning

Suggesting dialogue as a basic orientation for (English) language education implies certain programmatic interests. As for its theoretical grounding, my understanding of dialogue is based on a set of key convictions derived from a hermeneutics after Gadamer (cf. Kögler 1992), Mikhail Bakhtin's (1981: 291f.) notion of *heteroglossia*, a dialogic approach to ideology-critique (Zima 1989), and the cosmopolitan concept of a "complex dialogue" as suggested by Sayla Benhabib (2002: 8). It would go beyond the scope of this paper to discuss this theoretical framework in some more detail (cf. Delanoy 2002: 91-112; Delanoy

2017). Thus, I will confine myself to briefly introducing the key assumptions underlying this concept before applying them to what I see as key issues in current ELT debates.

This concept of dialogue rests on the conviction that all human understanding is limited because of people's implication in specific socio-cultural contexts and the hyper-complexity of the environments in which they live. Yet, and this is the second key belief, limitations can partly be overcome through engagement with different positions. Thirdly, a case is made for respectful engagement with other viewpoints. Fourthly, such a concept is power-critical in orientation and, therefore, aims for a removal of power imbalances. Fifthly, dialogue is an open-ended process, where, to quote Bakhtin (1981: 30) "there is no first word, and the final word has not been spoken". Sixthly, dialogue, is practised where existing expertise does not suffice to find satisfactory solutions. Dialogue, thus, is a creative approach, where new person-, situation- and problem-specific solutions need to be found in the light of changing demands. Also, dialogue is shaped by its participants, and a dialogic educational programme aims for the inclusion of as many people as possible. Finally, dialogue only works when its participants play by its rules. This is also the main weakness of this concept, since the idealism of the approach may well fall short of real-life practices.

Dialogue is created through language (in a multimodal sense). Indeed, it implies both a certain life-approach and specific language use. As for language learning, such an approach aims for language education, i.e. for interlinking socio-cultural with language-related learning aims (cf. Byram 2008: 6). To better illustrate such a concept let me briefly turn to a dialogic model for English language education, which I discussed in an earlier article (cf. Delanoy 2007). The model addresses four different directions for (English) language learning, which I see as key players in current ELT debates. One of the axes refers to two central thematic directions for language learning. As for the other one, the focus is on the languages to be learnt. The model looks as follows:

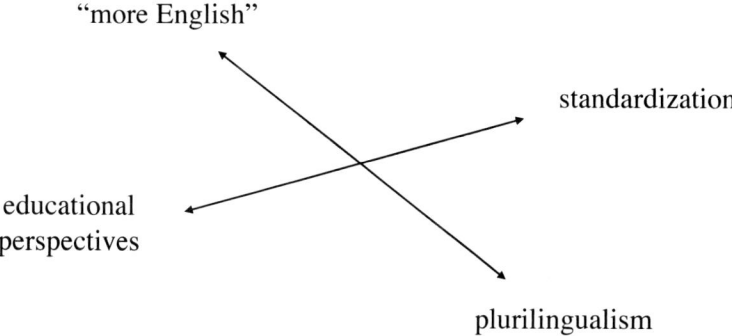

Indeed, the four perspectives can mark irreconcilable poles. Yet, a dialogic perspective wishes to avoid both stiff opposition and a pre-given hierarchy. The arrows therefore go both ways to indicate that each pole can serve as a critical perspective on and source of inspiration for the other. In addition, these arrows signal that all the directions represent important objectives for ELT, and that integration is paramount to prevent one-sided realizations.

As for the two thematic directions, educational perspectives meet current standardization practices. My understanding of education goes back to definitions as suggested by Rainer Kokemohr (2007: 21) and Hans-Christoph Koller (2012: 15-16). They argue that education should focus on issues where existing knowledge, beliefs and attitudes do not suffice to find solutions to present- and future-related personal, socio-cultural, economic, technological or ecological problems. On the one hand, such a programme stands in clear contrast to standardization, where pre-given norms play a central role in establishing clear and unambiguous parameters. On the other hand, the two orientations also interact. Creativity, for example, presupposes socio-cultural or language-related norms, and it may well lead to the creation of new rules and regulations. In other words, a dialogic approach is not opposed to standardization processes as long as they remain open to critical questioning and further development.

As for the language(s)-axis, the demand for more English can open manifold possibilities for international communication of global proportions, owing to the widespread use of English as a lingua franca. However, it can also foster an 'English-only' attitude, where proficiency in one foreign language is perceived as enough for transnational communication. Such development, however, would severely curtail the manifold lexical, conceptual and identity-related possibilities that different languages can offer to their speakers. Moreover, despite its dominance English language proficiency is not as widespread as one may believe (cf. Delanoy 2014: 64-65). Therefore, a case is made for inter-linking the demand for more English with a plurilingual agenda. My use of the term *plurilingualism* goes back to the *Common European Framework of Reference for Languages* (CEFR). In this document (2001: 4-5) plurilingualism is defined as constructive integration of learning experiences with different languages. Such plurilingualism can increase the general ability to learn languages, it can keep alive a wide spectrum of languages, it can raise language-and-culture awareness, and it can promote appreciation of different languages.

3. Drama pedagogy and (English) language education

In ELT debates, scholars have repeatedly referred to how drama can benefit language learning. For example, drama activities can lessen inhibition, thus heightening motivation to use the foreign language (cf. Surkamp / Hallet 2015: 8). Elektra Tselikas (1999: 41-42) argues that the use of drama activities leads to "Sprachnotsituationen" (communication emergencies), i.e. situations where existing language proficiency reaches its limits. For Tselikas such emergency scenarios can foster language learning, since the learners' strong emotional involvement urges them to find new means to express themselves. Franziska Elis (2015: 95) stresses that in such situations the focus is less on accuracy than on communicative success, and Andreas Bonnet and Almut Küppers (2011: 42) add that such a language learning approach ties in well with Merrill Swain's (1985) concept of pushed output. Finally, Almut Küppers (2015: 15) refers to the findings of the DICE-project.[1] The results show that drama activities in language learning contexts boosted the learners' self-confidence. Moreover, they had a positive impact on both learner empathy and perspective taking. Küppers' comments indicate that the language learning encouraged through drama aligns well with dialogic learning aims and intercultural learning objectives.

Another key competence for such learning is cooperation with other people. Küppers, Schmidt and Walter (2011: 7), therefore, make a case for linking drama and language learning to co-operative learning principles. Moreover, Bonnet

---

[1] The abbreviation DICE is an anagram for Drama Improves Lisbon Key Competences in Education.

and Küppers (2011: 42) argue in favour of a drama approach where strong involvement goes hand in hand with (self)-critical reflection. Similarly, Barbara Schmenk (2015: 43-44) draws attention to how drama in language learning can help develop critical language awareness, increase the learners' scope of imagination and foster aesthetic competence. For Schmenk (ibid.) the hallmarks of such language learning lie in its unpredictability, and the need for creativity to deal with unexpected development.

Schmenk's comments link back to the concept of dialogue and the definition of education mentioned above. In both instances, creativity plays a crucial role in inviting meaning making that goes beyond the tried and tested. Schmenk's comments also re-state what proponents of the performative turn in culture studies have emphasized. For example, Erika Fischer-Lichte (2017: 49) defines performance as a transitory and unique phenomenon, where the participants can make new experiences on cognitive, affective and somatic levels. Fischer-Lichte (2017: 327) makes a distinction between "Inszenierung" (preparation for a performance) and "Aufführung" (the performance as such), while in ELT-related drama pedagogy the term "Inszenierung" may include both stages (cf. Bonnet / Küppers 2011: 34). Indeed, I prefer Fischer-Lichte's terminology to keep apart the pre-performance work, i.e. the design of a scenario, and the actual performance. My translations for these two terms, therefore, are *scenario design* and *performance*.

In the light of my dialogic model such a performative approach, on the one hand, undoubtedly privileges the creative and non-fixable dimensions of language learning. Yet, such a focus must not be at the expense of less transitory dimensions. Jörg Volbers (2014: 77) argues that the main strength of performance-related perspectives lies in their focus on how new experience can come about. However, he (ibid.: 79) warns about one-sidedly celebrating openness end ephemerality without paying attention to the "harte Realität der Struktur", i.e. to the norms and systems regulating real-life communication. In other words, in language learning rules and standards for accurate language use are equally important for successful communication. The same applies to literary learning, where Carola Surkamp and Ansgar Nünning (2015: 221) stress that understanding drama also requires knowledge and awareness of its structures to understand the make-up and intended effects of drama practices. Furthermore, (inter)cultural learning goes hand in hand with a growth in awareness of value systems, thinking patterns and structures of feeling which – often unconsciously (cf. Bargh 2017) - regulate people's activities.

Indeed, performative competence has become a key competence in late-modern societies (cf. Hallet 2015: 53), where "elements of performance have permeated many areas of life" (Nicholson 2009: 44). Of course, performative competence is more than effective packaging. It also includes power-critical abilities that enable reflection upon performance practices. In sociology, Manfred Prischnig (2009: 114) argues that in late-modern societies decoration has become more important than substance. He adds that this may lead to the loss of ability to distinguish between surface and depth. Having lost that ability, people will continuously engage in performative acts, which only superficially promise empowerment, while in fact they substantially limit people's scope for self-realization and cooperation. In a performance society, culture-and-language education, therefore, aims for cognitive and affective depth when developing critical literacies.

Finally, a performative approach can also foster plurilingual competencies because of the multimodality of the communication channels involved. In other words, spoken and written language are in close interaction with gestures, facial expressions, body language, voice modulation and the participants' use of space. Moreover, depending on the texts, topics and activities used, the inclusion of different languages (national languages, dialects) can also play an important role in (English) language learning, as will be shown in the following sections.

4. Brian Friel's *Translations*

Translations is a play by the Irish playwright Brian Friel. The play is rich in potential for language and cultural learning. As for language learning, the play's title already signals one of its thematic concerns, namely that of translation. The play is set in Donegal in the 1830s, where British soldiers make an Ordnance Survey map of the area. A part of that project is to anglicise the Gaelic place names. Another key theme concerns multilingualism, i.e. the different languages spoken in the area, which include Gaelic, English and the classical languages Greek and Latin. Indeed, Brian Friel draws a complex picture of an area in transition, where personal, linguistic, political and socio-cultural perspectives interact in manifold ways.

In *Translations* the setting is the area around a small town in Donegal (Baile Beag) at a time when major changes are about to affect its inhabitants. These changes all refer to real events. As mentioned already, a new map is being made of the area.[2] From the British point of view, the aim is to gain stronger political, cultural, financial and military control over a colony. However, one of the English cartographers is a committed Hibernophile who tries his best to maintain links to the Gaelic language and the native culture. In addition, following legislation passed in 1831 (cf. McGrath 1999: 179), a national school system is being established in Ireland with a British syllabus and all the instruction now in English, thus replacing earlier systems with their focus on Irish traditions and Gaelic as the preferred means of communication. In fact, the main setting for most of the scenes is an Irish Hedge School on the verge of becoming obsolete. Such Hedge Schools were local initiatives, and they offered basic education (reading, writing, arithmetic) to a predominantly rural population. Moreover, in some instances, the students learned classical Latin and Greek, which for Irish people symbolized cultural superiority over the British invaders. These schools were illegal but tolerated because of their small size and lack of trans-local significance (cf. Pine 1990: 167f.).

In the play, people in Ireland/Donegal find themselves in an in-between state of development. On the one hand, old traditions such as tribal isolation or adherence to 'dead' languages stand in the way of a community's further development. On the other hand, the two main options for the way forward are either assimilation to British culture or emigration to America. Both options necessitate a breach with existing life approaches plus the study of the colonizer's language (English) to succeed in a new environment. The characters' responses to impending change vary significantly, with some longing for, others pragmatically accepting, others violently resisting change. The play invites exploration of different perspectives without privileging any of them per se.

Perhaps the most memorable scene in the play is when the British soldier and cartographer George Yolland and the local girl Maire Chatach meet after a dance. Both have fallen in love with each other; however, neither speaks the language of the other person. Brian Friel dramatically solves this problem by letting both characters speak English in the play, although only George speaks this language, while Maire communicates with him in Gaelic and some Latin. Thus, the viewer can understand more of what is going on than the characters themselves. At a first glance, the viewer may get the impression that love can conquer linguistic limitation; yet, on closer inspection, the audience soon learns

---

[2] Following a recommendation by a parliamentary committee in 1824, British cartographers together with an Irish scholar created such a map in the 1830s and early 1840s (cf. de Paor 1986: 235).

that the lovers differ in their desire (cf. Onkey 1997: 164). While George wishes to go native in Ireland, Maire is determined to leave Ireland and longs for a future outside the country. Moreover, the odds are against the two lovers, since such a union is anything but welcome, particularly in Maire's community.

The title of the play – *Translations* – refers to translation both in a linguistic and cultural sense. On linguistic levels, translation is practised when places are renamed and when a mediator translates between English and Gaelic, for example, by deliberately misrepresenting meanings to lessen their harsh implications (cf. Friel 1981: 31). In a metaphorical and cultural sense, on the one hand, a population has to translate itself into a new system, while, on the other hand, a romantic George longs for new roots in a Gaelic-speaking community. In both instances, no smooth transition to a new position is possible. Instead, the focus shifts to clashes of interest, misunderstandings and conflicts getting out of control. The play, therefore, merits a microscopic study of the shaky ground on which the characters are moving, thus raising awareness of the complexities involved in translation processes.

Such a perspective interacts well with the translational turn in culture studies (cf. Bachmann-Medick 2016a: 175f.). Translation, here, stands for the processes of identity construction experienced by people moving into new contexts. The focus is on breaks, conflicts, obstacles, unresolved issues, misunderstandings, failure, negotiations and new creations that accompany translation attempts (cf. Bachmann-Medick 2016a: 184-188, & 2016b: 121f.). This perspective focusses on in-between stages of development where the outcome is still unclear.

5. Assemblage theory as a research approach

Before turning to my teaching of Brian Friel's *Translations*, let me focus on a recently developed research approach, which helped me reflect upon this project. This approach is a dialogic variation on *Assemblage Theory*, the term *assemblage* going back to the philosophers Gilles Deleuze and Félix Guattari (1987). Building on their work Manuel Delanda (2016) further developed this notion into a theory of his own. He explains that the term assemblage is derived from the French *agencement* which "refers to the action of matching or fitting together a set of components ..., as well as to the result of such an action: an ensemble of parts that mesh together well" (Delanda 2016: 1).

In other words, an assemblage is a dynamic and well-working ensemble of interacting parts. To help illustrate this notion, Delanda (2016: 68) refers to an example given by Deleuze and Guattari (2018 [1987]: 470-471), namely that of an archer riding a horse in battle. The component parts in this assemblage are the warrior, the weapon (bow and arrow) and the horse. By interacting, these component parts can become a whole, and this whole can develop properties, which go beyond those of the parts in isolation. For example, together, archer, horse and weapon become a moving instrument of attack that can cross frontlines more quickly. Of course, to be successful as an assemblage the warrior needs to be a skilled rider and archer, the horse needs proper training, and the weapon must function well. Otherwise, these parts would not make up a successful unit. Delanda, however, does not focus on the skills and competences underlying successful performance. Instead, his focus is on the system in action, i.e. on its heterogeneous components, the acts of fitting them together, and the results of this enterprise. As for results, Delanda's main interest lies in the new possibilities emerging from the components' interactions.

When researching the use of drama in (language) education, assemblage theory draws attention to both the scenario design and the actual performance. As for scenario design, the focus is on the component parts and their combination. As regards the actual performance, the researcher studies the concrete interactions between the component parts with a particular interest in emerging new qualities. Of course, assemblage theory by itself does not suffice to understand why certain systems work well. Considering its limitations, structural and competence-focussed concepts are required as a complement.

For Delanda (2016: 9-10), assemblage theory is an approach rejecting "micro- and macro-reductionism". In other words, Delanda studies social wholes on a meso-level where the focus is neither on individual elements in isolation nor on what he calls "reified generalities" (ibid. 2016: 13), i.e. general and abstract concepts like education, ELT, language or culture. Assemblage theory looks at specific cases, discussing them as historically contingent and contextually situated social phenomena. Of course, micro- and macro-perspectives can act as a complement to such an approach. To my mind, this middle position is a useful starting point for studying concrete educational practices, since it shifts attention to complex and developing systems without foregoing the possibility to include more micro- and macroscopic dimensions. Like action research, such a perspective can offer insight into the workings of specific cases, while the general applicability of the research findings remains open to further investigation.

Barbara Schmenk (2015: 46) makes a case for educational research, which provides evidence for how drama activities can benefit language learning. She argues that such research should bring to light the personal insights gained by the learners, the conflicts and moments of surprise experienced by them, and their creative acts of meaning creation. For Schmenk (ibid.) such evidence is important as a counterweight to solely outcome-focussed language learning programmes. Indeed, assemblage theory is a suitable concept for such research because of its focus on an assemblage's emergent properties. In addition, assemblages in action are a communal effort, co-created by all the players involved. Indeed, in its communal dimension assemblage theory interlinks with principles of co-operative learning such as the search for and pursuit of shared aims, positive interdependency, assumption of individual and group responsibility, plus mutual respect and support (cf. Bonnet / Küppers 2011: 37).

Building on Deleuze's and Guattari's (2018 [1987]: 1-29) notion of the rhizome as a metaphor for (human) life-worlds, the creation of assemblages happens in hyper-complex and multi-centred contexts, which, in line with a dialogic perspective, can never be grasped as a whole. Thus, assemblages always run the risk of falling apart when colliding with unforeseen factors. However, the respective make-up of assemblages can heighten or lessen their prospect for success.

Delanda (2016: 22-23) introduces two central criteria, "territorialisation" and "coding", for studying the composition of assemblages. Territorialisation draws attention to the homogeneity of the repertoire from which the component parts are taken, and to "the degree to which an assemblage homogenises its own components" (Delanda 2016: 22). Coding refers to the degree of fixity of the component parts (ibid.: 23). When applied to the dialogic model for language learning as portrayed in section two, the model deliberately includes heterogeneous directions which may stand in opposition to each other (territorialisation). As for coding, the four directions themselves include different and contested realizations open to further development (cf. Delanoy 2007). From a dialogic perspective, heterogeneity and openness are important pre-requisites for constructive engagement with unforeseen development. Moreover, such a make-up is a pre-condition for bringing alive the creative potential of drama pedagogy. On the opposite, a monologic approach would opt for homogenization and clear fixing to either prevent change or channel it into a clearly defined direction. Such an approach may also be successful, yet, such success would contradict the aims pursued by a dialogic programme.

Finally, for Delanda (2016: 19) assemblages not only include human players but also material components (e.g. tools, media, and application software) and setting-related factors (e.g. classroom interior design, time-related factors). Assemblage theory, therefore, can help dialogic concepts move beyond their focus on human 'partners' in a dialogue. Such a perspective seems particularly relevant to (language) learning programmes in a digital age.

6. Teaching Brian Friel's *Translations*: Project design

The following activities were trialled in an ELT-focussed university course titled "Teaching Literature and Promoting Intercultural Competence". The course took place in the winter semester 2018/19 at the University of Klagenfurt, and the project was carried out on 16 January 2019. The students attending were either in the third or fourth year of their teaching-training programme. What made this group special was their familiarity with many languages other than English and German. The wide spectrum of languages included Albanian, Dari, French, Italian (different varieties), Maori, Serbo-Croatian (the student in question preferred this designation), Slovene, Spanish and Swedish, which the students had learned as a first or another foreign language. Thus, despite English being the language of communication tapping into this wealth of multilingual competence became an important objective for this class.

Briefly, the aims pursued were as follows:

(1) The approach to the text should be performative in orientation.

(2) Reflection should always follow performance to gain insight into the students' experiences with the textual stimuli and activities used.

(3) The activities should foster a differentiated understanding of the play.

(4) The activities should give recognition to the multilingualism of the students and raise awareness of the language-related issues discussed in the play.

The time set for the project was one 90-minute unit. The focus, therefore, was not on the whole play but on preparing the ground for optional student readings of *Translations*. The work plan included three activities, (1) translating place names, (2) a pre-performance drama activity, and (3) performances of Scene Two. Moreover, the course tutor developed two questionnaires to invite reflection on the classroom activities (see appendix).

7. Translating place names

In the first activity[3], the course tutor asked the students to translate some of the place names mentioned in the book into a language of their own choice (except for English). They were given three maps, one showing the *Baile Beag* area with the old Gaelic names, the other one with the names created for the new ordnance survey, and a third one with blanks for the new names to be created. Information was provided as to the literal meanings of the Gaelic place names and as to their pronunciation. Moreover, the students could use both the Gaelic version and the anglicised names as a basis for their own creations. For example, the information for *Baile Beag* included a literal translation (little town), the ordnance survey version (Ballybeg) and hints as to pronounce the Gaelic version ('balye'biog). Another example is *Lis na Muc* (literal translation: Fort of the Pigs; pronunciation: 'lish na 'mok) and its ordnance survey equivalent 'Swinefort'. Otherwise, no contextual information was given at that point for two reasons. First, explanation of the socio-historical context may have narrowed the students' scope of reference when creating their place names. Secondly, reference to a colonial enterprise would have introduced a note of seriousness that may have interfered with the fun and pleasure this activity can generate. Indeed, the students should experience the task as an enjoyable activity to promote a positive attitude to multilingualism.

When the students were done with their remapping, I invited them to pick one of their creations and write it on an A1 poster displayed on a flipchart showing the map with both the Gaelic and anglicised place names. Moreover, the students explained why they had opted for certain translations. Two short activities followed this activity to provide some insight into the play's socio-historical context. Moreover, these activities served as a bridge to the following tasks. First, the students were asked to slip into two different roles of cartographer, the first one being that of a colonizer and the other one that of somebody in love with Ireland. Secondly, pronunciation of the Gaelic place names was practiced by reading the names out either from the colonizer's or the 'lover's' perspective. Finally, the students received a questionnaire to invite further reflection upon the activities (see appendix). Participation was optional; the students answered the questions after the project and submitted their documents to the tutor either in paper form or via e-mail.

---

[3] The instructions for all the activities for this part of the project can be found in the appendix.

As an assemblage, its component parts included the three maps, the instructions for the activities and the different languages activated. Moreover, the course tutor and the students were key elements in this assemblage, with the teacher acting as task-designer and moderator, while the students assumed the roles of creative and reflexive cartographers. Other factors included the size of the class (17 students, one tutor), the age of the students (between 20 and 25) and their English language proficiency (very high). Moreover, the non-human components comprised photocopies, a poster, a projector, power-point images, smartphones (repeatedly used by the students for their translations) and setting-related factors like the time frame (30 minutes for this set of activities) or the architecture of the classroom (no desks, thus flexible in arrangement). For Delanda the component parts all play a crucial role for the success of an assemblage, and removal of one would make the system collapse. In my application of assemblage theory, the components can prove more or less important in specific situations. However, each of them may play a crucial role for the success of a concrete project.

As for the assemblage's make-up, I would argue that in some respect 'territorialisation' and 'coding' were low. As for the project's multilingualism, a variety of languages could enter the scene as 'co-players', and – as became noticeable in the students' creations – the borders of languages were also crossed in favour of hybrid varieties (e.g. "Baileville" as a mix between Gaelic and French for 'Baile Beag'). Moreover, the structure of this university course was open to experimentation, and changes to the syllabus were welcome in the case of emerging needs and interests. In other respects, however, there was a high degree of homogeneity as was the case with the students' level of English language proficiency. Indeed, without such expertise in the language, more scaffolding would have been required to facilitate engagement in the project. As regards 'coding', for example, there was a clear time limit for the project, which, as will be shown later, posed a threat to the success of the project.

As mentioned above, dialogue, performative approaches and assemblage theory all shift attention to the new possibilities emerging from the interactions between the partners involved. In this light, the responses showed that the students repeatedly experienced the activity as a novelty. One student, for example, pointed out that she "had never been asked to use [her] first language neither in school nor university settings before", thus positively commenting on the recognition of her multilingual identity. Many students referred to the enjoyment they felt when doing this activity, and, in some instances, they pointed to the mix between entertainment and serious reflection. For example, one student argued that she felt joy and guilt at the same time, when translating the place names, since she wanted to keep as much of the Gaelic original as possible without knowing enough about the language and the places to be renamed. Repeatedly, there was mention of the creativity invited by this activity.

As for multilingual and co-operative learning objectives, for one student the design of the activity "shows appreciation of the individual [student] and their language skills", and "it helps to get to know the others better". The activity also raised awareness of historical instances where place names underwent translation as in South Tyrol after WW1 or, more recently, in Carinthia. Finally, asking the students how the roles of 'colonizer' and 'lover' would affect their translations, they agreed that the perspective of colonizer implies the wish to exercise political, military and cultural control over a territory.

Delanda (2016: 4) argues that when an assemblage is in place it "starts acting as a source of limitations and opportunities for its components". Viewed in this light, the activity had helped create conditions conducive to further engagement with *Translations*. Student motivation was high and strong involvement was accompanied by (self)-critical reflection.

8. Simulating the scenario in Scene Two (Act Two)

The following activity, which I had tried out with a significantly smaller group before, was added to the work-plan in class. The students' positive response to the first set of activities encouraged me to include this activity despite the tight schedule for the project. In other words, this task also represents an 'emergent property' of an evolving assemblage.

This activity was a role play based on the following instructions:

Role A: You are a young British soldier who is stationed in 19th century Ireland. Your name is GEORGE YOLLAND. You like Ireland very much, and you have fallen in love with a young local woman who does not speak your language. Her name is MAIRE CHATACH (pron. ´Mora Cha´tach). You meet her after a dance, and you want to tell her about yourself, your love for Ireland, and your feelings for her. Now have a conversation with Maire.

Role B: You are young Irish woman living in a small village in 19th century Ireland. Your name is MAIRE CHATACH (pron. ´Mora Cha´tach). Near your village, a battalion of British soldiers is stationed. You like their language a lot, but you cannot speak English. One of the soldiers you find very attractive. His name is GEORGE YOLLAND. You meet him after a dance, and you want to find out more about him. You also want to tell him about yourself, and your feelings for him. Now have a conversation with George.

In a scenario similar to Scene Two in the second act of the play the students slip into the roles of George and Maire. For the role play the students had to use a language that the conversation partner did not understand. Where this was not possible, I asked the students to invent an imaginary language on the spot. As course tutor, my concerns were that the time allotted to the activity (about 15-20 minutes) and the invention of new languages may be asking too much of the students. However, from my observer's perspective the students experienced the activity as manageable and enjoyable.

Indeed, some student comments confirm my observation, since they repeatedly mention the fun generated by this activity. However, there is also reference to the difficulty of creating a new language ("It was fun to act out this scene, but it was hard to create a new language"). Moreover, the students commented on the frustration they felt when lacking the means to communicate, but also referred to their creative and successful attempts to make themselves understood with the help of paralanguage (e.g. pitch, intonation, volume) and body language (e.g. gestures, facial expressions, use of space). Again, some students positively referred to the multilingualism of the activity ("teaming up with students who speak other languages besides English showcases the big variety of languages that exists on our campus"). Finally, one student pointed out that he first doubted the usefulness of this activity for language learning ("How does this activity make me a better language teacher?"). However, his attitude soon changed, and he became appreciative of the task because it "pushed [him] out of [his] comfort zone", and because "it was interesting to experience how it feels when not speaking the same language, but desperately wanting to communicate with each other". In the light of drama pedagogy, this student refers to a 'Sprachnotsituation' (a communicative emergency) and the creative potential unleashed in such a situation.

9. Performing Scene Two

The final activity included two performances of Scene Two (Act Two). Before the performances, I handed out photocopies of the scene (cf. Friel 1981: 49-53). The first time the course tutor, slipping into the role of George, performed a dramatized reading of the text with a student who had volunteered to read Maire's part. The second time the students performed the scene in pairs (again as dramatized reading). In the short discussion following the performances, the course tutor drew attention to the different desire expressed by George and Maire, which becomes noticeable towards the end of the scene. Moreover, the students speculated about how the story may continue.

In my experience, acting the scene out with the student volunteer worked very well, in particular because of her confident and convincing performance. Her comments show that she also experienced the performance as successful. She points out that "[she] love[s] acting in general", and that performing Maire's part came "easy" and felt "natural" to her. Indeed, I felt a lot of energy coming from the students as audience, which greatly helped me in my efforts. This may indicate positive audience response, yet, there is no 'hard' evidence for such observation.

The students repeatedly commented on their own performances. Again, they pointed out the pleasure they had experienced. However, they also referred to the difficulties involved, such as getting into the role of the character, pronouncing the Gaelic place names (which also "disrupted the acting out"), and staying focussed on the text and the conversation partner at the same time. The activity also raised various questions concerning the characters and the plot. The students expressed the wish to learn more about how the story continues and about the play's socio-historical context. In one instance, the final development in the scene invited speculation. Here, another character (Sarah) sees George and Maire kiss and calls for another person (Manus) before she runs off (cf. Friel 1981: 52-53). The student in question wondered about the relationships between George, Maire and the two new characters ("Is Sarah George's girlfriend?"; "Is Manus Maire's partner?").

The questionnaire also asked the students how they, as future teachers, would work with this scene in an ELT context. On the one hand, the students repeatedly assessed my work plan as useful and transferable to their own pedagogical interests. On the other hand, they expressed some reservations and suggested some modification to the scenario design. First, they addressed the age and the English proficiency level of the target learners by pointing out that the approach chosen presupposes mature and linguistically proficient students. Secondly, there was reference to personality traits averse to a performative approach ("it would not make sense to do this with introverted students"), and to thematic concerns ("George and Maire are madly in love, this could lead to situations that students are not comfortable with"). Thirdly, there was mention of time constraints ("I would have needed more time to prepare"). Finally, two students expressed dissatisfaction with how the unit ended. The scenes were only performed by the pairs without the others watching. These students suggested that some pairs should have presented their work to the whole class.

Judging by the students' answers and by my reflections after the event, the students experienced this part of the project as significantly more challenging than the other activities, the main reason being the limited time available. For example, there was little time for role preparation and text discussion. As regards text discussion, the different desire expressed by George and Maire, for example, received mention only in passing. Moreover, the lack of possibility to perform in front of the class did not allow the students to go public with their creations. Finally, my course organisation – the project took place shortly before the end of the semester – did not permit further activity. Thus, the responses given and sent to me marked the ending of the unit.

With the benefit of hindsight, the scenario is certainly in need of improvement. I would even go as far as saying that the final activity could have wrecked a well-working assemblage. To my mind, improvement goes hand in hand with better time management. Moreover, addition of a pre-performance task seems appropriate to give the actors/actresses enough time to read the text before the performance and to work on their roles. Such preparation could include engagement with performances of the scene uploaded on YouTube, which would extend the range of component parts and enhance the assemblage's digital orientation. In addition, giving the students a chance to perform in front of the class would give stronger recognition to their effort.

10. Conclusion

The project gives concrete evidence for the possibilities which drama can offer to (English) language education. Indeed, in one of the response documents, a student aptly sums up the advantages of drama in this learning context. She argues that drama "supports active, playful, artistic but also self-reflective processes, and [that it] represents an interesting approach to dynamic language learning". From a dialogic perspective, the students' and the teacher's creativity, plus their shared and respectful search for constructive co-operation merit attention. In its plurilingual dimension, the activities helped promote appreciation of the group's multilingualism and critical language awareness. Finally, in the light of assemblage theory the new possibilities emerging from a certain constellation of different factors deserve mentioning. They include the novelty of the activities, the intensive feelings experienced by the players, and their manifold creations (e.g. new languages, translations of place names). Such a perspective, however, also shows that mismanagement of one component can jeopardize the success of a project.

In this article, assemblage theory serves as a means to study concrete educational practice. I chose this approach because of its systemic orientation, its inclusion of non-human factors and its focus on developing interaction processes. To my mind, assemblage theory interacts well with drama pedagogy, concepts of dialogue and educational perspectives for language learning. Assemblage theory can foster a systemic understanding of the factors conducive and averse to promoting new and dialogue-friendly learning and teaching experiences. Of course, the approach also poses limitations because of its disregard of structural and competence-related factors. Further discussion will show how novel and productive the approach is for educational research.

11. Appendix

Translating the place names: Instructions for activities (a)-(d).

- Translate the place names into a language of your own choice. Why did you create certain names?
- Imagine you are a colonizer whose job it is to produce a map of a colony. What would be your aims? How would you translate the place names?
- You have to do the same job, but this time you are person who has fallen in love with this other country, its language, its history, its people, etc. How would you then do your job?
- Read out the Gaelic place names either from the colonizer's or the lover's perspective.

Questionnaire (1): Translating the placenames

- Which language did you choose for your translations?
- What emotions/associations did the activity trigger in your minds?
- Did you use the Gaelic/English version or both versions as a basis for your translations?
- What was/were your concern/s when translating the place names? (e.g. to keep as much of the original meaning of the place names;

making your place name sound like the Gaelic/English one; making it easier for people speaking your language to find their way about in this area; any other comments)

- What were the main challenges/difficulties?
- Did your concerns/aims change when you slipped into the role of colonizer/lover?
- Any other comments.

Questionnaire (2): Acting out Scene Two

I. What did you like/dislike about this activity?

II. How did you want to present your part/your character (George/Maire)?

III. What do you think of the pre-performance activity where you and your partner spoke different languages?

IV. What were the main challenges when acting out the scene in the play? (E.g., getting into the role of George/Maire; pronouncing the Gaelic place names; not knowing enough about the context; other challenges?)

V. As for the scene/play, what has remained unclear to you?

VI. As for the scene/play, what would you like to learn more about?

VII. How would you work with this scene if you were the teacher? (Would you use the same activities/approach if you worked with this text in an ELT context? Why? Why not? What would you do differently?)

VIII. Any other comments.

Bibliography

Bachmann-Medick, Doris (2016a). *Cultural Turns. New Orientations in the Study of Culture*. Berlin and Boston: Walter de Gruyter.

Bachmann-Medick, Doris (2016b). From Hybridity to Translation. Reflections on Travelling Concepts. In: Bachmann-Medick, Doris (ed.). *The Trans/National Study of Culture. A Translational Perspective*. Berlin & Boston: Walter de Gruyter, 119-136.

Bakhtin, Mikhael M. (1981). *The Dialogic Imagination. Four Essays*. Austin: University of Texas Press.

Bargh, John (2017). *Before You Know It. The Unconscious Reasons We Do What We Do*. London: Windmill.
Benhabib, Sayla (2002). *The Claims of Culture. Equity and Diversity in the Global Era*. Princeton and Oxford: Princeton University Press.
Bonnet, Andreas / Küppers, Almut (2011). Wozu taugen kooperatives Lernen und Dramapädadagogik? Vergleich zweier populärer Inszenierungsformen. In: Küppers / Schmidt / Maik (eds.). *Inszenierungen im Fremdsprachenunterricht. Grundlagen, Formen, Perspektiven* Braunschweig: Schroedel / Diesterweg / Klinkhardt, 32-52.
Byram, Michael (2008). *From Foreign Language Education to Education for Intercultural Citizenship*. Clevedon / Buffalo / Toronto: Multilingual Matters.
Council for Cultural Co-operation, Educational Committee, Modern Languages Division, Strasbourg (2001). *Common European Framework of Reference for Languages: Learning, Teaching, Assessment*. Cambridge: CUP.
Delanda, Manuel (2016). *Assemblage Theory*. Edinburgh: Edinburgh University Press.
Delanoy, Werner (2002). *Fremdsprachlicher Literaturunterricht. Theorie und Praxis als Dialog*. Tübingen: Gunter Narr.
Delanoy, Werner (2007). Dialogue as a Perspective for (English) Language Learning. In: Kindermann, Wolf (ed.). *Transcending Boundaries. Essays in Honor of Gisela Hermann-Brennecke*. Münster: LIT, 49-69.
Delanoy, Werner (2008). Dialogic Communicative Competence and Language Learning. In: Delanoy, Werner / Volkmann, Laurenz (eds.). *Future Perspectives for English Language Teaching*. Heidelberg: Winter, 173-188.
Delanoy, Werner (2014). Mehrsprachigkeit, Englisch und Literatur(unterricht). In: *Zeitschrift für Interkulturellen Fremdsprachenunterricht* 19(1), 63-76.
Delanoy, Werner (2017). Building Bridges. Towards a Timely Concept for Culture and Language Learning. In: Onysko, Alexander / Graf, Eva-Maria / Delanoy, Werner / Sigott, Guenther / Dobric, Nikola (eds.). *The Polyphony of English Studies. A Festschrift for Allan James*. Tübingen: Narr, 163-176.
Deleuze, Gilles / Guattari, Félix (2018 [1987]). *A Thousand Plateaus*. London and New York: Bloomsbury Academic.
de Paor, Liam (1986). *The Peoples of Ireland. From Pre-history to Modern Times*. London: Hutchinson.
Elis, Franziska (2015). Mit dramapädagogischen Methoden sprachliche und kommunikative Methoden fördern. In: Hallet, Wolfgang / Surkamp. Carola (eds.). *Dramendidaktik und Dramapädagogik im Fremdsprachenunterricht*. Trier: WVT, 89-115.
Hallet, Wolfgang (2015). Die Performativität und Theatralität des Alltagshandelns. Performative Kompetenz und kulturelles Lernen. In: Hallet, Wolfgang / Surkamp. Carola (eds.). *Dramendidaktik und Dramapädagogik im Fremdsprachenunterricht*. Trier: WVT, 51-67.

Hallet, Wolfgang / Surkamp. Carola (eds.) (2015). *Dramendidaktik und Dramapädagogik im Fremdsprachenunterricht*. Trier: WVT.
Fischer-Lichte, Erika (2017 [2004]). *Ästhetik des Performativen*. Frankfurt/M.: Suhrkamp.
Friel, Brian (1981). *Translations*. London and Boston: Faber and Faber.
Kögler, Hans-Herbert (1992). *Die Macht des Dialogs. Kritische Hermeneutik nach Gadamer, Foucault und Rorty*. Stuttgart: J.B. Metzler.
Kokemohr, Rainer (2007). Bildung als Welt- und Selbstentwurf im Fremden. Annäherungen an eine Bildungsprozesstheorie. In: Koller, Hans Christoph / Marotzki, Winfried / Sanders, Olaf (eds.). *Bildungsprozesse und Fremdheitserfahrung. Beiträge zu einer Theorie transformatorischer Bildungsprozesse*. Bielefeld: Transcript, 13-69.
Koller, Hans Christoph (2012). *Bildung anders denken. Einführung in die Theorie transformatorischer Bildungsprozesse*. Stuttgart: Kohlhammer.
Küppers, Almut / Schmidt, Torben / Maik, Walter (eds.) (2011a). *Inszenierungen im Fremdsprachenunterricht. Grundlagen, Formen, Perspektiven*. Braunschweig: Schroedel / Diesterweg / Klinkhardt.
Küppers, Almut / Schmidt, Torben / Maik, Walter (2011b). Inszenierungen. Present tense incarnate im Fremdsprachenunterricht. In: Küppers, Almut / Schmidt, Torben / Maik, Walter (eds.). *Inszenierungen im Fremdsprachenunterricht. Grundlagen, Formen, Perspektiven*. Braunschweig: Schroedel / Diesterweg / Klinkhardt, 5-17.
Küppers, Almut (2015). Interkulturelle Kompetenzen, Dramapädagogik und Theaterwissenschaft. In: Hallet, Wolfgang / Surkamp. Carola (eds.). *Dramendidaktik und Dramapädagogik im Fremdsprachenunterricht*. Trier: WVT, 145-164.
McGrath, F.C. (1999). *Brian Friel's (Post) Colonial Drama. Language, Illusion and Politics*. Syracuse / New York: Syracuse University Press.
Nicholson, Helen (2009). *Theatre and Education*. New York: Palgrave Macmillan.
Onkey, Lauren (1997). The Woman as Nation in Brian Friel's Translations. In: Kerwin, William (ed.). *Brian Friel. A Casebook*. New York / London: Garland Publishing, 159-174.
Pine, Richard (1990). *Brian Friel and Ireland's Drama*. London: Routledge.
Prischnig, Manfred (2009). *Das Selbst, die Maske, der Bluff. Über die Inszenierung der eigenen Person*. Wien: Molden.
Schmenk, Barbara (2015). Dramapädagogik im Spiegel der Bildungsstandards GeRS und Kompetenzdiskussionen. In: Hallet / Surkamp (2015), 37-50.
Surkamp, Carola / Hallet, Wolfgang (2015). Dramendidaktik und Dramapädagogik im Fremdsprachenunterricht: Zur Einleitung. In: Hallet, Wolfgang / Surkamp. Carola (eds.). *Dramendidaktik und Dramapädagogik im Fremdsprachenunterricht*. Trier: WVT, 1-18.
Surkamp, Carola / Nünning, Ansgar (2015). Kategorien, Fragen und Verfahren der Dramenanalyse im Zusammenspiel mit szenischen Methoden. Plädoyer

für ein Sowohl-als-auch von textzentrierten Zugangsformen. In: Hallet, Wolfgang / Surkamp. Carola (eds.). *Dramendidaktik und Dramapädagogik im Fremdsprachenunterricht.* Trier: WVT, 221-239.

Swain, Merrill (1985). Communicative Competence. Some Roles of Comprehensible Input and Comprehensible Output in its Development. In: Gass, Susan / Madden, Carolyn (eds.). *Input in Second Language Acquisition.* Rowley/MA: Newbury House, 235-253.

Tselikas, Elektra I. (1999). *Dramapädagogik im Sprachunterricht.* Zürich: Orell Füssli.

Volbers, Jörg (2014). *Performative Kultur. Eine Einführung.* Wiesbaden: Springer.

Zima, Peter V. (1989). *Ideologie und Theorie. Eine Diskurskritik.* Tübingen: Francke.

List of Authors

Grit Alter is professor for teaching English as a foreign language at the University College of Teacher Education, Tyrol in Austria. Her research interests lie with literary and cultural learning, children's literature in language classrooms, textbook studies, critical media literacy, and critical pedagogy. She is currently involved in projects in curricula studies, visual literacy, and diversity-sensitive teaching.

Max von Blanckenburg is postdoctoral researcher at the Chair of Teaching English as a Foreign Language at Munich University (LMU). His research interests include the role and potential of rhetoric in foreign language education, literary and performative teaching and learning as well as digital literacies.

Werner Delanoy is associate professor of ELT in the Department of English and American Studies at the University of Klagenfurt. His main areas of research are inter- and transcultural learning perspectives, literature teaching, cosmopolitanism and global education, language learning and contemporary British culture and literature.

Annette Deschner works at the Institute of Transdisciplinary Social Sciences at the University of Education Karlsruhe. Her areas of research are CLIL, multilingual didactics and cultural studies. She worked as a teacher at a bilingual grammar school in Baden-Württemberg.

Maria Eisenmann is professor of EFL teaching at the Julius-Maximilians-University Würzburg. Her primary research interests lie in the fields of digital literacy, literary learning, drama pedagogy, global education including individual differences. She has published widely in the fields of foreign language education, digital and literary literacy in the EFL classroom.

Christiane Klempin is the head scientific project coordinator at *FU Berlin*. She was also a research assistant in English didactics at *FU Berlin* (2015-2020), Potsdam (2019/20) and Greifswald (2014/15). Her main focus is to investigate effectiveness of (English) teacher training, e.g.b on reflective abilities (PhD), drama-related attitudes/instruction skills of teacher trainees (habilitation).

Christian Ludwig is a researcher and speaker in the field of ELT. He is particularly interested in using literary texts and digital media as well as enhancing students' foreign language learner autonomy. He currently works as a guest professor for TEFL at the Freie Universität Berlin, Germany.

Christiane Lütge is professor at the Ludwig-Maximilians-University of Munich (LMU), where she holds the Chair of Teaching English as a Foreign Language (TEFL). Her areas of expertise in research and teaching include digital literacy and literary learning as well as global citizenship education in EFL. For several years, Christiane Lütge worked as a teacher of English and History.

Frauke Matz is chair of English language education at the Westfälische Wilhelms-Universität Münster, Germany. Her research interests lie in the field of teaching methodology of literature, with a special focus on young adult fiction, the role of cultural studies as well as alternative forms of summative assessment in the EFL context.

Lisa Peter is senior lecturer in Shakespeare Studies and European Projects Manager at the Shakespeare Birthplace Trust. Her work ranges from teaching Shakespeare to school groups and universities to adult learners, and she leads on all offers for language learners and teachers from around the world.

Laurenz Volkmann, PhD, is full professor of Teaching English as a Foreign Language at Friedrich-Schiller-University Jena. He has a long teaching experience both at schools in Germany and at universities in the USA, the UK, Chile, India and in various German states. He has edited and co-edited numerous books, published around 300 academic articles and co-authored the standard textbook *Teaching English* (2015).